As a single man, I found myself deeply cared [...] *Solo Planet*. In many circles these things are not often seen or approached well. I think this book was written for that set of followers like myself who feel a calling to righteous singleness, and not just as a holding pattern for marriage. I think discipleship on this level can really make a difference in the global church, as people want to find support as single followers but also want to be all in for the Kingdom and all the opportunities that are in front of us. This book does a good job of covering a wide variety of cultural differences and related hardships that Christian singles face. I was most impressed. I feel a lot of grief about this personally, and reading the stories within made me feel seen and appreciated.

COURTLAND HOPKINS, Native InterVarsity, IVCF USA

Anna Broadway has written an astonishingly broad-ranging analysis of Christian single life that is at once astutely sociological, deeply personal, sincerely prayerful, and boldly ecumenical. It is a mature achievement that deserves serious attention from clergy and lay leaders alike.

DAWN EDEN GOLDSTEIN, theologian, canon lawyer, and author of *Father Ed*

This is a challenging book in all the right ways. While I cannot endorse everything in the book (from a strictly ecclesiological or theological position), still . . . it challenges us to look past preconceived notions of how one is to live in the church—not to idolize the married state, or better, not to see singles only as a problem to "fix" by getting them married (or in my tradition, sent to a monastery, as beautiful and holy as monasticism is). . . .

It's too easy to overlook the young (or not so young) singles in a parish, thinking that they will have their social/communal needs met outside of church (but do we really want that?). It's even easier to forget the widows and widowers or divorced people who may be suffering in silence. One is also challenged to remember those who have same-sex attraction. Each church and parish *will* be faced with this issue. While you may not endorse all the ways other churches or individuals have approached this issue, this book reminds us strongly of everyone's basic humanity, being made in the image of God. Their struggles need to be remembered and treated with dignity.

Without shrinking from the difficulties and problems the single life carries with it, whether singleness is seen as a calling or a "curse," the tone of the book is one of hope and encouragement and a call to deepen one's spiritual life and commitment to the Lord, which is really the point of the church after all. This book has challenged me to open my eyes and to see parish life through different lenses.

FR. PHILIP KONTOS, St. Herman of Alaska Orthodox Church, OCA

Anna Broadway has written an astonishingly broad-ranging analysis. A smart, convicting book whose stories from across the globe on singles and their lives throw open a welcoming invitation to churches and believers to embrace the unmarried with joy, acceptance, warmth, and love. Anna Broadway's tour de force of worldwide research is sure to help God's Kingdom reimagine a more integrated church with room on every pew—and at every table—for all. Brave, exciting, and worthy of attention and action. May many read and heed.

PATRICIA RAYBON, Christy Award–winning author of *My First White Friend, I Told the Mountain to Move,* and the Annalee Spain Mystery series

Anna Broadway asks the hard questions of Christian singleness: How can you thrive as a single when you have not chosen it? How do you deal with desire and longing? Through an incredible journey across the globe, she interviews Christian singles on six continents. With their voices and her sensitive insight, she guides us on a journey of understanding. The journey leads us to our core—God and His community—which brings renewal and hope. Highly recommended.

DR. MICHAEL O. EMERSON, Chavanne Fellow in Religion and Public Policy at Rice University and author of *Divided by Faith* and *People of the Dream*

I have watched Anna Broadway undertake this labor of love, *Solo Planet*, over the course of her long journey across the globe, into strangers' homes, and inside gatherings of local congregations near and far. In this culmination of that journey, readers will find a holistic, faithful, probing, and challenging call for all Christians to love one another better as brothers and sisters, regardless of marital status. Those called to minister "solo" are no less a part of the family of God, and *Solo Planet* offers a holistic and helpful approach to enacting this truth.

KAREN SWALLOW PRIOR, PHD, author of *The Evangelical Imagination*

For the first time in history, I'm told that single Christians (of marriageable age) outnumber those who are married. In her book *Solo Planet*, Anna addresses the situation head on, interviewing single people from an amazingly broad spectrum of life circumstances.

Anna takes an honest look at the common yet seldom-addressed situation(s) of single Christians and points out both the many challenges and the sometimes-overlooked benefits of single life. She also reminds the reader of the importance of gratitude for all of us, and the necessity for each of us—married, single, or consecrated—to orient ourselves more and more fully to God's will: "Our hearts are restless, until they rest in Thee." While our theological perspectives differ at points, churches and church leaders would do well to prayerfully consider the issues she raises.

ED HOPFNER, director of Marriage and Family Life for the Archdiocese of San Francisco

I've read a lot of discussion of single Christians' lives and vocations over the years, but almost all of them stick to one narrow subcommunity or topic: They look at singleness for Black evangelical women or English-speaking Catholic laypeople; they explore theological questions but not practical challenges, or vice versa. *Solo Planet* is the rare exploration of the unmarried state that isn't about one small, siloed group or question. And yet it doesn't feel unfocused or vague. In gentle, vibrant prose, Anna Broadway offers empathetic reflections for never-married, widowed, and divorced Christians, as well as challenging our churches to understand single people's needs and cultivate their gifts. I truly appreciated Broadway's commitment to seeking out the voices of the global church. *Solo Planet* doesn't feel lonely. It depicts a teeming, questioning, prayerful world, where those who are most overlooked might have the most to share. Even when I did not share every aspect of Broadway's view of a situation, I truly appreciated her commitment to seeking out the voices of the global church.

EVE TUSHNET, author of *Tenderness*

Anna Broadway has a keen insight into how singleness and service in Christ's Kingdom go hand in hand. In *Solo Planet*, Broadway also welcomes in the voices of a diverse, global community of others who have walked the paths of discipleship and singleness at the same time—bringing many fresh and personal perspectives to the vital roles singles play in the church. *Solo Planet* is an honest and, at times, quite vulnerable book. I highly encourage Christian leaders, whether single or not, to engage this book with open hearts and minds to be encouraged and challenged by the many ways God is at work among Christ followers who are single all over the world.

ERIC COSTANZO, pastor and coauthor of *Inalienable*

Anna Broadway has put in the years and the miles to report the deeply personal stories of what's happening with single Christians around the globe. *Solo Planet* goes beyond the familiar presentation of issues that affect many in the West to show how loneliness, finances, housing, food, and more present very real challenges to single people across six continents and all kinds of Christian believers. That these simple concerns of how to flourish while unpartnered have application for every human shouldn't be a surprise, but it's rare a Christian book goes beyond denominational boundaries or singular theologies to listen to those for whom sexuality, race, poverty, and other differences impact their experiences of finding acceptance, love, and a place within Christian life. Offering simple questions to help reflect on and own the issues raised, *Solo Planet* is a great place to start to understand the big-picture situation and the tiny, heartfelt details that make up so many single Christians' experience of faith and life.

VICKY WALKER, author of *Relatable*

Across the US and even across the world, 60 percent of churchgoers are women. That single statistic (pun intended) tells you marriage and child-rearing cannot be the only model for Christian life. Broadway tells the story of single Christians and points toward ways churches can include them more fully in the faith community. The book is never negative or judgmental about families at all, but rather realistic about the world we live in and the nature of religious organizations. Broadway encourages churches to look deeper when they think about the nature of Christian commitment.

ARTHUR E. FARNSLEY II, author of five books, including *Flea Market Jesus*

Accessible, charming, and wise, Anna Broadway's *Solo Planet* sheds much-needed light on the question of how the church can best integrate and include singles . . . and how singles empower and enrich the church. I especially love that Anna's work includes the global church, not just the American one, and the stories of her adventures traveling and interviewing singles worldwide are delightful. It's refreshing to see the diversity of opinions, beliefs, and ideas about church, singleness, and sexuality throughout our broader community. We don't always agree with each other—you won't agree with everyone in this book—but we are called to love one another. This book helps move us toward understanding each other better.

MATT MIKALATOS, author of *Journey to Love* and coauthor of *Loving Disagreement*

Every single Christian is single for at least some season—if not all—of their life. So how can the church live up to the biblical call to truly be God's family of married and single people alike?

Drawing on a vast array of voices, Anna Broadway helps us see both the struggles and the victories of the global church in this area while casting a vision for what it means to be the family of God in everyday life. This is a valuable work of practical theology for the church today!

BRANSON PARLER, author of *Every Body's Story*

SOLO PLANET

*How Singles Help the Church
Recover Our Calling*

ANNA BROADWAY

NavPress

A NavPress resource published in alliance
with Tyndale House Publishers

NavPress.com

Solo Planet: How Singles Help the Church Recover Our Calling

A NavPress resource published in alliance with Tyndale House Publishers

NavPress and the NavPress logo are registered trademarks of NavPress, The Navigators, Colorado Springs, CO. *Tyndale* is a registered trademark of Tyndale House Ministries. Absence of ® in connection with marks of NavPress or other parties does not indicate an absence of registration of those marks.

The Team:
David Zimmerman, Publisher; Deborah Sáenz Gonzalez, Acquisitions Editor; Elizabeth Schroll, Copy Editor; Olivia Eldredge, Operations Manager; Eva M. Winters, Designer

Cover photograph of people in city copyright © by CACTUS Creative Studio/Stocksy.com. All rights reserved.

Cover photograph of church copyright © by Volodymyr Shevchuk/Adobe Stock. All rights reserved.

Cover photograph of mother and child copyright © by Santi Nuñez/Stocksy.com. All rights reserved.

Author photo copyright © 2023 by Brian Adams. All rights reserved.

The author is represented by the literary agency of DeFiore & Company, www.defliterary.com.

All Scripture quotations, unless otherwise indicated, are taken from the Holy Bible, *New International Version,*® *NIV.*® Copyright © 1973, 1978, 1984, 2011 by Biblica, Inc.® Used by permission. All rights reserved worldwide. Scripture quotations marked ESV are from The ESV® Bible (The Holy Bible, English Standard Version®), copyright © 2001 by Crossway, a publishing ministry of Good News Publishers. Used by permission. All rights reserved. Scripture quotations marked FNV are reproduced from First Nations Version, copyright © 2021 by Rain Ministries, Inc. Used by permission of InterVarsity Press, Downers Grove, IL. All rights reserved. Scripture quotations marked NCB are taken from THE NEW CATHOLIC BIBLE®. Copyright © 2019 by Catholic Book Publishing Corp. Used by permission. All rights reserved. Scripture quotations marked WEB are taken from the World English Bible.

A portion of the introduction and conclusion originally appeared in the August 2021 *Plough* online article "Can Christian Singles Thrive?" A portion of chapter 2 originally appeared in the June 2021 *Christianity Today* online article "It's the Summer of Weddings. Here Are Other Milestones We Can Celebrate."

All stories shared in this book are used with author-obtained permission.

For information about special discounts for bulk purchases, please contact Tyndale House Publishers at csresponse@tyndale.com, or call 1-855-277-9400.

ISBN 978-1-64158-685-6

Printed in the United States of America

30 29 28 27 26 25 24
7   6   5   4   3   2   1

For JMF, JG, TI, DG, and all those living an unchosen singleness. And for all the friends who've shown me your family has room for me, too.

CONTENTS

INTRODUCTION

Why Another Book on Singleness?

THE WOULD-BE PRIEST CAME HOME to a surprise. Rather than the empty house he'd left, he found a strange woman there, sitting on his bed. His relatives had brought her there in hopes of changing his mind, he learned.

As of 2019 estimates, more than four in five Kenyans are Christian, almost a fourth of them Catholics.[1] But Fr. Bassols's family didn't approve of his plan to enter the priesthood. First they tried persuading him. "You will never see the foot of your blood," one relative warned. In other words, he would never have his own child.

When their words failed to persuade him, they smuggled in the woman, hoping entrapment and the allure of a female body might do what words could not.

Fr. Bassols's family demonstrates a very common view of human fruitfulness. To have a successful life, we think, you must marry and/or procreate. The Bible calls children a sign of God's blessing, after all (Psalm 127:3). How can single people fully enjoy God's favor if we can't receive such gifts from Him?

Everyone spends at least part of life alone. This single-ness foreshadows heaven, where Jesus said people won't marry

(Matthew 22:30). Yet Christians around the world still tend to treat nuclear-family life as the norm.

Many factors keep people from marriage, but the church continues to emphasize "Be fruitful and multiply" (Genesis 1:28, ESV) more than "Seek first his kingdom and his righteousness" (Matthew 6:33). And when it comes to church growth or decline, we often talk more about babies and aging than the call to "make disciples of all nations" (Matthew 28:19).[2]

This skewed, myopic picture of earthly life contributes to significant theological problems and a widespread failure to be the church singles and marrieds alike need. And it likely contributes to singles' decreased church attendance.

According to the 2022 American Religious Benchmark Survey, the share of singles who never attend church increased almost 50 percent from 2018 to 2022. As the survey authors summarized it, "The pandemic appears to have pushed out those who had maintained the weakest commitments to regular attendance."[3]

Traditionally, the church has offered one alternative to marriage: full-time ministry or missionary work. That's not a practical option for people who lack the skills, means, or, in some denominations, the "right" sex. Nor is it as feasible for those who become single later in life. And it's certainly no comfort for those angry over missing out on sex.

Singleness raises hard questions for Christians. We need to face them. Can Christian singles thrive when the partners we've lost can't return, our sexual desires cannot change, and God seems unwilling to provide the companionship for which we deeply long? Does Jesus offer a full life to people like us, too? Is the God of those who didn't choose our singleness, widowhood, divorce, or sexual identity still good? Or is a full life only guaranteed for married, straight, and nondisabled[4] people?

I begin this book weeping over another romantic disappointment. Behind my grief lies a new possibility: I may never bear children. I turn 44 in just a few months. Were this a different book on singleness, I don't know how I could go on. But this is a book about singleness when your most cherished dreams have died and yet longing persists for what you have lost or never found. This is a book about the kind of community God desires for His people. This is a book about how God provides even when we struggle with His plans for our life.

Within this book, you'll read stories of single people from all over the world. As you do, ask yourself: *Where is God in these stories? How does God glorify Himself through singles?* If we do that, these stories will help us recover a more biblical view of Christian life and community.

The demographics problem

The global church has at least eighty-five million more women than men among adults 30 and older. In the US church, women outnumber men by twenty-five million.[5] Even if some of those women have or find spouses outside the faith, that leaves millions who can't ever marry. The church has yet to face that reality.

Instead, most Christians I met on my trip around the world seemed to believe nearly all people would wed. Marrieds and singles alike seemed largely unaware of or unwilling to reckon with the church's significant demographics problem.

And the gap may be worse than it seems. Not all Christian men can or will marry. Those who do marry may not seek Christian wives. In her 2019 book *Relatable*, Vicky Walker reports that two-thirds of women she surveyed deemed a Christian spouse "non-negotiable."[6] Only half the men she surveyed were equally committed to a Christian wife. As Walker notes, that further reduces the options for Christian women.

The sex gap gets far worse as age increases. Factor in genocide, war, mass incarceration, and other factors, and women's prospects for marriage get worse yet.

By contrast, most Christians treat heterosexual marriage as the primary narrative axis in life. While in the Middle East, I heard a sermon on Ephesians 5. Wives, I learned, are God's "greatest gift outside salvation." (I don't remember what husbands were.) *And singles?* I wondered. *What of us?* Beside me sat a long-divorced grandmother.

Finally, the preacher remembered us. "Singles," he said, "take hope. You might still marry too." Even the grandmother?

Later in the trip, I heard of worse teaching. A young gay man in the American South asked his pastor for resources on singleness. In answer, the pastor said that Paul had misjudged God's timing. If the apostle had known the millennia remaining before Jesus' return, he'd have probably changed his comments on singleness.

When clergy treat singleness like that, they gravely mislead those under their care. But the problem goes beyond them. Other singles reported a lack of church role models or culturally relevant materials. And many complained that married people were mostly the ones teaching classes or special events on singleness.

All this reflects and reaffirms a false and unbiblical hierarchy. Marriage is normal and singleness abnormal, the thinking goes. Thus, too many Christians conclude that it's singles' fault that we haven't married.[7] I even heard that explicitly from a pastor. I was to blame for not having a husband, he said. I wouldn't be surprised if more women hear that than men.

What almost no one seems to consider is that singleness might actually show obedience. When women outnumber men in the church, that leaves three options: polygamy, marrying a non-Christian, or staying single. Which would you like us to choose?

Our theological problems

Misguided views of singleness contribute to significant theological problems for the church. First, and most obviously, we proclaim an incomplete theology of singleness. At its worst, this raises the question of life without marriage only in the case of gay people.[8]

Second, we weaken our theology of blessing. Christians often interpret the desire for (heterosexual) marriage as a sign of God's plans for your life. But what about the many Christians who long for justice? That desire often goes unfulfilled, at least in this life. As the book of Job shows, what God allows can raise many hard questions.

Third, treating marriage as the norm distorts our theology of purpose. All too often, Christians seek life's meaning from the narrative arc that marriage provides. (I wrestled with this in my first book, *Sexless in the City*.) But Jesus commanded all believers to seek first God's Kingdom. *That's* supposed to provide the ultimate narrative and meaning of our lives, whether married or single.

Last, the emphasis on marriage and family contributes to a flawed theology of church. The New Testament shows the church growing through evangelism. But many Christians—and churches—focus on growth by procreation. Some even teach this explicitly.[9] We also misunderstand church. Some see it as a social club. For others, it is a building or weekly event. All these miss the New Testament's clear vision: a family.

These theological problems help create a significant integration problem. When Christians treat singleness as a temporary "problem," we tend to segregate singles on the margins. The integrated church God wants requires that we accept singles as a permanent feature of life.

Our perspective problem

Pursuing God's vision for community requires a perspective change for singles, too. Most of the Christian resources we might turn to presume a young, nondisabled, heterosexual, and probably Euro-American single. This trains us to prepare for marriage or seek a contentment that verges on suppressed desire. When singles consume such offerings, we reveal something of our own beliefs and desires.

Looking back on some things I read in my early twenties, I'm struck by the parallels to dieting and shopping. Oh, how I hoped this method or that mindset could finally bring the change for which I longed. Could this new thing save me from the self and life I so despised?

It never did. How many times did I come away from some "new" perspective feeling trapped, depressed, and frustrated by all that I couldn't change? I daresay even singles with a healthier perspective sometimes fall into viewing this season as life-without. But notice the focus: It's on *what we don't have*.

The Bible does not mince words about such a focus. Just a few pages into Genesis, two perfect people start focusing on the one thing they *don't* have and can't do. Next thing we know, they've decided the thousands of things they *can* enjoy aren't enough. They simply must have the one thing that's forbidden.

They disobey God, seize the one thing they don't have, and promptly experience the first vestiges of shame. The entire human story ever since has been of our struggle to live when our lives are marked by death and the brokenness sin creates. Focusing on what you don't have can yield disastrous results.

What seeded Adam and Eve's fall? A sudden discontentment with God's incredibly generous provision for them. Paradise itself was not enough when they focused on the one small thing they couldn't have.

The apostle Paul lacked far more than pre-Fall Adam and Eve did. Yet he still found contentment. "I have learned in whatever situation I am to be content," he writes to the Philippian church. "I know how to be brought low, and I know how to abound. In any and every circumstance, I have learned the secret of facing plenty and hunger, abundance and need. I can do all things through him who strengthens me" (Philippians 4:11-13, ESV).

Paul had much less sweetness than Adam and Eve enjoyed. In some ways he faced far more trouble than they. Yet he managed to be content. What was his secret? I think it lies at the start of his letter. "I thank my God in all my remembrance of you," Paul writes (Philippians 1:3, ESV).

Similar words appear throughout his letters. Elsewhere he urges his readers to "giv[e] thanks to God the Father for everything" (Ephesians 5:20).

Early during the COVID-19 pandemic, I fell into a deep despair that may have verged on depression. My housemates had all moved to other places. My church had stopped meeting in person. I knew almost no one in the new town and state I had moved to just months before. Some days I'd hardly done anything by sundown.

Then one day, I started trying to blog about things I was thankful for.

As I did so, I discovered part of what makes gratitude so powerful. When you give thanks, you focus on *what you have.* Though many studies have shown the benefits of being grateful, it has added benefit for Christians. We believe every good gift comes from God (James 1:17). Gratitude focuses us on God's provision and generosity. Gratitude reminds us that He's good.

The journey ahead

This book started well before COVID, but it shares something in common with that gratitude lesson. As a woman who faces a possibly lifelong season of singleness, I have almost never heard or read something that shows me what *I have* in this season. Yes, I may have unsatisfied desires, but that's not all.

I—and you, whether once, now, or someday single—also have many things. We eat, sleep, and work. We have friends and housing, joy and sorrow. We don't just *have* in marriage and *lack* in singleness. We have and lack *in both seasons* but in different ways.

Many Christians dislike calling singleness a gift—with good reason. So let's flip the question: What gifts do single seasons bring? How do such times help us enjoy God and serve others? How can singles thrive, even if we didn't choose this life? And how can every Christian help the singles in his or her life thrive?

To answer those questions, I quit my job and packed up my life in the United States so I could do full-time fieldwork around the world. Over the next seventeen months, I interviewed 345 Christians from nearly fifty countries.[10] I'm not sure an organization exists that would sponsor, much less fund, such research. I therefore self-funded the project, using most of the small savings I had at the time.

Breadth over depth

Research on singleness tends to center on women of European ancestry. I believe we miss a lot of who God is when we focus on such a narrow slice of experience.[11] And, personally, more of God is the only way I can face the hardest things life has yet thrown me. So I've tried to include all of the church in this book.

To better reflect the global church, I divided my time among sixty cities across six continents. In all but Australia, I visited countries across each continent. I tried to account for differences in climate, geography, and the wealth or poverty location can bring. For practical reasons, I mostly stayed in cities.

I also aimed to interview about five people per city. My schedule didn't allow for many more than that. Nor could I linger, given my small budget. Many times I had just six or seven days to learn a new city, connect with a local church, set up interviews, and complete them.

All of the church

All who read this book will disagree with at least some of those quoted. My sources disagree with each other, too—on everything from baptism and communion to what calendar and Bibles to follow. In at least one region I visited, Christians are now at war with each other.

That's the paradox of joining God's Kingdom: We can't

control whom He invites. The movement of the Holy Spirit in Acts makes clear that God's invitations shock everyone. So I hope this book unsettles you. As I once heard Tim Keller say, possibly quoting someone else, the church does not bring together natural friends, but natural enemies. When we manage to love each other anyway, it's a miracle that testifies to Jesus' presence among us. Only Jesus could build a family from people this dysfunctional and divided.

The following chapters draw on conversations with men and women of all ages, marital histories, and major strands of Christianity. In keeping with the Bible's own approach to storytelling, I chose people based on whom they claimed to follow, not how they lived. Christians define their ties to the church differently. Some believe faith starts with a childhood baptism. Others tie it to a prayer of commitment. When I call people Christian, then, I mainly do so in a sociological sense. Only God can know the state of the heart.

As both a journalist and a committed student of the Bible, I could not choose people based on my view of their virtue or salvation. Instead, I aimed to get a good cross section of traditions and perspectives. Interviews included Palestinian teenagers and Sudanese refugees, single pastors and foster parents. I talked to people with and without disabilities and members of various sexual minorities.

Interviews entail a snapshot of people at the time. For most, five or six years passed between our interview and publication of this book. In that time, some have died, others have married or moved to new countries. I only include updates where relevant.

Most interviews took place in English. For Spanish and German, I spoke enough to ask my questions. I recorded nearly all interviews in those languages and had native speakers help translate them later.[12] (Learn more about my approach in the methodology section at the end.)

All of life

Some of my topics may surprise you as much as my sources. I don't believe faith ends at the church doors or at sundown on the day you worship. "Love the LORD your God with all your heart and with all your soul and with all your strength," Moses commanded the Israelites (Deuteronomy 6:5). Later, Jesus expressed the same idea: "If anyone would come after me, let him deny himself and take up his cross and follow me" (Matthew 16:24, ESV).

Such a commitment calls us to live increasingly integrated lives. No part of our lives should remain untouched by the love of Christ. Every part of life provides a chance to experience God and show His love in new ways.

That's why I also include some stories that may disturb you. I interviewed real people, which means they showed and reported human flaws. Some things I heard or witnessed deeply troubled me. At times, I probably couldn't get past my culture. Other things would probably trouble most people.

Here again, I've tried to follow the Bible's lead. I can't name a major human sin it leaves out. So when people courageously shared their painful stories, I included them where it made sense. Abortion, child sexual abuse, and suicide all appear in these pages.

In doing so, I hope to remind us that no darkness can withstand God's light. As Jesus said, "In this world you will have trouble. But take heart! I have overcome the world" (John 16:33).

• • •

This book argues that seeking and showing the goodness of God in *every person's single seasons* requires all of the church, both single and married alike. I hope Christians around the world read this in community: single and married, young and old, laity and clergy. However you come to this book, I hope you leave it hungrier for Jesus. May God use these pages to increase our picture of who He calls His church—the bride of Christ—to be.

One practice that consistently deepens *my* hunger for God is prayer. So throughout the book, I'll encourage you to reflect on four questions. Take a few moments now to pray about what you've just read and how you come to it. If you're not a person who follows Jesus or considers yourself religious, welcome! Hopefully these prompts inspire fruitful reflection for you, too.

What do you **grieve** in the season you're in?

What do you **have** in this season?

Is there something you need to **confess or repent of**?

What can you **give** because of this season?

PART ONE

SOCIAL AND EMOTIONAL LIFE

CHAPTER 1

COMMUNITY

How the Gospel Redefines Family

JOSH, 27, A PROTESTANT LIVING IN THE San Francisco Bay Area, made a decision. He'd let his friends come help clean his apartment.

Josh hadn't let many friends inside his space—a studio apartment—apart from his brother.

Born into a relatively secular family, Josh became a Christian at 22. Since his baptism at an East Bay Presbyterian church, he had become very involved in ministries and other events there.

At first, he drew on his many strengths. A well-paying job let him buy fancy boba drinks for a church potluck. Sometimes he played classical piano pieces before the service.

Soon, much of his social life revolved around church relationships. One of the deepest evolved with one family. Almost every week, Josh played tennis with the middle child, Scott. Sometimes Scott's dad Jonathan, a founding pastor at the church, joined them.

Such regular contact lowered Josh's guard. One day, someone in the family learned he struggled with organization. Josh's brother had moved out, and the mess in the apartment had grown harder to conquer.

"Why don't we come help?" Scott's mom, Catherine, suggested. At first, Josh balked. Letting them into his messiness seemed like too much. But Catherine kept bringing it up. And all three kids embraced the idea.

Finally he agreed. He didn't own enough chairs for everyone to sit on, but he'd let them come.

The Saturday they came over transformed his space. It shifted his view of community too.

Josh started to join the family for casual dinners sometimes, including their ritual of reading aloud. His own parents live within an hour's drive. But the St. Clairs now feel to him like part of his family too. They feel the same way about him.

•   •   •

Relationships like the one Josh and the St. Clairs share embody much of the best in Christian community. But evidence of such tight integration between singles and married people proved rare in my interviews. I set out on my research expecting to learn that Christians in other cultures handle singleness better than Americans do. To my surprise, I found otherwise. While cultural forms vary, nearly *all* of the church struggles to integrate singles well.

For the global church to become a more integrated body, we have to rethink how God's family forms community. Fortunately, we already have a great model for that.

In this chapter, we'll look at how God calls us to integrated diversity, interdependence, and shared welfare. As we proceed, I encourage you to think about how this applies in both your church, if you have one, *and* your own relationships.

Certainly, most churches could improve how they integrate singles. I hope this book helps provide some insights on that. But the smallest unit of any given community is the individual relationship. And God can bring fruit from even seemingly small changes.[1]

Whether you're single or married, working on even one relationship with someone different from you will bring more of God's Kingdom here on earth.

Recovering the church's best model for community

Christians have a brilliant and practical model of community: the human body. In his first letter to the Corinthians, the apostle Paul insists that God formed a diverse earthly body *for good reason*. Yet far too often, the church forgets or ignores what this teaching means.

To help us start to think about singles' place in Christ's body, let's go back to Paul's analogy. If you have the time, read and pray through 1 Corinthians 12 a few times. For now, I'll walk us through three key sections, one at a time. We'll then reflect on the relationship Paul describes.

First Paul paints the macro picture. "The body is one, although it has many parts; and all the parts, though many, form one body. So it is with Christ. For in the one Spirit we were all baptized into one body, Jews as well as Greeks, slaves as well as free men, and we were all given the same Spirit to drink" (1 Corinthians 12:12-13, NCB).[2] In this first section, Paul repeats the idea of *integrated diversity* several times. Yes, he says, our differences include things as big as race and wealth. Still he insists: God made us one.

Sometimes Christians embrace unity by trying to deny people's differences. In the next section, Paul explains why our differences actually *help unify* the body:

> If the whole body were an eye, how would we be able to hear? If the whole body were an ear, how would we exercise a sense of smell? But God arranged each part in the body as he intended. If all the members were identical, where would the body be? . . .
>
> The eye cannot say to the hand, "I do not need you," any more than the head can say to the feet, "I do not need you."
>
> I CORINTHIANS 12:17-19, 21, NCB

Here we start to see more of God's purpose. He didn't just assemble a diverse body to make things hard on us. He has our good in mind! Viewed the right way, our differences knit us together in *interdependence.*

Last, Paul addresses the challenge of inequality. When we start to see our differences, it often stirs up insecurity. But "God has so designed the body as to give greater honor to the more humble parts, in order that there may be no dissension within the body and each part may have equal concern for all the others. If one member suffers, all suffer together with it. If one member is honored, all the members rejoice together with it" (1 Corinthians 12:24-26, NCB). Yes, we get different lots and gifts in life, Paul says. But bodily unity persists when we remember our *interconnected welfare.*

Of all three things I've highlighted, this last one may be the hardest to accept. Especially in hyperindividual America, we delight in independence . . . or the illusion of it. But think about your own body for a minute. What happens when you get a sinus headache? Stub your toe? What happens if a cut doesn't clot or heal properly? Even small things can divert most of your attention and energy to healing what's ill. In more serious cases, the entire life of the body hangs in the balance.

The same truth holds for the church. We all have an interconnected welfare. If you're single, the health of married couples affects you. If you're married, the health of singles affects you—and that doesn't necessarily mean finding spouses for them. If you're a man, the health of God's daughters affects you. And if you're a woman, the health of God's sons affects you.

Integrated diversity

All human beings struggle with how to handle our God-given differences. In *Cross-Cultural Servanthood*, Duane Elmer says people in Western cultures often treat differences as bad. "If something is unlike me, I respond with suspicion, distance, frowning, critiquing and trying to change it (or change *you*) to look like me."[3]

Singles often feel demeaned and left out in Christian communities. But when churches get integration right, it provides a wonderful foretaste of God's community.

How we get it wrong: shaming, denying, or trying to change what's different

Christians around the world struggle with the temptation to seek first our cultures' values. Worse yet, we often spiritualize these cultural values! Thus, marriage becomes a "reward" from God.

Writer Katelyn Beaty calls this idea a sexual prosperity gospel.[4] Yet while Christians often call singleness a "gift," I've never heard it called a reward.

Language like this contributes to a feeling that singles have less worth or God loves us less. Two Protestant British women I interviewed together conveyed what many singles told me.

Theodora, 36, said her previous (charismatic) church centered on marriage. "Singleness was viewed as, like, a terrible thing. The goal was to get out of it and get married as soon as possible."

The leadership reinforced that marriage was normal, singleness abnormal. "All the role models of the faith would be married," Katy, 31, added. She, too, grew up charismatic. "It just makes you feel like you're constantly waiting to be picked off the shelf."

Many Christians and churches treat singleness as a less mature state than marriage. Across all three major Christian traditions, groups or programs for singles tend to assume youth. Filipina Protestant Rebecca, 55, said her Quezon City church focuses only on young singles. "There is no group that would cater to older women."

The assumption of youthful marriage often yields suspicion of older singles. "People think, 'If you haven't got married yet, it's because something happened to you,'" said a Spanish Catholic woman in her forties.

When we get it right: richer community

When Christians *do* build integrated relationships, they often find rich community. "I love it when I'm part of something like that and just treated as normal," said Australian Protestant Bec, 42. "It doesn't need to be a special dinner party."

Chris, a British pastor then working in Hong Kong, saw this in his church's small groups. The healthiest ones had both single and married people. One such group that also had diversity in age "has really flourished," he said. The younger people sought out an older married couple's advice on various challenges. Some of the group's leaders were "the most secure of any of the singles we've had."

Without each other, singles and married people tend to have smaller conversations, Chris said. "When singles connect with just singles, they talk about relationships and work." Married couples have similar struggles. "When you get together, everything revolves around your kids," Chris said.

Put the two in community, however, and everyone's conversations become larger. Exposure to other people's challenges draws you out of yourself and deepens empathy. Single and married people can discover surprising common ground too.

For years, I thought the pain of waiting was unique to singleness. Being in small groups with married couples has shown me how much waiting they, too, have: For illness to resolve. To find a new job. To finally conceive or buy a house.

Interdependence

Paul's metaphor shows that God gave us complementary differences. Together, we can do more than on our own. But Christians often see differences as a threat.

How we get it wrong: jealousy, suspicion, and independence

I remember one Sunday when a new woman showed up for worship team. She even had a better voice than mine! Immediately I bristled. Would I still have a part to sing? In my fear, I saw her as competition.

Singles often face similar fears. From Basel, Switzerland, to

San Antonio, Texas, I heard stories of married people's suspicion about singles—especially women. This may increase with age, when the sex-ratio gap between women and men gets larger. By age 65, women outnumber men in every country I visited. According to data IndexMundi compiled, it's most acute in Ukraine and Russia, where women outnumber men two to one in the 65-plus cohort.[5]

American Catholic widow Olga, 76, said she's sometimes left out at her San Antonio church. "I think it's that the wife has an insecurity."

Friends might even get jealous on a wife's behalf, such as Olga's married aunt. She and her husband often include Olga on trips and other outings. After someone saw her dancing with her uncle, they warned Olga's aunt.

"One evening somebody told her to be careful with me because I would probably try to take her husband away," Olga said.

Men experience this too. During my time in Atlanta, a pastor told me the Black church in America often has especially acute sex gaps. American Protestant Ronnie, 64, said he experienced this firsthand as a younger man. A church elder once told him, "You're saved, you're single, and you're employed. They see you talking to the women, you're a player. You don't talk to the women, you're gay."

A widowed Orthodox priest, 77, said dinner invitations largely stopped once his wife died.[6] "They don't understand that you need some adult companionship during the week and also that it's difficult to invite yourself into people's houses," said Fr. T., as he asked me to call him. He's lived in the same American Midwest parish for decades.

Some cultures take an especially harsh view of widows. During my trip to India, I stayed with an older Protestant widow named Rupani. "Christians will have a lot of Hindu customs," she told me. Rupani, 87, once heard a Christian friend warn a paid household helper not to let anyone "put the evil eye" on her new grandchild. Apparently, people see widows as cursed in a way and fear they could pass this to others.

"I was so shocked," Rupani recalled. "I said, 'But aren't you a Christian? Who can put the evil eye?'" Even leaders can fall prey to such thinking. Another time, Rupani attended an event where the pastor only invited married people in. Not singles or widows.

Whether clergy accept or challenge their culture has a real impact. In Nigeria, a young Pentecostal widow I met in Lagos said a pastor was the only reason she got to attend her husband's funeral. Florence, 34, said her in-laws tried to bar her from it. They blamed her for her husband's death and told the pastor she'd abandoned him.

Fortunately for Florence, the pastor insisted on hearing her side of the story. Once he did, he believed her. If not for his help, she wouldn't have been able to attend her own husband's funeral.

Kwabena Asamoah-Gyadu, president of Trinity Theological Seminary in Accra, said this happens in Ghana, too. "It's very, very common for a widow to be accused of the death of the husband," he said. "It's even worse if you do not have children. People have gone through very, very despicable things because of that." In at least one case, he said, in-laws forced a wife to stay in the same room with her dead husband for days.

Some pastors might address the issue. However, every church I visited struggled with areas where the Bible challenged cultural practices. Unless we closely study the Bible, it's easy to confuse what God wants with what our culture dictates. Culture often wins.

• • •

Competition in community can take another form: busy schedules. People in urban centers all over the world spend hours each day getting to and from work. By the time they get home, many have little time to sort out dinner, do other basic chores, and go to bed. In the morning, they start all over again.

"The busyness of people's lives tends to take over," said Canadian Protestant Patricia, 52. When her friends' kids were young and living at home, "it was kind of like, oh, they have this or that activity," she said. "Something always prevented more interaction with them."

When that happens, the burden of planning to meet often falls on single people. Many people told me how exhausting this gets. "I'm a person who likes to continually reach out to people," Patricia said. But even she grew weary of it.

"Sometimes you get to this sort of stubbornness with yourself. 'Why am I the one who's always doing this?' But if you don't, the friendship dies. So you have to decide and choose. 'Am I willing to put in more effort?' The comment often is, 'Oh, Pat, it's so great that you continue to call.' But if you wait for the other person to call, you could wait a long time."

What a single chooses to do may depend on her energy and her mood that day. "It's just that you make choices," Patricia said. "You decide."

In some cultures, a "dating" approach to friendship makes the challenge of busyness worse. We assume meeting friends requires a dinner or drinks out and spending money. We assume friendship takes disposable income and several hours of free time per visit. Viewed that way, many of us can't see friends very often.

When we get it right: vulnerability and collaboration

When we change our expectations for seeing friends, it can open up a lot of time in our schedules. As Josh's experience with the St. Clairs shows, sharing our routines can be powerful. The St. Clairs didn't do anything special when Josh came to dinner; they just set an extra space at the table.

I've had many such meals myself. Before my research, I spent a decade in the St. Clairs' church. I don't know how many times I've visited them and had Catherine offer me leftovers to eat. With that simple, humble act, she put me on equal footing with her family.

American Protestant David, 32, a single pastor in Los Angeles, said he loves how an older family he knows makes him part of daily life. On visits to their home, he might help them cook or work on other tasks. He values that.

"Sometimes they're worried about me, like, 'Are you bored?'" he said. "I love more community-based, hospitality-based cultures." He cites central Asia as an example of this. "Doing chores might not seem like quality time, but those things build relationships. Those things bless one another."

And we all have to do them. In fact, we all spend a lot of time doing chores. What if we started to view those moments as equally good times to visit with friends? On visits back to my former home in the San Francisco Bay Area (where I still have a storage unit), I now try to see more friends around errands and chores. One friend and I caught up on a Costco run. We talked while she filled her cart and I looked for items I couldn't buy in Alaska.

Other friends and a very long-suffering aunt have spent hours helping me hunt through my storage unit. Not only do we get to catch up, but their presence also transforms a potentially lonely and unpleasant task into something much better. It was the same when a friend recently joined me for an unplanned trip home to turn off the oven. Alone, I'd have given in to self-pity. With company, the mishap became a fun adventure.

Toward the end of my research, I heard a story I didn't understand at the time. While in Canada, I met with Ray Aldred, director of the Indigenous Studies Program at Vancouver School of Theology. We discussed how to approach interviews with Alaska Native and First Nations people. While advising me, Ray, who is Cree, brought up mutual relationship. Then he said something that at first seemed unrelated: "Wild horses share food. Domestic horses don't."

Not until months later did I understand. Too often, relationships involve an unspoken power dynamic. Either one party ends up always taking from the other, or one person prefers to give in ways that maintain a sense of control. As long as Josh shared out of his tennis expertise, his relationship with Scott and the St. Clairs probably felt safe in some way. Letting them come help clean his apartment changed that.

Shared welfare

In an interconnected body, all the parts work together to help when one part suffers. But in a disconnected body, we sometimes have no idea when other parts suffer.

How we get it wrong: segregation

Disconnection within the church can take multiple forms. Sometimes it starts with a good intention: programs for different ages and stages. But because of what we saw earlier, too many church singles programs leave out older people.

Filipina Protestant Lalyn, 36, said she doesn't fit any of the typical "buckets" at her Protestant church. She was too old for singles groups, too single for older groups. "I'm not able to join the older fellowship because it's for couples," she said. "I don't know where I belong."

Wealth can create another form of segregation. Many people live in spaces too small to host friends. In cities like Hong Kong, people often have live-in helpers. One Catholic Filipina helper I met had a college degree. Her Hong Kong job paid more than she could make at home. But she still had to share a tiny room behind the kitchen with another helper. It barely had room for their twin bunk bed and a small fridge.

The only way the women could see friends on their day off was outside home. Weather can make it hard to meet outdoors—whether heavy rain or extreme cold. When friends earn different incomes, it can be hard to meet at a restaurant.

A church group I met with in Tanzania said marriage improved women's economic standing.[7] Married couples all over the world also enjoy savings in many forms. For example, Anchorage households pay a flat water charge, no matter how much they use. The garbage company charges based on bin size, but singles still struggle to fill the smallest one. All this can make group meals a challenge.

"I budget quite well, so it doesn't look like I don't make a lot of money," said a Canadian Catholic, 24. Robin, as she asked me to call her, doesn't like it when people want to split a group dinner bill evenly. That usually costs her more. "I don't feel pressured to go along with the group," she said. But it sounded like money sometimes limits her ability to socialize with friends who want to eat out.

Talking about differences in wealth isn't easy. But differences don't go away just because we ignore them. The early churches of Acts achieved their remarkable community because they *talked* about the inequality. They became a spiritual family because those with more shared with those who had less.

Getting it right: ways to share

When we acknowledge our shared welfare, the needs and joys of some become everyone's concern. This takes many forms.

For friends, it might mean meeting for a walk. Or they may cook dinner or have the poorest friend choose the restaurant. Maybe sometimes a richer friend treats. Chris, the pastor in Hong Kong, said his church let helpers meet in their space. That gave them an indoor space that didn't require a purchase.

My old church in California provided childcare for many events. That gave parents—especially single parents—an equal chance to attend. My Alaska church provides a van service. They also encourage those with cars to offer rides to others.

Recognizing our shared welfare can also mean rethinking our conversations. At a large South African small group I attended, we discussed friendship between married people and singles. Many in the group seemed surprised to hear what each had assumed about their other friends. Single friends often assumed their married friends were too busy to meet. Married people assumed singles would be bored doing something with their family.

A Canadian Protestant church intern in Toronto, 28, said he sees this during the after-service coffee hour. "Most people hate talking to married people. They don't know how to talk to them," said Kingsley.

Chris, the pastor, echoed this. "It's very difficult when you're single to break in" to the married circle, he said. "It's like this little castle, unless the married people put down the drawbridge."

In one group discussion in Dar es Salaam, Tanzania, several people said single people don't have much to offer their married friends. Through a translator, they said you need firsthand experience to give a married person advice. Needless to say, they weren't Catholic!

Chris argued otherwise. "You actually need people outside your marriage that you can share and talk with," he said. "I don't think you actually need to be married to understand the basic issues of marriage. All the issues are basically the same. My selfishness is my selfishness. My heart issues were exactly the same when I was single as when I'm married. They just come out in different ways."

What would happen if more churches thought along those lines? I imagine groups for mothers often address issues like identity, patience, and time management (not to mention dealing with difficult people!). But single women, especially those who work full-time, face those challenges too. What would happen if women came together around their challenges rather than their present roles or contexts?

"In Christ Jesus you are all sons of God, through faith," Paul wrote. "There is neither Jew nor Greek, there is neither slave nor free, there is no male and female, for you are all one in Christ Jesus" (Galatians 3:26, 28, ESV). When we honor that equality in our friendships, there's no telling how Father, Son, and Holy Spirit might show up in someone different from you.

• • •

As we finish this look at community, take a few minutes to think about your relationships.

What do you **grieve** about your relationships?

What kind of friendships and community do you **have** right now?

Is there something you need to **confess or repent of**?

What can you **give** through relationship?

Travel as a Single Woman

FROM THE START OF PLANNING THIS RESEARCH, I faced a grim possibility. I could get raped. Not assaulted, or even violated. Raped.

I didn't dare soften the worst possibility. I had to face the full, awful risk my trip held. Was I willing to research this book even if it cost me *that*?

By the standards of many previous generations, and not a few modern cultures, I set out to do the unthinkable for a woman. I planned multiple months of globe-spanning travel *alone*. On some of my Middle East stops, women marveled at or envied my travels. Many of them would spend their whole lives under men's protection and power.

The men in my life gave me their blessing to set out with God alone beside me. I ultimately visited seventy-five cities in forty-one countries across six continents. God alone explains how I made it home so relatively unscathed.

I spoke only one language fluently: English. German I spoke passably but could use in only two or three countries. I learned most of my limited Spanish on the road.

I had good health but almost no self-defense skills. I've never served in the military or learned to throw a punch. My sole safety training consisted of a two-hour training in Krav Maga, an Israeli self-defense method. I learned it's sometimes okay to fight dirty. I did not learn how to do so. The only tip I used afterward was to put my back to a wall any time I stopped to look at my phone, especially in public.

I didn't even pack lightly should I have to flee at some point. My backpack always weighed close to or slightly over the airline's bag limit (usually fifty pounds or twenty-three kilos). The suitcase I deemed my "carry-on" whenever possible weighed close to thirty pounds (about thirteen kilos).

Beyond luggage, I also had bags. On my left shoulder, I slung a giant canvas tote bag. I sometimes passed this off as my "purse" when needed, though it often weighed close to twenty pounds. To balance it out, I had another ten or more pounds packed into the real purse that hung from my right shoulder. Another small bag often hung beneath my coat. This led to some very sweaty train-station transfers. I often prayed I wouldn't sprain an ankle.

If my trip were an animal tale, you'd have to cast a chick or duckling as me. Who else packs sourdough starter for a world trip? Who packs *sewing* patterns and carries a piece of art to share with each host along the way? I'm sure many people shook their heads at me. They weren't wrong to do so.

But I'd learned something from two earlier trips to India. The summer I turned 22, I spent ten days in Andhra Pradesh on a short-term mission trip. Many people prayed for us. Despite significant cultural differences, I had a powerful experience of God on that trip. (See more in my first book, *Sexless in the City*.) I left India with a newfound love for the best of its culture.

Seven years later, I took a shorter trip to Mumbai, alone. This time I visited a college friend. I tried but failed to find Christians to connect with during my short stay. And since it was a vacation, not a mission trip, I didn't ask many people to pray.

As my flight descended the first day, I got the worst sinus headache of my life. It lasted for days. Things got so bad I finally saw an ayurvedic doctor. Not until I saw and heard the chanting plug-in device in the exam room did I wonder what spiritual environment I'd entered. I spent all of that short session in desperate, silent prayer.

After I left, my headache improved. But that night I had a strange dream about an animal trying to bite me. I prayed as if it were a demonic attack.

At my lowest point, I thought, *I could fall into a sewer drain and no one would find or miss me.* It was an awful feeling. I've never been so ready to fly home from a trip. And I've never traveled the same way since. No matter where or why I go, I always connect with the local church. As much as I can, I ask people to pray.

Maybe I should have been more afraid or cautious in my research travels. I had a lot to lose. But memories of another trip helped anchor me. The summer I turned 33, I went to Peru— alone, but mostly visiting family or friends. Toward the end, a friend offered me a city tour on my most feared mode of transportation: a motorcycle. I didn't even get to wear a helmet.

As I considered my fate that day, I faced a weighty question: Did I trust God? He might let me come home maimed or dead.

Or He could let me have a great adventure, safely. He was good either way, but I couldn't foresee His will. Did I trust Him?

Setting out on this trip was no different. It just involved a much longer journey.

CHAPTER 2

CELEBRATIONS

Rethinking Communal Gratitude

THE MEAL DIDN'T START AS A CELEBRATION. Monica and her friends from a Bucharest rock-climbing gym had gathered to cook dinner again. This time, though, they decided to have Andrei lead. Born with cerebral palsy, Andrei normally sat and watched the others cook. He could walk and even run, but he often felt self-conscious about his disability.

From an early age, Andrei had felt judged for the ways he's different. "I *am* different," he said. "I run differently, I walk differently, I cut potatoes differently." In response, he tried to avoid attention—even at the group's dinners. "I just stayed in my seat, did what was comfortable."

Monica said the others reinforced this without meaning to. "In our culture, there's this mentality of 'Don't ask him to do that. Don't you see that he's disabled?'"

All that changed the night they asked Andrei to lead the cooking. The more he tried, the more he learned he could do. Monica's encouragement helped, he said. "She doesn't consider different bad." When she saw how Andrei cut the potatoes, she said, "Wow, I like that."

The dinner became a celebration of Andrei's newfound skill . . . and something more.

The friends weren't all Christians. But two of them, Monica and another friend, had previously formed a close bond with some other Orthodox women. Monica calls them her "agape group." For several years, they ate together most Sundays.

Monica and her friend sought something similar with the rock-climbing gym crowd. At first, it was just about fun adventures, like the times they tried to make sushi. But as Andrei began to participate more fully, the group's bond grew deeper.

Sometimes they talked about faith. Monica and her friend from the first agape group shared honestly. And little by little, more people in the group began to come to church with them. Even Andrei, who hadn't attended since childhood.

•　　•　　•

For many people, celebrations laud relational milestones: marriages, births, anniversaries, kids' birthdays. These are certainly good things. But when they're *most* of what we celebrate, it leaves out singles and those who don't or can't have children. This drives home a message that married people *have*, while singles *lack*. That married people have things to celebrate, while single people do not.

But celebration shows gratitude. For Christians, it's part of how we thank God for His providence. Celebrations also show us who we are. In Romans 12:15, Paul says Christians should share each other's joys. If we see and celebrate God in only married people's lives, we miss a huge swath of divine activity. Doesn't God do marvelous, amazing, wonderful works in single people too?

Of course He does! To see more of our creative God, we have to rethink what we celebrate.[1]

An easy place to start broadening your celebration is by following the church calendar. Orthodox and Catholic Christians celebrate some different feasts than Protestants do. Because of that, I'm going to focus on five main seasons that all three traditions share: Advent, Christmas, Lent, Easter, and Ordinary Time. The Orthodox call these Nativity Fast, the Nativity/Theophany season, Great Lent, Paschal season, and the post-Pentecost season.

Together, these seasons remind us that *all* Christians, single and married alike, belong in God's family. We all have much to celebrate. We all have many ways to rejoice and weep together. For even when we weep, we weep with hope in God's future goodness.

Advent: the season of longing

Most singles I interviewed want to be married. That means we're very familiar with longing. For many of us, especially in the United States, the weeks before Christmas stir up that longing even more. That's when the cards start arriving. And the pictures appear online.

The form changes with technology, but family photos remain a constant. Several women said they struggled with this custom. "It has really challenged me to see my worth not where I'm at in life, but to see myself with the eyes of God," said Rosina, 42, a single Protestant pastor in Europe. She asked that I not identify her country.

For others, it raises questions of maturity. "Sometimes I ask myself, 'What if I'm single forever?'" said G., 34, an American Protestant who wanted to use her first initial. (We met in North Africa,[2] where she hosted me.) "At some point, do I start sending Christmas cards?"

If one sent such a card, what to put on it? "The normal format does not work," Rosina said. She usually sends a photo from the year, along with a short, handwritten note.

G. had a similar approach. But her globe-spanning travels made the choice more difficult. "I don't want to be rubbing it in," she said. Sending a Christmas card as a single person was probably "a bit snobby," she thought.

For a Japanese Protestant, 36, the family photo cards come around New Year's. "Since that's something I wish I would have, the cards kind of spotlight what I don't have," she said.

"I think it distracts me from being mindful of what good I've received," said Yoshiko, as she asked me to call her. "That can be destructive. It's not that I haven't changed or that I didn't receive anything for that year." If she sends a card of her own, it might have a family picture. "That lets others know we've had another good year."

Married or not, year-end photos can become a serious business. But at least in the United States, you sometimes get that rare gem: the *themed* year-end card. (These often have some humor.) The typical, family-focused cards inadvertently convey, "You're in the club if you have a family too." But the more creative, themed cards send a different message: "You're in the club if you get the joke."

Years ago, I lived with several singles who went to a different church. I knew two of their church friends from the goofy Christmas cards on the side of our fridge. For several years, the two bachelor roommates sent an annual Christmas card.

On year two, one man's girlfriend joined the card. They gave themselves a family name that combined all three last names. Perhaps to cement the tradition, the couple eventually married. The husband moved in with his wife, naturally. But the couple continued their annual card tradition with the now-former roommate.

Each year they get more creative. They've spoofed exercise videos and magazine covers. One year, they were a dance group. Another time, a rock band. After twelve years, they made a calendar.

The couple now has two children. The other roommate has stayed single. But he's firmly ensconced in their now-epic Christmas card tradition. Beneath all the humor, it tells a very biblical story about what God's family looks like. If most cards whisper, *Long for a family like this*, the Yoopers' card has a different message: *Long for friends like these. Long for community like this. Long for the God who makes such community.*

Christmas: God is with us

Christmas should be one of the most joyful times of the year. During this season, we celebrate God's coming to dwell with humans. In Jesus, humans could see, smell, touch, and hold God for the first time. So, naturally, God's enemy does everything he can to drag our focus elsewhere.

The busyness can look different whether you're single or

married. Some people said the holiday frenzy actually makes them grateful for singleness.

"There are never any fights about where to celebrate," said Chris, 43, an Australian Protestant.

"It's way less complicated 'cause you're not balancing two families," said Tina, 32, an American Catholic living in Iowa.

Sometimes, though, singleness means your family expects even more. Tina's family expected near-perfect attendance at holiday gatherings. "I only got away with Thanksgiving at a friend's because of the new baby," she said.

For Rosina, the busyness comes from her work as a pastor. "It's a big gift to me, too, to have all the services," she said. In this, Christmas holds a tension. "The church is not the most single-friendly culture."

But in God's mercy, our failings can't thwart His expansive plan for the church. "They are feasts for everybody," Rosina said. "Christmas is Christmas for everybody."

Our celebrations don't always show that. Christmas programs tend to highlight families. So do Christmas Day observances. Some singles said they have only a parent to celebrate with. They wondered what Christmas will look like when that person dies.

"The only holiday I could say is lonely is Christmas," said Kenyan charismatic Maureen, 39. Most of her family is Muslim and doesn't celebrate Christmas. Only her mom shares Maureen's faith.

Other singles live far from family and can't afford to travel. To avoid spending Christmas Day alone takes rethinking with whom we celebrate.

One simple idea to consider: a drop-in meal that anyone can attend. Melody, 36, said Protestant friends in Vancouver host an "open brunch" on Christmas Day. Anyone can come, "which is amazing," she said. "It feels like 'Oh, there's a place for me.'"

Anyone could host such a gathering. "We sometimes think families' responsibility is to provide space," Melody said. "We can't expect it. We singles also need to provide this thing for ourselves."

Lent: forty days to lament and repent

During the next major season after Christmas, Christians spend forty days in lamentation and repentance. Many also fast from something during Lent. (We'll talk more about this in chapter 6.) Some churches even stop using the word *hallelujah* until Easter.

"Lament helps us move toward receiving joy," said Kim, 32, an American Protestant living in Canada. "We see that in the Psalms: 'Those who sow in tears will reap in joy.'"[3]

Kim once helped her Vancouver church with a course on singleness. In it, they discussed how lament and celebration fit together. "I don't think in this life you can honestly have one without the other," she said. "Sometimes the celebration is not for here, but we hold on to the someday."

"For those of us who are single," she added, "it's important to find those places where you can grieve, lament, take your hurt to God and say all the things." Shortly before our interview, Kim went through a deeply painful breakup. "We insist hope and joy are the endgame, what we're moving towards, what undergirds us," she said. "Lament helps us stay open to hope and joy."

In 2020, American Protestant musicians Poor Bishop Hooper— a married couple—started writing new songs for all 150 psalms. In an interview with *Christianity Today*, the couple discussed how the sad psalms affected them.

"'When I sing the laments, even when everything in my life is great, it opens my eyes to intercessory prayer. To see that the world is a broken world,' [husband] Jesse Roberts said. 'There will always be something that I can lament over.'"[4]

In *A Sacred Sorrow*, Michael Card goes further. "If you and I are to know one another in a deep way, we must not only share our hurts, anger, and disappointments with each other (which we often do), we must also lament them together before the God who hears and is moved by our tears. . . . If I am not interested in your hurts, I am not really interested in you. Neither am I willing to suffer *to know* you nor to be known by you."[5]

One year, I told my prayer team I planned to fast the weekend of Valentine's Day. The second day, a married friend texted me to say she was doing a partial fast with me to pray for me and one other person. Few acts have moved me like her cosuffering sacrifice that day.

Whatever our lives look like, Lent helps all Christians weep with those who weep. For those of us who mourn, it helps us find company in our sorrow.

Easter: Jesus' victory over death

All Christians celebrate Jesus' resurrection, though the date and length of the celebration varies. For some Christians, Easter Sunday also includes a renewal of baptismal promises. These typically include promises to renounce sin and Satan and affirmations of the Apostles' Creed.

For each promise, the priest or pastor asks a question about commitments or beliefs. The baptized respond, "I do." Colin, 47, an American Catholic, said this holds special importance for him as a single man.

Many Catholics said they struggle with the question of vocation. "Single people get really lost and fall through the cracks," Colin said. "My sense of vocation comes from the baptismal vows."

Like many Catholic and Orthodox Christians, Colin was baptized as an infant. But he finds the Easter vow-renewal meaningful.

After our interview, Colin texted me: "It's baptism that gives us our identities, not our marital status." When he reminded me that baptismal vows also take the form of "I do," this made much more sense. If repetition shows importance, how appropriate that Catholics reaffirm baptismal vows far more often than they do their marital vows!

Colin said renewing his baptismal vows points him back to Jesus' last words on earth: "Go and make disciples of all nations, baptizing them in the name of the Father and of the Son and of the Holy Spirit, and teaching them to obey everything I have commanded you" (Matthew 28:19-20).

"That's my vocation. And anybody can do that, any Christian can share the good news of Jesus with people."

Most of us can list things we *say* we believe or value. But our actions often reveal somewhat different beliefs and values. How Easter compares to your other celebrations shows a lot about what you value most.

Ordinary Time

After the season of Pentecost, the church enters what some call Ordinary Time. (The Orthodox celebrate a few more feasts during this season.) Many ordinary moments merit thankfulness and celebration, but Christians often default to certain milestones. For some singles, these can be some of the year's hardest events.

Birthdays

"Birthdays I avoid like the plague," said Martin, 59, a South African Pentecostal man who attended a church for motorcyclists. Even as a child, he didn't like birthdays, he said. "If somebody has a birthday, I don't wish them a happy birthday." He hopes this makes them forget his.

"It's pretty screwed up," Martin conceded, "but at least I know why I do it." In part, it's probably a denial of aging, he said.

Many women find birthdays a burden. "You're the one who has to plan the celebration," said Dani, 40. For that reason, the Australian Protestant didn't do much to celebrate her fortieth birthday. "I think it's part of my nature," she said. "We don't like asking people to celebrate things with us because it feels like a bit of an imposition or a 'Hey, look at me.'"

Rosina agreed. "If you don't do anything, nothing's going to happen."

I suspect planning gets harder with age. In your twenties, fewer friends have married. People get together often. It's easy to celebrate birthdays when you're already planning to meet. But standing plans tend to evaporate once more people marry and have families.

Sometimes, in that mystery of divine providence, God Himself makes the plans. Laura, 44, said, "God always gives me special things on my birthday, without me planning." I met the Argentine Christian in Jerusalem. Laura didn't specify a tradition. She had moved to the city from England for several months of volunteer service.

On her most recent birthday, Laura worked all day in a Jerusalem bakery. The day before, a wedding party celebrated until midnight. But the couple left behind the cake and cupcakes. So all the other people working sang to Laura in all their different languages. It ended up being like a big party. "It really made my day," she said.

"God is good, and He knows what makes us happy," she said. "I was tired from working all day. I couldn't prepare for myself anything, so He made everything for me. It was very unforgettable."

In my Anchorage church, the pastor always asks if anyone has a birthday that week. If so, we sing to them. Some churches also offer a blessing. When we celebrate others' lives and births this way, it affirms our bonds as a spiritual family.

Graduation

After a child's birth, graduation is one of the next major events that communities often celebrate. We seem to assume most learning happens in youth, however.[6] This may be why singles in some communities and cultures struggle with graduations. Several of those I interviewed said they didn't feel supported when they reached major educational milestones.

When Jamie, as she asked me to call her, finished medical school, she invited lots of people. Only one came to the ceremony.[7] "Everybody else had family things," the 33-year-old Protestant said. "So I never actually had a graduation party. That was very sad for me."

"On Facebook, you post a photo and hundreds of people will 'like' it and post congratulations." But it's not the same as having others show up in person to help you celebrate.

Jamie, who is Indian Canadian, had two things working

against her. First, she has four degrees. Her family thinks that's "too many." Second, she hasn't married. "In the Indian culture, having a daughter in her thirties who's single is a shame to the family." That extends to their diaspora community in Canada. Within that culture, Jamie said, it's embarrassing for parents to celebrate an unmarried daughter.

A few months after she graduated, someone at her Protestant church found out. "Why didn't you tell us?" they asked. But Jamie told me she didn't want something done out of pity. It's hard to figure out when and how to interact with others. "Singleness hits you in other ways—not just you sitting and feeling lonely," she said.

Dani told me of a similar disappointment when she got her doctorate. "I love the people who came, and I was so glad to see them," she said. But despite three months' notice, only a few people came to celebrate one of her life's costliest and greatest achievements. Dani drove home fighting tears.

In hindsight, she thought she should have told her friends how important the event was. But that, too, hurts. You don't have to say how much a wedding or birth matters; people grasp that.

To Melody, whose friends host the Christmas brunch, this shows a small view of celebration. "The only things in the Christian church that are celebrated are relationally based," she said. "We need to also celebrate when someone is sober this long." I think I also heard of a church celebrating when an adult man learned to read.

"As single people, we kind of get left out of the celebration game completely," Melody said. "What can we declare and know that God is for us and that our community is for us?"

Other celebrations

For Kat, 25, an American Catholic, small celebrations happen most often with a group of friends from a former job. Over the past four or five years, the mostly Christian group has developed a regular routine of gathering. They've celebrated completion of major craft projects and looking at the stars together. Once, they even celebrated when one person found replacements for a beloved set of cups that all broke.

"We don't have to do big things in order to have a life full of joy and full of love," Kat said in a phone interview. "We don't have to have these ground-shaking moments in our lives all the time in order to share time and company and be exuberant in our lives.

"So much of what I see in the world is this idea that we have to reserve ourselves. We have to reserve celebration for things that are often either focused on material success or married life and children."

Kat's friends see it differently. "There's a recognition that we should celebrate not just big events, but small things. We can bring specialness; we can bring joy and happiness into small things we do."

Steve, 27, an Orthodox Palestinian I met in Jerusalem, said something similar. "It's not only celebrating anniversaries and birthdays," he told me. "It's also something you've worked hard on, something you've wanted a long time."

When Steve got a raise and promotion at work, his brother wanted to throw him a party. But Steve calls himself the quietest one in most groups. He tried to have his brother accept a beer at home instead. The scale of celebration didn't matter. To him it was more important that "you have other people that would be happy for you and with you."

For Malin Lindroth, a Protestant Swedish writer, those moments are book releases. She has a party each time a new book comes out. "Maybe I appreciate them more than other writers," she said. "I think you get better at celebrating little stuff along the way."

Nicholas, 31, an Orthodox American, said he learned this helping his dad recover from an aneurysm. His dad had lost so many skills that at first someone always had to be with him. "We realized we had to look at the smaller victories in his recovery."

The aneurysm caused numerous physical and cognitive problems. His dad doesn't always get Nicholas's name right or know when to use words like *wife* versus *sister*. But recently, he'd correctly identified someone he hadn't seen in a long time.

Such moments prompt family celebration, Nicholas said. If things are going well, he might take his dad out for a ride in the car. Even Alaska's largest city, where they live, offers wonderful mountain views. If a drive doesn't work, they find another way to celebrate in the moment.

•　•　•

One of the most important celebrations of my early adulthood involved a great disappointment. Two years after moving to New York City, I reconnected with an old crush via the internet. Eventually, I found an excuse to visit his part of the West Coast. We had dinner. I met his family.

Thinking he wouldn't pursue me unless I lived closer, I interviewed for two jobs near him. (I had been unemployed for several months.) Before I went home, the man's mother prayed about my job search. She asked God to plant me where He wanted to plant me.

Her prayer unsettled me. But it prompted one of my own. No

matter what the two companies chose, I asked God to help me rejoice. (The first had already told me no.)

I didn't hear back until I'd returned to New York's wintry chill. The second firm chose someone else too.

My stomach dropped when I heard. A long stretch of depression loomed up in front of me. How would I support myself now? Worse, how could I hope for romance with that man when he lived three thousand miles away? If nothing happened with him, would I even marry?

Then I remembered. *You wanted to rejoice in this news.* I did. I'd even asked God to help me. But how could I rejoice in what seemed like the worst possible outcome?

In the end, it took a small party. Numbly, I made a short shopping list, then pulled on my winter garb. If I had to celebrate bad news, then I'd have to make cake. And drink sangria.

After that, something strange happened. My spirits lifted. I made the food and drink of celebration. Then I ate and drank to God's will for me, and the good I couldn't yet see.

Over the next several months, the man and I grew apart. But I also grew closer to God. I got that miracle in the writing world: a book deal. And almost two years after those jobs fell through, I moved to California. My book paid for that move. And a California church planted one year after my "bad" news became one of my richest communities.

God really *did* have my good in mind. Celebrating that goodness, even when His plan seemed cruel, helped me trust Him until I *saw* His goodness at last. Many times since, I've recreated that memory in the face of new doubts. I pull out a glass. And I pour a small toast. Then I drink to the goodness I can't yet see.

• • •

What do you **grieve** when you think about celebration? Are there parties you've long hoped to hold, but never gotten to? Who might need you to grieve with them?

What do you **have**? How can you celebrate what God *has* given you? Can you celebrate the good you don't yet see in God's provision?

Is there something you need to **confess or repent of**?

What can you **give**? How could your celebrations point others to God and enlarge your shared picture of Him?

How to Get into Russia without a Visa

I STARTED MY TRIP IN THE EASIEST REGION: Europe. Great mass transit, frequently spoken English, and no visas to obtain. Well, *almost* no visas.

As I'd read once, and noted in a multipage Google spreadsheet, Russia required a visa. European travel had always been so easy that I soon forgot this.

Instead, I fretted over the ongoing strain between that country and mine. Could those tensions affect my border crossing? What about other in-person encounters?

I *didn't* consider how enmity translates to paperwork and bureaucracy. It turned out I couldn't even *apply* to visit Russia until I made a friend there. A friend who could sponsor me.

Unfortunately, I learned of this just two weeks before I'd hoped to visit Russia. As person after person told me, singleness lets you make faster decisions. So I often didn't start arranging things for the next city until shortly before I wanted to visit. This almost doomed my Russia visit.

Then I joined a free walking tour in Bucharest. During a break, talk turned to the 2018 World Cup. Several in the group had tickets. We all came from different countries, but at last I had to ask: "What did you do about the visa?"

"Oh, you don't need a visa," a tall, blond backpacker told me.

"You don't?!!"

"No, you just buy a ticket. Then they issue you something called a Fan ID, and that gets you into the country."

Hope started to stir in me. Would I get to visit Russia that summer after all? *And* see a World Cup game?

That night I joined the online ticket queue. By that point in the sporting match, sales had slowed. They only predicted a forty-five-minute wait before I could use the website!

The moment arrived. I had never bought sports tickets online, but I started to figure out the matrix of dates and prices. After several error messages, I finally got a ticket for a game the week I wanted to visit Russia. And it cost less than a visa!

A few days later, I boarded a night train for Moscow, entry paper in hand. The guard at the wee-hours crossing spoke little English. Thankfully, a bunkmate spoke some of both our languages. He helped translate my team-country answers into Russian.

Just as someone warned me before I left Bucharest, I needed more than the ticket. I also needed to memorize its key details: the date, teams, and so on.

Once I gave the border guard enough correct answers, he stamped my passport with a train-entry icon. We continued onward to Moscow.

Not until the day before the game did I learn the guard had spared me a question I couldn't answer: *where* my game was.

I, great sports fan that I am, thought the World Cup worked like the Olympics. As everyone knows, the main events occur in and around one main city. (Right?) Hadn't Brazil just hosted the World Cup in Rio de Janeiro?

It had. But I hadn't watched any games or read much coverage. The day before my Sunday match, my Moscow host asked what time the game was. I checked my ticket. "Six o'clock."

"Ah. Church isn't until three," she warned me.

I pondered this. Normally I try to treat Sunday as a Sabbath, but it had emerged as a key day for meeting potential interviewees. This usually happened *after* the service.

Sensing my dilemma, my host pressed further. "Do you know what stadium it's at?"

I had to check the ticket. "Ekaterinburg."

"Hmm." My American host had only lived in Moscow a few months. "I know Ekaterinburg is a city, but I'm not familiar with that stadium."

This time I consulted my official World Cup booklet. The booth where I got it had run out of English copies, so mine was in French . . . which I don't read.

Eventually, I found Ekaterinburg in a list of stadia including that of St. Petersburg—so far north of Moscow that I'd later take a night train there.

With a sinking feeling, I suddenly recalled the graphic of Russia I'd seen in a German train magazine. I can read some German, but I'd been too lazy and uninterested to look closely. I mistook that German piece for a travel feature on places one might *visit* while in Russia for the World Cup.

I now realized it showed all the Russian cities *hosting* World Cup matches. My Sunday night match? Not in Moscow. Not even close to Moscow. Almost twenty-four hours east by car, in fact.

And that is how I got into Russia for far less than a visa would have cost but missed attending my World Cup game in Siberia.[8] Even most Russians laughed at that.

CHAPTER 3

LEISURE

What We Need to Really Rest

LANRE HAD REACHED A CRISIS. Nearly every month, the Nigerian Pentecostal man, 27, got sick. His doctor said his blood pressure was too high for someone so young.

"I was losing control of my time," the young marketer told me. "Before you know it, I'm divided in different parts." Like many in his country, Lanre worked for himself. To survive in the largest city of Africa's most populous country, you have to hustle. So, like many on that continent, Lanre didn't really take vacations.

As the firstborn—and a son—Lanre felt a particular drive to succeed. Especially in the African countries I visited, young men said they needed money to marry. (Some of this related to cultural practices.)

Like many people, Lanre had to balance financial goals with day-to-day needs.[1] He sometimes helped a younger sister in college. In some African countries, people joked to me about what they called the "black tax."[2] The continent has a growing middle class. But wealth is rare enough that, when someone in your family does well, relatives expect them to help all of you.

Lanre was one of the more successful ones. With all these pressures, he often found it hard to say no. And once he says yes, he feels a commitment to follow through. His duties at church compounded this.

When I asked about Sabbath, Lanre said he doesn't do "*work* work" on Sundays. But clearly, his church "work" kept him busy. Even hearing from God had grown difficult.

At last, the signs of burnout became acute. "I thought I might drop if I continued," Lanre said. So even though he had to give up two weeks' work and income, he took a vacation.

• • •

Workaholism tempts anyone who's willing to seek security in wealth or find their meaning in work. When singles struggle to rest, it often involves different challenges from those that married people face.

Many of us have no kids to pick up. No one calls us to ask, "When are you coming home?" Sometimes bosses expect us to work more hours than those with families. Even if they don't demand this, we ourselves can struggle to stop.

Other singles work long hours because of great need. Single parents often struggle to cover all their monthly costs. Even those who can think beyond necessity often have to save longer for a house than a married couple might. Many other things often cost more for one than when a couple or family can share them.

All this makes the fourth commandment that much more radical. *God calls us to rest.* He calls for a rest from work every seven days. And He calls us to rest in community. As I learned, that goes beyond weekly church attendance.

For the global church to become a more integrated body, we have to rethink how God's family rests. In this chapter, we'll look at three things that can help singles (and, really, all Christians) become better resters: land, companions, and equity.

The challenge and importance of connecting to land

One of our greatest resources for rest took me by surprise: the earth. I did not expect to discuss land in this book, apart from describing my travels. I'm writing about community and human relationships, after all. I didn't think the earth offered much that's essential to existence, apart from food and water. I certainly didn't think I needed the earth to connect with *God*, even though He made me from the ground and will return me to it someday.

God has used this book to teach me otherwise. Through it, I've come to see a major theme in the Bible that I'd overlooked. Just as we'll learn with food, the earth plays a significant role in how God wants us to connect with Him. It's especially vital for learning about and trusting God.

Our yearning for the earth

My interviews suggest that singles can have a harder time connecting with God through creation. "Beach vacations are for couples," as one woman put it.

I sunburn easily and swim poorly, so at first I didn't notice how often people seek to vacation at the beach. But it came up in many interviews. Africans seemed to vacation less than people on any other continent. But even they talked about the beach. In landlocked Nairobi, Kenyans said if they *did* go away, they might visit coastal Mombasa.

In South Africa, a woman who worked in a township near Johannesburg planned her first-ever vacation in Durban. It has beaches. "I want to have some me time. To just find myself again," said a Protestant single mother, 28. "I want to hear the air blow me away from the left and the right."

Several singles said they find the beach hard to visit alone. As one Spanish Catholic woman put it, "Who is going to look after my things?" You can't take your phone or money into the water with you. You can only take your body and whatever clothes you wear.

Indeed, swimming is one of the most elemental ways we experience God's creation. That's probably part of why God chose baptism as a sign to mark our commitment to Him. To plunge yourself into water, you have to let go of everything else. In perhaps his greatest act of faith, Peter stepped into very deep water toward Jesus. No human effort could buoy him up.

Centuries earlier, God worked one of His greatest miracles by moving aside the body of water that stood between the Israelites and freedom. And when Jonah seemed to face the worst fate—immersion in the sea—God did it again, this time providing safety beneath the water.

Why we need the earth

During the past few months of writing, I've been shocked by how much I worry. Despite all that God has done for me, I fret constantly about getting my deepest needs met. In those few, fleeting moments when I manage to trust God, I feel light. I can rest.

But that's hard, no matter how faithful God's proved Himself. So lately, I turn to the Bible's advice on worry. What does Jesus say about how to fight it?

> "This is why I am telling you not to be troubled about getting enough to eat or drink, or what to wear. Is eating, drinking and clothing yourself all there is? Does your life not have more meaning than this?
>
> "Look to the winged ones who soar on the wind. Do they plant seeds and gather the harvest into a storehouse? No! But your Father from above gives them plenty to eat. Do you not know he cares even more for you? Can worry add even one more step to the length of your life's journey?
>
> "Why do you trouble yourself with what to wear? Have you seen how the wildflowers grow in the plains and meadows? Do you think they work hard and long to clothe themselves? No! I tell you not even the great chief Stands in Peace (Solomon), wearing his finest regalia, was dressed as well as even one of these.
>
> "If Creator covers the wild grass in the plains with such beauty, which is here today and gathered for tomorrow's fire, will he not take even better care of you? Why is your faith so small? There is no need to say, 'What will we eat? What will we drink? What will we wear?' This is what the Nations who have lost their way have given their hearts to, but your Father from above knows you need these things.

"If you will make Creator's good road your first aim, representing his right ways, he will make sure you have all you need for each day. So do not worry about tomorrow's troubles. It is enough to trust Creator to give you the strength you need to face today."

MATTHEW 6:25-34, FNV

Take a minute to reread that once or twice. Maybe take a deep breath in between. Chances are, we could *all* stand to pause and reflect on Jesus' words. I've spent most of my life reducing this text to poetic metaphor. I've read it as if Jesus chose birds and lilies as colorful symbols. So when source after source kept telling me how they relaxed in nature, I missed the earth's role. How could land matter so much? People vacation in cities, too, after all.

But then I remembered the book of Job. For more than thirty chapters, Job and his friends debate the cause of his sudden heartbreak. His wealth gone. Ten children killed in a house collapse. His health vaporized in painful boils. And all this in a couple of days. What kind of God would do that? Or had Job somehow earned this? Round and round they go.

Finally, in chapter 38, God speaks. He spends four chapters calling Job, in vivid detail, to closely examine the earth and its creatures. That's it. That's the majority of God's answer: "Look at My creation."

If Job wants to reckon with Who God is, he must get closer to the land God's made.

What's more, most of people's greatest encounters with God in the Bible occur close to the earth. God appears to Moses in the wilderness (Exodus 3). He gives the Ten Commandments at Mount Sinai (Exodus 19–20). Elijah has his showdown with King

Ahab on Mount Carmel (1 Kings 18). And later, when Elijah asks to die, God takes him away and meets him at Mount Horeb (1 Kings 19). Is all this just a coincidence?

• • •

Many singles I met struggled to find consistent rest. Many of the *people* I've known struggle to rest. Getting better at it starts with remembering who God is.

At the start of drafting this book, I really struggled. Then I noticed that my prayer life seemed to correlate with the writing. In weeks with few prayer walks, things ran behind. With more prayer walks, things went better.

Until today, I would have told you the secret was getting more time with God. And that's probably true. But I secretly thought, *It's my work to seek out God that matters. My work makes the difference.* Then today, for my second walk, I took the path through a lush, forested area near a creek. I'm told bears sometimes catch salmon there. The path by the creek parallels a neighborhood street. But in summer, trees hide much of the city. As soon as I enter the path, my shoulders ease. My eyes pick out the pink fireweed that breaks up the dense, lush greenery. I relax a bit.

In prayer walks, I don't just seek God. In prayer walks, I draw nearer to the earth, one of God's primary ways of showing us Who. He. Is. "Since the creation of the world God's invisible qualities—his eternal power and divine nature—have been clearly seen," Paul writes in Romans 1:20. *The earth* is why he says humans have no excuse for rejecting God.

And I think *that's* the real reason my writing improves. If we let it, time nearer the earth can remind us of God's bigness and our

smallness. Of His generous provision for ants and lilies and birds
. . . and us. True rest starts with remembering that.

The challenge of resting in creation

For all that the earth helps us connect to God, it's risky to do so
alone. The more vulnerable we are, the greater the dangers.

Canadian David, 54, used to take long walks in his city,
Toronto. Ever since his parents died, David, who has Down syndrome, has had a live-in caregiver. He used to walk alone for up
to two hours at a time. Now he no longer leaves the building on
his own.

The area near David's building has some uneven ground,
including a ravine. When he left for his last walk alone, one winter, his caregiver warned him to be careful. Stay on the sidewalks,
she said. Stay out of the ravine.

It's not entirely clear what happened, but David fell. A man
helped him up, but he fell again. The man then walked with him
as far as the other part of the valley, where he left David. The way
home continued through the valley, which David had to walk
alone. He didn't get home until after dark.

Even nondisabled men face greater risks alone. One of my closest friends in Alaska is a very capable hunter and outdoorsman.
But when he goes into the woods to forage, he takes a friend. He
did the same for a long and perilous kayak trip down the Yukon
River.

Women face these dangers in rural *and* urban environments.
Eunice, 51, a Korean Protestant, said she always takes precautions
when traveling alone. When booking a hotel room, for instance,
"I normally put two people there, just in case," she said. "I might
be exposed to danger, being a woman there alone."

Even though it costs more, she's come to accept the unfairness as the price of being single and female. Being a woman also limits where we go. I would have felt very vulnerable in some Middle Eastern countries. Other women said similar things. In some places, I couldn't prayer walk at all. When I got held up at knife-point, it happened on a short walk alone, along a beach.

Companionship matters

Traveling with others can make all the difference between harm and safety. Companionship can also make the difference between taking a trip and staying home.

Why it's so good to travel with others

Committed friends or married people can make rest more possible for single people. Chris, the pastor we met in chapter 1, said he and his wife had invited a couple of single parishioners to join them for a recent family vacation. After the trip, Chris noticed that their relationships with each other seemed much deeper.

Dani, who shared about celebrations, said it was a big deal when friends invited her to ski with their extended family. "Being asked to be part of their family was such an honor, a blessing. There was no way I was going to turn that down," she said.

An American Protestant living near Los Angeles said it's worth the extra cost to travel with married friends. True, he can't split room costs. But Robert, as he asked me to call him, gets a lot out of it. "It's really good to travel with somebody that loves his wife, and you see that every day for however long," he said. You could pretend during shorter visits, but not for a longer time.

"It's very humbling. 'Wow, that's a lot of work.' You're watching how much they cooperate." Sometimes, in fact, Robert, 56, thinks it's too much work. "It's like watching a guy that goes to the gym all the time," he said. Ultimately, though, he's found it "very encouraging. You see how similar and different you are, and you appreciate your singleness sometimes," he said.

Including single friends can create a deep sense of belonging. Kevin, 59, a gay Protestant man from New Zealand, said his straight Christian friends constantly invite him to vacation with them. Once he spent two weeks visiting a newly married friend and his wife in Germany. "They desperately, desperately try to spend time with me. Simply because they love me, and they want me in their lives.

"They tell me very clearly that when they have children, they still want me to be part of their lives because I will be a positive influence on their children."

Friendships like these provide a beautiful picture of the integrated family God wants His church to be.

Why it's hard to travel with others

Traveling with others can have many benefits. But sometimes singles struggle to find companions. Planning a trip with others only multiplies the challenges we discussed in chapters 1 and 2.

Kim, who shared about lament, said that vacations had become much more difficult since her last relationship ended. Ironically, a recent trip with a male friend had only drawn out the difference.

"I was glad to have him," Kim said. But she found herself making constant comparisons with how much more she enjoyed trips with her previous partner, a woman. "With her, it felt like family." With her guy friend, things felt much less permanent.

"It's not that I don't think it's possible to travel with other people, or even that it wouldn't be good," Kim said. "But in conversations I've had with other single people, it's that you don't really have those people where, every summer, you're going to go to this place." Any new trip involves a whole new set of inquiries. Could you do it? Who might go? Who's interested enough to put down money?

"It's so much work to get people together," Kim said. "Sometimes I'm probably just feeling sorry for myself, and I acknowledge that." But as for many other singles, the burden of planning sometimes proved too much for her. Without the shared commitments of annual plans, it's often too hard.

For others, it goes beyond want to necessity. Two interviewees who use wheelchairs said they could only travel with others. An older Protestant man I interviewed in Jerusalem said he never got to leave the city anymore. "People never think to ask, 'Would you like to come with us?'" said Tony, who was 80 at the time.

How to make rest more equitable

Rest for singles can involve significant inequalities. One of the most basic occurs when your siblings marry and the family ends up living in different places. The single person's voice can start to carry less weight in family travel plans—especially if all the rest have married. The others' votes now represent multiple people, while you still speak for just one.

"I feel this enormous obligation to go home," said G., my host in North Africa. Living there meant that G. had to fly back to the States to see her family. "I spend a lot of money and time every year—twice a year—going home."

Admittedly, the travel costs are unequal. Most people can host one person in their home for at least a few nights. It's quite different to squeeze in a family. And it's much cheaper for a single person to fly somewhere than four or five people. When relatives can drive to each other, travel costs aren't as different.

But when the single ones *always* do the traveling, they can bear more burden—and financial cost—for the relationship. Some families solve this problem by taking a cruise together or renting a house at the beach. But having a blood relationship is no guarantee of having similar wealth as adults. Siblings enter different professions. People use money differently. And some get an easier path in life than others.

"Those of us who come from not-wealthy families are not able to travel much," said Rebecca, whom we met in chapter 1. "We need to save for the whole year to take a long trip. The downside of being single is that you need to save for your travel, not like if you have a husband to share the cost with."

Since unrelated Christians don't often vacation together, inequality can show up differently in churches. Married people more commonly own homes. In many places, homes also come with a yard. If you're in a Bible study where some people have more land than others, what would it look like to share that? Could you offer part of your garden space to a single friend who lives in an apartment?

Churches can do this too. In Anchorage, one Episcopal church built an outdoor labyrinth that winds past wild roses and other flowers. It's open as long as the snow's not too deep. Their generous use of that land has blessed me more than once.

Sometimes singles can provide this for each other. A wealthy, busy career woman in Singapore let me stay at her apartment three separate times during travel in that region. At least part of the time, she was traveling for her own work.

An overworked young Orthodox Ethiopian student once spent four hours a day commuting to and from home. The eighth of nine children, he couldn't afford to live near his school in Addis Ababa. Abebe, as he asked me to call him, also worked part-time to help support his mother.

Then in his teens, Abebe said his fatigue made it harder to learn. In addition to his subjects, he had to learn the two languages used in his classes: Italian and English. (He grew up speaking Amharic and Oromo.)

Life changed when a teacher learned about the situation. As he had done for several others, a single Italian man named Fulvio offered Abebe a room near school. For free. For one of the first times in his young life, Abebe could rest.

Other people steward company benefits in that way. Paul, 52, an Indian Pentecostal man, said a friend once invited him along on a work trip to Pondicherry.[3]

At most, Paul had to pay for his own transportation there. The rest of the trip his friend's company covered. When they went to a restaurant, Paul could order what he wanted—at least up to a limit. "I used those moments to just cherish the allowance that was there," he said.

Another time, the same friend gave him a similar experience as a gift. He and his wife invited Paul to join their Goa trip.

"He paid for the trip, in fact," Paul said. "If I tried to buy an ice cream, he would not allow me to pay." That freed Paul to sit and meditate on the seashore.

"There's no substitute for discovering God in nature," he said. "You begin to discover how emotion can be shared in nature.

You see a bird, you begin to enjoy the bird, to love the bird." You can even gain perspective. "Nature fixes itself," he said. "We don't allow this in a mechanical society. We want it to be dictated the way we want it." But in nature, things happen the way God wants them to happen.

•   •   •

As we come to the close of our look at rest, take some time to reflect on land, companionship, and equity in your life.

What do you **grieve?** Do you have enough space to name that? Or do you need to make more time for reflection?

What do you **have?** Where do you find rest in this season? What does your nearest land—even if it's a houseplant—show you about God?

Is there something you need to **confess or repent of?**

What can you **give?** Where might God ask you to commit to others? Do you have the means to help a person poor in rest get more of it?

By Motorcycle, Rickshaw, Ferry, and Jeepney

ALL MY LIFE, I'VE FEARED MOTORCYCLES. When I was young, my family once visited a man who'd recently survived a serious crash. His scarred face left a deep sense of danger that kept me far away from motorcycles for most of my life. Even after surviving motorcycle rides on a couple of previous trips abroad, I was not prepared for all that researching this book required.

I knew Europe's trains and subways from prior trips. But I'd never had to learn the complexities of seat reservations. That ignorance stranded me in Vienna for the night. Fortunately, God provided a Christian Airbnb host. We had a lovely time sharing tea and testimonies in our mutually limited German.

Things got harder once I left the European Union. I've used subways all over the world. Kyiv's and Moscow's train stations were some of the hardest to figure out. Google Maps's instructions used romanized station names. Local signs and maps used Cyrillic. Two-word names became the key that helped me match station names in my English train booklet with the Cyrillic I saw on signs.

Then I crossed the Mediterranean. On my ferry ride south, I learned almost too late that I should have entered the visa line as soon as I boarded the ship. Otherwise you might not get your passport stamped before the boat reaches port.

Apparently, family groups could send one person to process all their passports. As a solo traveler, I had no one to hold my place in line if I needed to go to the bathroom or retrieve something from a bag.

As the trip continued, travel got more crowded. Many countries have informal buses. They called these matatus in Kenya, dala dala in Tanzania, and something Amharic in Ethiopia.

I managed to board one on my own in Cape Town, South Africa, but it took a lot of querying fellow passengers. In that city, few white South Africans use the service. (I think they called it a minibus taxi?) Once I found the sprawling transit center, I had to comb through the snaking queues for dozens of routes until I found mine.

Then, for a few rand (about fifty-three cents in 2018), we clambered in until the back bench filled. Once it did, the conductor took out a board to fill the aisle of the next bench. He packed us in until all seats and boards were full. If more people boarded, they sat on the floor.

In some countries, people also stood next to the conductor in the open doorway, holding onto the roof as we traveled. This practice extends beyond African countries. In Manila, outside riders grabbed the back of the Philippines' distinctive Jeepneys.

My riskiest ride almost made a motorcycle look safe. One night I took a bicycle rickshaw in New Delhi. You couldn't hail these by app, so a local friend helped negotiate the price. Then I climbed aboard the unlit vehicle and hoped for the best.

We should have had an easy ride along a fairly busy highway. But it turned out the shop I wanted was across the highway. Or so my driver thought. We made a series of U-turns and salmon runs to cross the many lanes of traffic. Then we did it again. The shop was on the first side after all.

Thankfully, we survived. On my long-ago first visit to India, I passed a less fortunate cyclist. I can still see his flattened bicycle in the roadway. Some locals had carried his body parts to the shoulder. They were still crowded around his remains when we passed.

Air travel almost calmed me by comparison. Then the Boeing 737 MAX crashed near Addis Ababa. I became a far more nervous passenger during takeoffs, no matter the carrier. Statistically, I know, air travel is many times safer than car travel.[4] But I read too much about how flawed computer systems helped down the doomed Boeing planes.[5]

Few things terrify like the prospect of a machine in charge. We want a human in control. Often the safest person for that seems to be ourselves. After all, the more control I *seem* to have, the better I imagine my life will go; the safer my possessions and body.

In fact, far more of life than I'd like to admit depends on how God chooses to show His goodness. In His providence, I survived every one of those many local transit rides. Then I ended my time on the road for good with a harrowing seven-day drive from Seattle to Alaska.

At the end, I realized I was wrong about control and motor transit. It's not enough to pray about motorcycle rides or just when I'm a passenger. Thanks in large part to a bad skid while crossing the Rockies, I now pray every time I put my car in motion.

CHAPTER 4

EMOTIONAL HEALTH

How God Transforms Our Pain

EARLY IN HIS FIFTIES, Fabio reached a new low. After years of disappointment, he stopped asking God for marriage.

"My relationship with God was in crisis," he said. "I had difficulty trusting Him as a Father. And also for this reason, I stopped sharing the deepest wishes of my heart, thinking that He didn't want to take care of them.

"I said, 'I don't want to ask You for something that You don't want to give me.'" Fabio, an Italian Catholic, asked for help enduring his loneliness and unfulfilled desire.

This approach did not ease his pain or change his desire. So for almost three years, he labored under the added pain of distance from God. Then his mother died. Fabio was now an orphan—alone but for some aunts and uncles and cousins.

"I fell down into a big night, a strong night," Fabio said. "When I lost my faith, I lost my hope. I lost also my wish to live."

His mother had been his anchor. His father's death in Fabio's youth had made them especially close. Even once Fabio moved to a city an hour from Rome, they talked every night. He visited her every week.

"When I lost my mother, I became really desperate," he said. "My job was really all I had."

For almost a year, he soldiered on. Then, a few weeks before our interview, Fabio faced his first Christmas alone. At first, he hoped some relatives might invite him over. But none did. Several friends invited him to join them, but this didn't help. "I don't know why, but at the moment, I wanted an invitation from my family."

Perhaps, like many people, he saw relatives as better than friends. And if he joined his friends and their families, it would remind Fabio of all he lacked.

"At that moment, I couldn't feel the love of God. God is not with me. My aunt is not with me. God doesn't love me; my house is empty. I have only my dogs."

•   •   •

Fabio's anguish echoes the pain many singles shared with me. Unchosen singleness can contribute to many emotional challenges. Depending on age and culture, these can include loneliness, anger, depression, powerlessness, and hopelessness.

I, too, have had times when death seemed easier than living out my life alone. I wasn't exactly suicidal, but the thought of my present pain lasting for decades more seemed unbearable.

What does emotional health mean when life brings such deep pain? First, it's important to acknowledge the complexity of our emotions. The best and most nuanced sermon I've ever heard on this was by my then-pastor, the Protestant writer Tim Keller. In it, he covered five different things that can contribute to a "wounded spirit," as he called it.[1] Depending on the cause of our pain, we might need different kinds of medicine.

But all emotions are deeply bound up with the spiritual. What are most of the Psalms, after all, but prayers that bring hard emotions to God? Whatever our feelings or their causes, I'm convinced we should bring them to God first. "Lean not on your own understanding," Solomon writes. "In all your ways submit to [God], and he will make your paths straight" (Proverbs 3:5-6). If we need more than prayer, won't God point that out when we seek Him?

Over the past decade, God has used a particular type of prayer to help me address a host of emotional troubles. When He helped me start to face my racism, I had to do some public confession (scary!). Later, dealing with some early childhood wounds led to starting ballet lessons. Other times, I've felt led to work on forgiveness, recount God's past faithfulness to me, or share my food with others.

I've been so helped by listening prayer that I want to use its main postures as a guide for our discussion of emotional health. I'm deeply indebted to Rusty Rustenbach and The Navigators for developing the booklet I've now almost memorized. Rustenbach gives more detail in his book, *A Guide for Listening and Inner-Healing Prayer*.

The basic process I've learned from Rustenbach and others goes like this:

1. Name the painful emotion you're feeling. Ask God to help you experience it in His presence.

2. Identify the root. Where did this come from? Often, a recent event stirs up much older wounds.

3. Ask God what you came to believe in that older wounding. In the midst of pain, we often accept and believe lies about ourselves, God, and others.

4. Ask God to reveal the truth about the situation. He might illumine relevant Scriptures (see Acts 8:26-36). Other times God speaks more personally (Acts 9) or uses agreement among believers to provide confirmation of the truth (Acts 15).

5. Choose to accept God's view of things. Repent of and renounce your belief in the lie(s). Sometimes healing also requires forgiveness, dealing with others' harsh words about us, or our own vows and strategies to prevent pain.

Wherever you are as you read this chapter, and whatever emotions it stirs up for you, I can't think of a better thing to offer you than this model for bringing hard emotions to God. Emotional health doesn't mean an absence of pain. It means learning how to bring pain to God.

That's important whatever your present life stage. When you're single, it's easy to think marriage will fix challenges like loneliness or rejection. When you're married, it's easy to blame problems on your spouse and demonize them.

But when we blame our circumstances, that only increases our sense of powerlessness! It also denies our own responsibility for how we handle challenges. It's much harder to show Jesus' love when we're trapped in our own fears and pain.

Emotional health frees us to love others more generously and wisely. The Bible offers hope that, with God's help, we can all grow more skilled in handling hard relationships and emotions.

In the next few pages, we'll look at how to bring God some of the hardest emotions singles face: loneliness, shame, and powerlessness.

Name it: loneliness

It's taken Ronnie, whom we met in chapter 1, many years to cry. He grew up believing men and boys don't cry. Several prison sentences only reinforced the need to bury his pain.

But toward the end of one of those sentences, Ronnie took advantage of a chance to escape. He had earned the right to leave the prison for shifts at a work-release job. Because it was less secure, escape proved easy.

Soon after getting away, Ronnie called an old friend. He didn't share much, just said that he needed help. His friend agreed to give him some money but said Ronnie had to pick it up from his parents' church.

"I didn't go there to go to church," Ronnie stressed. But his friend's mom welcomed him so warmly that Ronnie stayed for the service after all. When they invited people up to receive Jesus, he went forward. He got baptized.

"When I came up out of the water, I just had a whole different feeling. I think that lasted for four or five months. And then I started having this internal struggle because I was living a lie."

God began calling Ronnie, like Jonah, to go back to what he'd run from. Just over two years after he escaped prison, Ronnie finally turned himself in to the police.

Despite his newfound faith in God, he continued to struggle. More than twenty years passed before Ronnie left prison for the last time. By the time we met in Atlanta, he'd been free for more than a decade.

As his faith has grown, Ronnie's gotten better at taking his pain to God. "When I feel that depression coming on—that isolation or whatever you want to call it—I go to the concordance and look for a passage. Sometimes I even cry, depending on what type of day I had. If I had one of them bad days, since I'm home alone, I can cry."

Facing the pain takes time, Ronnie said. "It took you years to ingrain those lies in your head. How are you going to undo that in a few lessons?" Little by little, he's learning that when he hurts, he can let himself cry.

Identify the root

As Swedish novelist Malin Lindroth told me, loneliness comes in multiple forms. We all face what she called "existential loneliness." This might be one reason loneliness is such a common emotion. It's also an emotion single Christians seemed more used to taking to God.

"Loneliness can be a negative loneliness, or it can be loneliness where there's a dwelling of God in us," said Fr. John, a Catholic priest I met in Argentina. Fr. John, 44, called that sense of being alone, but with God, "inhabited loneliness."

"It's just like how a couple of people who love each other don't feel alone when it's just the two of them," he said. "There are moments when I do feel different weaknesses or tired, or difficult experiences from time to time. But I believe it's an opportunity to grow in that relationship with God. Some of that bitterness makes way for another type of sweetness."

Malin said other forms of loneliness point to loss or unmet needs. "The destructive loneliness, it's a feeling of lacking, and the sense that this is threatening in some way," she said.

Many singles attributed their loneliness to the lack of someone to share things with. "The reality is, we were not created to be alone," Ronnie said. "It's not just the sex part, it's the companionship—getting up in the morning, either she's making coffee for me or I'm making coffee for her or we're making coffee together."

Ask God what you came to believe

When you've never married, it's especially easy to think a spouse would meet all sorts of needs. Of course, people in a hard marriage might think singleness would provide a similar cure! Whatever your current life stage, take a minute or two to bring your loneliness before God. What have you come to believe about it? What do you think would fix it?

Over my decade of practicing listening/healing prayer, I've found that the lies I believe often twist a truth. This isn't surprising. After all, the enemy used a very similar strategy with Eve in Genesis 3.

Ask God to reveal the truth

In the midst of loneliness, it's often easy to think, *I'm alone.* Gifty, 53, a Ghanaian Protestant woman I interviewed in Accra, felt that way after she and her husband separated. "Things became so difficult," she said. Together they'd had three children, but her husband apparently didn't help with any of the expenses after the separation. "We didn't have money, we didn't have clothing, we didn't have food to eat," Gifty said.

"That's where I trusted in God." Tempted to believe she was all alone, Gifty instead trusted Jesus' promise "I will never leave you nor forsake you" (Hebrews 13:5, ESV).

"I put my trust in the Lord. And with Him, everything became possible," Gifty said. "Through God, I've been able to care for my children."

Accept God's view

As Gifty trusted God, He provided more and more of her needs. She found work at a hospital. She's also become a leader at church and joined the choir. "It helps me a lot," she said, echoing what others said about singing or playing songs that worship God. "We sing, and I forget about my problems."

Across traditions, Christians saw loneliness as a reason to spend more time in prayer, read spiritual materials, or seek deeper connection with other believers. Cuban Catholic Nalda, 54, said she does a multiday retreat when she starts to feel like an outsider in her community. She tries to find a place where she can hear God's Word and get encouraged by other Christians.

How do you handle loneliness? How could God use you to show others they're not alone?

Name it: shame

Many singles also deal with shame. From Russia to Egypt, Christians said they faced a lot of cultural pressure to marry. When that didn't happen, or the marriage didn't last, they faced shame and blame.

Identify the root

"Because of the societal expectations, you feel stigmatized, you feel shame because we're in a shame-honor culture," said a Lebanese Protestant man. He asked me to call him Youssef. Because of his wife's mental illness, they had separated several years before. They divorced in 2020. "I don't feel ashamed because I am single," said Youssef, 34. "It is because I was married and I am not married anymore, regardless of the reasons."

Others said they struggle with shame related to their body and sexuality. Cătălina, 35, an Orthodox Romanian, struggles with her previous sexual relationships. "From a human perspective, it's experience," she said. "When I'm coming in front of God, it's like a full backpack."

What causes you shame? How do you handle it?

Ask God what you came to believe

For me, shame often feels like a crawling sensation. I start to feel so repulsed that I wish I could get away from who I am. What I've done or fear others think seems inseparable from who I am.

If you're dealing with shame in your life, take some time to bring this before God. What have you come to believe about yourself? What do you believe about your actions? Who do you believe is responsible?

Ask God to reveal the truth

Years ago, someone gave me the book *When People Are Big and God Is Small* by Edward T. Welch. I never finished it, but I never forgot the title. If you look at your causes of shame, someone's opinion likely looms very large. God's view may seem quite small. But who has the right to judge you?

If you're struggling with shame, ask God to illumine the parts of His Word that talk about this. If you're not comfortable with listening prayer yet, look up instructions for lectio divina—an ancient way of reading Scripture. Or, read and pray through a passage like Hebrews 9 or 1 John 3.

Kevin, the gay man who often vacations with his friends, said he wears a rainbow-colored Jesus fish on his collar. It helps him remember and share what God's done for him. "I'm an evangelist by nature," Kevin said. "And Jesus has taken my shame. Why would I want to hang on to it?"

I interviewed people with many views on sexuality; for Kevin, following Jesus means celibacy. "In order to follow Him, we need to surrender our lives, lay them down," he said. "My cross is rainbow-colored. I have given everything up in terms of my sexuality, which is, I'm gay, same-sex attracted.

"My cross is rainbow-colored. That shows that I have laid down my desires and intentions to be in a relationship with another man. I will carry this cross until final sanctification because I love Jesus."

What would happen if Jesus took your shame?

Accept God's view

Kevin has found it very costly to love Jesus. But he's also found great freedom. "If Jesus has taken my shame, I can instead broadcast to the world that here is an example of Jesus taking my shame. And no, He has not chosen to change my orientation, just like He chose not to remove Paul's thorn," he said.

"Instead, He has encouraged me to try to learn how His grace is sufficient. And if Jesus' grace can be sufficient for me, then perhaps it can also be sufficient for you."

How would your relationships change if you lived as if Jesus' grace really is sufficient?

Name it: powerlessness and rejection

I did not consider powerlessness an emotion until I started using The Navigators' prayer guide. But feeling powerlessness often goes along with feeling anger, despair, and hopelessness.

For singles, it often comes up in the context of barriers to marriage. These challenges most often involved either money or some aspect of their body: race or ethnicity, weight and/or height, disability, and so on. Other times, singles live or worship in a place with more of one sex than the other. This can create intense competition. As a result, people often feel less desirable to others as a romantic partner or spouse.

Identify the root

In South Africa, Protestant Kholekile, 36, said men like him struggle to provide the wealth expected for a marriage. Under the custom there, called ilobolo, couples' families work out what the man will pay to marry the woman.

Traditionally, they would agree to a certain number of cattle. "My family would bring cattle to your family," Kholekile said. "That provides evidence that the two families are in relationship because of their two children."

Nowadays, the cows are mostly symbolic. Families calculate a price for each. "I call it a get-rich-quick scam," Kholekile said. "Guys pay a ridiculous amount of money for the lady they want to marry." If a man can't afford what the family asks, it might be hard for the couple to marry.

In other places, women's families face pressure to pay a big dowry. Grace, 53, an Indian Pentecostal, said her parents had tried to arrange a marriage when she was younger. But the man's family wanted too much.

"They wanted gold beyond our limit," she said. For the wedding, they wanted a very expensive hotel.

Grace and her parents discussed the terms. They were glad the man came from a Christian family. India's Hindu majority can complicate marriage for Christians. But Grace had three younger siblings in school. She and her parents decided the dowry was too high. The other family turned elsewhere.

"I was not interested in marriage after that," Grace said. "I really was disgusted."

Tina, whom we met in chapter 2, faces a very different challenge. Even at her lowest weight, she's always felt "too fat" for men on the dating apps she's tried. "In our culture, being an obese woman is extremely difficult," she said.

Like Grace's family, Tina helped host me during my travels. During an interview in her home, she said several friendships have also gone painfully. "I've had a string of really good guy friends who have turned out to not be interested," she said. In one case, it took a year to figure out whether he wanted romance or not.

"When you have those experiences, too, it reinforces this idea that men are going to be interested in you for your personality, but they're never going to want to date you," Tina said. "It adds so much anxiety and stress that it makes it really difficult to conceive of someone being interested in being with you."

A Catholic woman I interviewed in Panama City said she

didn't think a man would ever marry someone like her. She uses a wheelchair.

Where have you felt powerless? How do you handle it?

Ask God what you came to believe

When I feel powerless, I'm often tempted to despair. I usually respond by seeking control. In recent months, God has shown me that I believe I have to be in control for life to go well. If I'm out of control, I believe, life will go horribly.

Rejection may be one of the most painful things a person can experience. However you connect to the stories we've just heard, take some time to bring your own rejections to God. Ask Him what you came to believe in those moments. The enemy loves to hammer our sense of worth when people reject us.

Who have you let define your worth? What have you based your worth on?

Ask God to reveal the truth

Sometimes it hurts too much to seek God. Fortunately, God relentlessly seeks His lost sheep, as Jesus described in Luke 15.

Fabio spent his Christmas with a priest friend in Lourdes, France. The place had meant so much to him in childhood that he'd gotten confirmed there. But over the years, he stopped going. Lourdes became a memory of happier times with loved ones now gone.

He returned with low expectations. Each day, he went to the grotto just once. "I had a heart of stone," Fabio said. His prayers sought only peace about his mother's death. Nothing else.

Nor did he approach the shrine's famed baths, where many

claim they've been healed. Fabio had promised a friend he'd bathe there. But fear and the near-freezing temperatures kept him away until the day before he went home.

Then at last he entered the waters. "I don't want to say that this bath was the miracle, but it was a sign of my acceptance, my decision to ask God's help," Fabio said. After three years, he let God crack open his heart's door again.

Fabio entered the waters, shivered, and climbed out. He dressed and went to confession. This one went differently. Fabio began in French, assuming it was the priest's native tongue. But after he mentioned being Italian, the priest said he was too.

They switched to their mother tongue. "Something arrived deep in my heart," Fabio said. He had not cried once in the year since his mother's death. But speaking Italian, he wept.

The priest cried with him. Then he told Fabio of God's love.

"All my life was rebuilt in that moment, in front of my eyes. He explained to me that God never let me alone," Fabio said. Instead, the priest helped Fabio see how God worked in Fabio's pain to give Himself more deeply.

"You are not alone because God is with you, even if you never have a wife, a family, children," the priest said. "You will never be alone until the end of your life, no matter how many years you live. Every day of your life, you will always be the son of God and God will be your Father."

How has God met you in your deepest pain?

Accept God's view

The priest gave Fabio several things to consider when he went home. His work teaching at a public high school wasn't just a job but a mission. "In reality, you have a family," the priest said. "At this moment, your students are your children, and your friends are your brothers and your sisters. Stay close to your friends, especially the good friends. God gave them to you."

The priest also encouraged him to reopen his desires to God. "He convinced me, 'You can still ask for a wife, for children, for a family.' I said, 'No, please; I'm at an age where I can't be a father.' The priest said, 'No, it's not true. Everything is possible for God.'"

Fabio went home.

"I returned with a new feeling," he said. "A new life, a new joy. A new way to see my past, my present, my future." He still didn't like his singleness. "But at the moment, I feel that God asked me to love what I have, to love what I am, to love what He gave to me. Maybe I'll ask Him for something more, but I'm starting with loving what I have now and what I am now. I have a big hope in my heart for the future."

If you really believed God meets *you* in your deepest pain, what would change?

•   •   •

When I finally reread Fabio's story, while writing this chapter, I needed to hear it myself. Later that day, it dawned on me: I had first tried to start my research in Rome. More Christians identify as Catholic than any other tradition, I reasoned. Where better to start my research than in the seat of Catholicism: Rome?

But nothing worked out. Instead, I had to start in Switzerland. Several weeks later, I tried again. And Rome fell through again. Finally, at the end of a Christmas return to Europe, Rome worked out. A brand-new contact connected me to Fabio.

He went to Lourdes in December. I flew to Rome in January.

We talked one week after Fabio's return. If things had gone according to my summer plan for Italy, I would have never met Fabio. You and I would not have heard the story he shares in these pages.

From my research and own experience, much of singles' emotional struggles revolve around powerlessness. *Why can't I get my way?* we rage. *If God would just follow my plan, I'd have a much better life right now.* I probably slip into such thinking daily, if not hourly. Yet time and time again in my research, God proved to have perfect timing.

As the priest's words did for Fabio, those reminders help renew my hope and capacity to thank God for what He's given today.

•　•　•

Whatever state in which you come to this chapter, take a moment to reflect on your own emotional health.

What's hard right now? What do you **grieve**?

What do you **have**? What can you thank God for?

Is there something you need to **confess or repent of**?

And whom and what can you love right now? What can you **give**?

PART TWO

LIFE ESSENTIALS

CHAPTER 5

HOUSING

How Shelter Shapes Our Character

LILI LEFT WORK IN SHOCK. She no longer had a job. Things were already tense with the aunt she lived with. What would her aunt say to this news?

Lost in thought, Lili didn't notice a friend until the woman called out to her. Several months before, they'd discovered her friend lived near Lili's work. After that chance meeting, their friendship deepened.

The women found they had more in common than just the Catholic church where they met. Both were past the typical age of marriage in a Mexican culture that prizes family. (Lili was 57 when I met her.) Though the other woman was wealthier than Lili, they found it easy to talk.

So Lili's friend soon learned the bad news. "Why don't you stay here tonight?" she suggested. Surprised and relieved at the chance to delay a quarrel with her aunt, Lili agreed.

The next morning, her friend surprised her again. "What if you just moved in here?"

At first it seemed too good to be true. How could Lili lose her job *and* find a way to escape the longtime conflict with her aunt? How could she afford to stay with her friend?

But after many years living alone, the wealthier woman valued the chance for companionship. Lili moved in eleven years before our interview.

It took three years before I fully understood what Lili had told me the day we talked in her small stucco home. I spoke enough Spanish to ask questions, but not enough to fully understand the answers.

With the translator's help, I learned Lili spent the next decade sharing the small house with her friend. She found work cleaning homes. Meanwhile, her friend's health declined. She didn't do what the doctor suggested to manage her diabetes. Eventually, they amputated a leg. The woman died a few months before I met Lili.

"That's how I got this house," Lili concluded. At some point in their decade as roommates, the other woman changed her will to leave Lili the house.

Until that point, my translator hadn't believed my vague memory that Lili lived alone. How could a house cleaner afford to do that in Mérida? "That's one in a million, believe me," she said when we reached that part of the recording.

As further evidence of how remarkable this was, Lili hadn't yet put the house in her name. Based on what we'd learned, the translator and I think she couldn't afford to pay for the legal change.

But with the will in her possession, Lili didn't worry. God had provided a house for her anyway.

. . .

Shelter plays a profound and mysterious role in how creatures connect with God and each other. Even many animals have homes, as Jesus once told a would-be disciple.[1] Years before the Israelites could pack up their Exodus tents, God had them build Him a mobile home: the Tabernacle.

Jesus later taught His followers that how they shared their homes with strangers was how they treated Him.[2] And when He prepared the disciples for His departure, Jesus promised that they would live together. "My Father's house has many rooms. . . . I am going there to prepare a place for you" (John 14:2).

These texts imply that sharing a roof is sacred. The space in which we live reveals us like few other things. Living with and near other people creates a powerful bond. It weaves us together in mutual responsibility. Even a person who'd never spoken to his roommate would hardly refuse to notify someone if the other person died.

Perhaps this is why one of the first Catholic priests I talked to reframed what I'd always thought of as a marriage text. When God says, "It's not good for man to be alone" (see Genesis 2:18), that applies to housing, too, Fr. Fred said. A Nigerian priest whom I met in Valencia, Spain, he said living in a family plays a critical role in our formation. According to Fr. Fred, family teaches us to share, help with chores, care for the sick, and give up things for the good of others.

I think that's why he believed so strongly in living with others.

In many ways, those four skills typify the love-in-action Jesus called all His followers to practice. If they're habits worth learning in childhood, they're worth continuing as adults.

For the global church to become a more integrated family, we have to rethink how housing fits into the life of God's family. In this chapter, we'll look at how sharing, helping, caring, and sacrifice can deepen our community and our understanding of shelter. As we do so, I encourage you to reflect on how you share your own roof.

The controversy of sharing

How we view different housing arrangements has much to do with cultural values and how we define *maturity*. Sweden and Japan lead the ranks of countries where living alone is common. In other parts of Europe and Asia, however, people more commonly report living with either roommates or relatives. In Arab countries, children generally live with their parents until they marry.

Of the 345 people I spoke with, 212 described their housing situation. Of those, 41 percent lived with one or more relatives and 39 percent lived alone. Most others lived with people they weren't related to (18 percent). A very small minority lived in intentional community or didn't have housing.[3]

Where sharing is expected

Some cultures value shared housing so much that they virtually require it. Outside the United States, adults often live with parents. In fact, in Singapore, it's very hard for young adults to avoid it. The city-state comprises an island, which means extremely limited housing. Singapore has a long history of expanding its size through "land reclamation." This comes at an extremely high cost. Sometimes the fill also needs years to settle before it can hold new buildings.[4]

To help address its housing limits, the government doesn't let single Singaporean citizens buy public housing flats until they're at least 35.[5] Eighty percent of Singaporeans live in such housing.[6]

Married or engaged couples and widows can buy at a younger age, if they have the means. Young divorcees can't. Renting and buying a car cost a lot too, so many young Singaporeans live with their parents as a way to save money.

"I think the housing thing is a huge issue," said a Protestant who asked me to call him Tony. "I have a lot of peers who would like to be independent." He, too, lives with his parents. But unlike in many cases, his parents take a more hands-off approach. When they were young, they moved to Singapore to get away from Tony's grandma. She followed them anyway. That experience gave them greater empathy for Tony's situation.

Singles I interviewed in Cairo said they're also expected to live with parents into adulthood. This most affects single women. Egyptian Protestant Nardeen, 24, said men might live alone. "It's not an option for the girls."

In Egypt, single adults' relationships with their parents also change less. In most other countries, singles who lived with their parents said adulthood changed that relationship. Many of them contributed to household expenses, for example.

But in Egypt, Nardeen said, a more equal relationship comes with marriage rather than age. At one wedding she attended, the couple offered to open their home to others as a resource. "Married couples have more freedom to serve God because they have their own home, so they make their own rules. They can open their home to people who are seeking prayer, seeking advice."

"As a single person living with your parents, that's not always the case," she said. "You have to have your parents' approval to go out." Even a visit to serve required their blessing.

Shared housing also has a practical benefit: safety. In both Egypt and India, I heard that living alone could be dangerous. "There is no safety," said Grace, whom we met in chapter 4. "It's very risky for women to live alone." She had a ground-level bedroom in the multistory home where her widowed mother lived.

"If men think, 'She's alone,' they'll start stalking you."

Sabrina, 27, a Sudanese Catholic living in Cairo, said that her skin compounded her risks as a woman. "When you go in the street and you're Black, they say some words to you—especially if you're a girl."

To keep herself safe, she lives with two other women. She also watches when and where she goes in the city. "I make sure that the timing is safe. I make sure that the roads I'm taking have some people on them so nothing like this would happen to me."

Where people suspect sharing

Cultures that prize independence can view sharing with more wariness. A few months into my research, *The Atlantic* ran a cover story on "the sex recession." It tied "populist discontent" in Europe to "adults who have so far failed to achieve the milestones of adulthood."[7] This failing? Living with their parents.

"It's definitely perceived as being either a slacker or unambitious," said American Protestant Josh, 23. At the time of our interview, he lived at home in Delaware. He paid his parents rent, but said, "I definitely feel like living with your parents is kind of shunned on."

David, the man who liked doing chores with friends, agreed. "I get a good amount of questions in terms of 'Oh, when are you going to move out?'" But not from his parents. He said they rarely raise the issue.

David moved back home after grad school. "There have been moments when I have prayed and wrestled with whether I should move out, but I never felt a strong push."

Like Josh, though, David said living with his parents makes it harder to have friends over. "It's much more difficult with my parents," he said.

In Japan, Christians cited multiple reasons singles often live alone. Notions of maturity seemed one reason—especially for men. "I have parents an hour away from here, but I'm almost 30," said Protestant Kentaro, 29. "You have to be independent at that point."

Living alone also lets you eat what you like, leave the toilet seat up, and make noise whenever you please. Protestant Keiko, 47, said their culture also values the way living alone avoids possible tension. "Sharing a room or house is not common in Japan," she said.

In a later email, she said, "Sharing itself is quite common in Japan." People even share public bathhouses with strangers.

Housing they see differently. "In Japanese culture, people think sharing might cause trouble," she said. "Maybe we need more private areas. And I think it's, in a sense, difficult to share. We've grown up in different families."

Earlier in adult life, she'd had roommates, partly for financial reasons. By her thirties, though, Keiko could afford to pay rent and utilities on her own. When we spoke, she'd lived that way for sixteen years.

When people want to share

Other singles told me they'd like to share their space but find it hard. Chinese Protestant Kate, as she asked me to call her, had lived with others in the United States. She found it harder in her homeland. "I don't mind having a roommate, but I haven't found a good one. It's not that easy to find a roommate here."

It sounded like Kate, 43, would have liked living with a Christian. However, she also wanted to live near work. "The traffic here is terrible. To find a sister with a similar economic situation is not easy," she said.[8]

Some Christians find a different way to share their space: hospitality. South African Pentecostal Juliet, 40, said she often hosts others. "I tend to have people in my space a lot," she said. For example, she'd hosted a family of four in her Cape Town apartment for a couple of weeks.

Though of European ancestry, Juliet said, "I think my dominant culture is more Asian." As a younger adult, she did missions work on that continent. Her time there changed her view of housing. "We always had people coming to stay," she said. "I was living off missionary support, so it was God's money anyway."

Singles like Juliet played a huge role in my fieldwork for this book. Of the eighty-one hosts I stayed with, twenty-six were singles living alone. Another five of my hosts were singles living with one or more relatives.

The complexity of helping

Sharing more of life with others and helping with more than just rent or a mortgage deepens relationship. "For me, that's very positive," said a Dutch Protestant woman who asked that I call her

Joke. "You know when you come home, there's someone you can talk to," she said. We met over coffee one day in Jerusalem, where she had lived for many years.

Though Joke, 53, once hoped to marry, living with others gives her a rich sense of community. Her neighbors are also "very good as a community at taking care of each other," she said. "I think that's also why for me singleness is not as lonely." Having so many others around, people who care about how she's doing, provides belonging.

For Kat, whose friends celebrate ordinary moments, housemates help her stay healthy. "I will always choose to live with somebody else," she said. "I don't do well living on my own. Because I have depression and anxiety, it can be incredibly difficult for me to socialize and take care of myself unless there's somebody else that I can be accountable to and be accountable for."

Unlike Joke and Kat, however, other singles struggled with the long-term uncertainty of roommates. Almost anyone who's lived with many people has had at least some roommates move out to get married.

"The frustration as you get older, when you share with people, is you're living in a perpetual state of temporariness," said Chris, whom we met earlier. "Just simple things like wanting to get the carpets cleaned is a big deal."

The year he turned 40, the washing machine died. His housemate wasn't working. "It was pretty clear that I was going to have to buy it," Chris said. "That sort of triggered this self-analysis. 'Do I buy a washing machine that serves me and my housemate? Do I buy a washing machine that might someday have to wash children's clothing?' It triggered all these thoughts."

In the end, he realized: "I don't want to spend my whole life in a temporary state." When we spoke, he'd been living alone for more than a year and loved it.

The high cost of caring alone

Many people don't have the option to live alone. Some don't have enough money. Others need help with certain tasks. American Protestant Barb, 66, was born with hydrocephalus. This condition can damage the brain and sometimes proves fatal. In her case, it led to legal blindness and eventually a wheelchair. She's always lived with others.

At one time, she shared an apartment with fellow college students. "That was okay," she said.

Another shared apartment didn't work out as well. "It was a little rough for them, because at that point I was always on crutches. They had to see how much they would have to help me," Barb said. "It worked, but it wasn't all that great."

The arrangement only lasted about a month. At the time of our interview in Delaware, Barb was living in an assisted care facility.

Other singles with disabilities I talked to lived with relatives or had in-home help. David, the walker we met in chapter 3, still lives in the apartment he once shared with his parents. After his mother died, a woman who'd already been helping his parents with him moved in. I met David and his caregiver at the Protestant church she takes him to. He'd been baptized as a child, she said.

In most places I visited, people didn't seem set up to welcome a Barb or David into shared life. In some countries, people with disabilities have to beg on the street to survive. In the United States, we seem to think only relatives or paid medical staff should provide the intense help some people need. Many people choose to abort a child with disabilities.[9] In all this, cultures overlook what people with disabilities have to offer.

Caregiving can exact a high cost, no question. I understand why many people hire someone to do it—whether it's caring for an infant, an elderly person, or someone with a disability. But certain views of community make caregiving that much harder. In the United States, we idolize the nuclear family. This puts all the work of childrearing and house maintenance on two adults. That's a heavy burden, in the best of cases.

David Mahaffey, Orthodox bishop of Alaska from 2014 to 2020, said he saw this frequently in a prior parish. "It's almost like one member of the family had to commit to taking care of the surviving mother or father," he said. This duty typically fell to an unmarried adult child.

Once someone made this commitment, the surviving parent often didn't die until the adult child was in their fifties or sixties. I met several men and women in this situation.

Mexican Catholic Francisco, 82, said he never married because of caring for his parents. All his brothers married, but he didn't think he could seek that.

After his mother died, he and his father lived alone. They paid for help with household chores, but Francisco still felt obliged to help his father. In the years since his father died, he's mostly lived alone. Francisco said you have to be very careful whom you let in your house. Yet it's also dangerous to live alone once you get sick, he acknowledged.

For Nicholas, whom we met earlier, the call for help came at 26. His father had suffered an aneurysm. A medevac to Anchorage ensued. (Many rural Alaskan communities live off the road system.) The older man spent three months in the hospital and almost died multiple times.

After his release, the man who helped Nicholas grow into manhood had to relearn it all himself. Walking, talking, even breathing. "Once they told me they needed help, it was a no-brainer," Nicholas said. His father's role as an Orthodox priest only made the call more important. "I felt that much more responsibility," he said.

The fifth of six children, Nicholas experienced less of his parents' earlier alcohol abuse than the older children. His parents quit drinking when he was three. Until then, "it was heavy drinking and fighting. I was kind of saved from that."

Involvement and eventual leadership in the Orthodox Church profoundly changed his parents' lives. But their youthful struggles took a toll on the four oldest children. Nicholas said none of his older siblings could help his parents navigate their dad's illness and newfound disability. They all had their own troubles.

So Nicholas quit his job. The church helped him and his parents find a home in Anchorage. By the time of our interview, he'd been helping his parents for five years. His dad has made progress, but both parents had to stop working. Their retirement covers some but not all the household expenses.

"It was up to me to do everything else." He said he wants his parents to have the most comfortable life possible. Despite steady work in Anchorage, he still often lives paycheck to paycheck. A recent trip back to his home of Saint Paul Island had the air of luxury. The remote Aleutian island cost him a paycheck to visit.

"I wanted to smell that salt air. I wanted to hear the seals and see the birds," said Nicholas, whose family is Aleut. He finally had enough tenure at work to get three weeks' vacation a year. That meant he could take enough time off to go.

The blessing of sacrifice

Caregivers like Nicholas can only get away when others come alongside them. That's the thinking behind one type of intentional community. When I use that term, I refer to people who choose to live together on purpose. In other words, they don't live with others to save money or stay safe. They certainly don't live with others because it's easier. Rather, intentional communities usually form around a shared belief that it's *good* to live together. Though these arrangements often prove somewhat temporary, they usually involve commitments beyond a lease.

Not surprisingly, some of the singles who lived in such settings were priests or consecrated Catholics. An Anglican option, the Community of St. Anselm, involves a one-year commitment. The archbishop of Canterbury started the program for young adults in 2015. Some choose to live together at Lambeth Palace in London, while others commute.

An ecumenical group of men in Nashville, Tennessee, aims at something more long-term. "One of our goals is to make celibacy much more normal and accessible and ordinary," said Pieter Valk, a founder of the Family of Brothers Monastery.[10] To make it more accessible, singles need long-term support, like committed housemates.

Pieter, who is gay, has challenged the Protestant church for "asking only gay Christians to consider celibacy."[11] For celibate Christians to thrive, they need ways to meet many of the needs this book identifies. One of the biggest needs? Commitment.

Pieter said that commitment plays a huge role in spiritual formation. For people in a marriage, that's "the primary place where their sanctification happens," Pieter said. The spouse says, "'I can't stand to be around you another year if you don't deal with this.'"

Single people rarely have relationships close enough and committed enough to provide such feedback. To assist in providing that, the monastery he helped start includes weekly confession and accountability.

Living with others does not guarantee the kind of relational depth Pieter describes. But it's hard to develop such closeness *without* living together. I think that's one reason sharing a roof is so sacred.

Of the few I've met who live in intentional communities, none said explicitly that they wanted a chance to share, help with chores, care for the sick, or give up things for others' good. But then, no one cites those as reasons for wanting marriage or a family either.

Yet at the heart of it, living in intentional community means committing to those things. Isn't marriage itself a form of intentional community? It's just that other forms are so rare, we tend to think they're altogether different from marriage.

For three years, I lived in an intentional community that combined single and married people, Protestants and Catholics. Each time I go back to the Bay Area, I stay there. On one visit, I met a new couple that had moved in downstairs. Each time he met me, Mike, the husband, reintroduced himself. Several years ago, he had a brain injury that caused severe memory loss.

Because of a friend who cares for a disabled son, I have some sense of how heavy a load Mike's wife, Maria, carries. But in the beautiful providence of God, she doesn't have to care for him all alone, as many others do. Because of the roof God's provided for them, many other hands have the privilege of sharing, caring, helping with chores, and giving up things for the good of Maria *and Mike*.

They do the same in return. "Everyone's lives are enriched," Maria said in an email. "Mike and I aren't merely receivers of our housemates' caring and helping. He can't remember specifics, but our housemates know he cares for them, encourages them, and prays for them."

For more Christians to love and live like that, we have to rethink how housing fits into the life of God's family.

• • •

As we come to the end of this chapter, take a few minutes to reflect on shelter in your life.

What do you **grieve** about your housing?

What kind of shelter do you **have**? In many cultures, housing is tied to wealth. How is God calling you to steward what you have?

Is there something you need to **confess or repent of**?

What can you **give**, whether in the present or the future? Proverbs 11:10 says, "When the righteous prosper, the city rejoices." How can you share your housing, whatever it is, in a way that makes others rejoice?

Staying with Strangers

PLANNING A YEARLONG TRIP involves immense detail. I had to move. Store my things. Deal with my car. Figure out insurance. And taxes! With all that, I overlooked emotional health.

Because of traveling alone, I had no human to share it all with me. My "community" changed every week or so. But I learned international travel early—and as an extension of family life.

My parents moved to Singapore right before I left for college. For several Christmases after, I had to fly abroad to visit my family. With that start to foreign travel, it seemed only natural to plan future trips to places where my friends moved. I often got a free place to stay. And they got to see a friend from home. (More than once, I brought them things hard to find abroad.)

When it came to my research trip, I decided to try staying with local Christians as much as possible. Since I planned to stay just a week in most places, I hoped even many strangers might say yes.

In return, I always offered to help however I could. I watered plants, washed many dishes, and often did some cooking for hosts. Sourdough bread, guacamole, and pizza all proved popular.

Not every culture sees hospitality the same, of course. But almost every time I had to use an Airbnb instead, something good came of it. More than once, I got a Christian host. In Panama City, my second Airbnb host of the week provided the contact who led to *all* that country's interviews.

One Addis Ababa host connected me to the Italian Catholic man through whom I later made contacts for interviews in Bethlehem and Rome. One of those Roman contacts in turn led to a priest who helped with interviews in Bogotá.

I initially grieved ending up at that Airbnb. To me, it seemed like a failure of my community. But it eventually led to seven interviews across four countries! Almost every time housing didn't go as planned, God had something even better in store.

Most often, though, I found housing through friends or churches or friends of friends. I met my Kenyan hosts' son in Switzerland, at L'Abri. People I met in Kyiv and Seoul proved vital contacts for my stays in Lagos and Bengaluru. An American I randomly met one Sunday in Rome later helped me find housing in Bogotá. Of my eighty-one hosts, the majority were Christians who opened their homes to me.

God always provided, as I told my prayer team. His timing often built my faith. My Bucharest housing came together the morning I left Germany. Had I not gotten stuck in Vienna en route, my host would have accepted me on barely one day's notice.

In Spain, I split my time between two apartments. The first stay ended on a Sunday, so my host drove me to a church whose pastor I'd emailed. I walked in with all my bags in tow. I didn't know where I'd stay that night. Thanks to the pastor's help, though, and a very hospitable teacher—herself a foreigner—I left the service with the key to an apartment.

It's still humbling to think how much kindness so many strangers showed me, and how many shared whatever they had with me. By God's kindness, my greatest troubles on the road all occurred in the otherwise hospitable country of Brazil. In São Paulo, I stayed with a family my sister-in-law knew. In the end, they let me stay with them almost six weeks total. I did my best to thank them, but only God can fully repay that debt.

Initially, I admittedly thought this approach would help contain costs. And it did. I spent much more on food than housing, even with cooking many of my meals. But ultimately, staying with so many previously unknown Christian siblings around the world proved most important relationally.

Staying with my global church family gave me a much richer cultural experience. And it made for much deeper conversation, despite my usually short stays. Those visits played a vital role in helping me stay grounded and resilient despite my often-grueling pace. And they deeply shaped how I write about community, friendship, and housing in this book.

I'm forever grateful to all those whose hospitality helped make this book possible. I hope their sacrifice and courage bless you, too.

CHAPTER 6

FOOD

*How Meals Connect Us to God
and Each Other*

THE PRIEST STOOD IN HIS SMALL student apartment in Bengaluru. A set table lay before him as he recited the daily mass. Even indoors, South India's humid heat found its way to him. But Fr. Jerin dressed the same for these private masses as he would have at his home parish, further south in Kerala. Alone or with others, he wore the long, white clerical dress and the wide, embroidered stole for that church season.

He continued reading aloud. Reaching a line for parishioners, he paused, then recited their part too. Then he read his own part, then theirs again—all the way through all the service's prayers and the psalms. If someone had submitted a special prayer request, called an intention, he read that, too.

Then at last, the climax of the service arrived: the eating of the host and drinking of wine. In this moment, Catholics like Fr. Jerin believe they consume the body and blood of Jesus Himself.

Fr. Jerin picked up the plate with the host—a smaller one than he used to serve multiple people. Back home in his Kerala parish, he'd break a special wafer large enough for attendees to easily see. Then he'd add the pieces to all the other smaller wafers. Today only one small wafer rested there. He ate. Theology doesn't change even if you must eat the Eucharist alone. Then he picked up the small chalice that only his lips would touch and drank the wine alone too.

After mass ended, Fr. Jerin closed the liturgy, took off his vestments, and returned to his studies. During the four years he spent in Bengaluru for school, he did this almost every day.

● ● ●

Food plays a profound role in how we connect with God and others. According to Genesis 1 and 2, food was one of the first things God provided for Adam.[1] Food also figured in humanity's first sin. This pattern continues today. The only meal Christians share across all three major traditions? Communion. But we eat at a divided table. I couldn't take communion at an Orthodox church because of my baptism. Catholic and many Protestant churches have similar restrictions on people outside their traditions. Some Protestant churches offer a more open communion.

In his commentary on Acts, theologian Willie James Jennings says, "We have not sufficiently reckoned with how God works in and with our hunger."[2] I don't think I've ever heard a sermon on Christian eating. Have you? Nor do most discussions of singleness look at our relationship with food. Yet as one woman told me she'd heard, "Eating by yourself is harder than sleeping by yourself." If we ignore food, we miss a significant part of singles' lives.

How we eat has the power to create both deep communion and deep loneliness. Jennings argues Peter's Acts 10 vision has great significance. Not by accident does God show Peter forbidden animals. Not by accident does Peter see them while hungry! Jennings says God thus invites Peter "to enter in, become *through eating* a part of something that he did not imagine himself a part of before the eating. This new eating grows out of another invitation to eat, one offered by his savior and friend: 'This is my body, which is given for you' (Luke 22:19)."[3]

Have you ever thought about food in this way? I hadn't, until this book. But for the global church to become an integrated body, we have to consider how food fits into God's plan for community.

In this chapter, we'll look at four biblical practices and teachings about food: fallen eating, fasting, feasting, and gleaning. Together, they remind Christians that spiritual birth trumps physical birth. We ultimately belong to the family Jesus formed through His death on the cross.

Fallen eating

Sin ruptured God's good plan for food and community. If God meant food to connect us, fallen eating probably looks a bit different for single versus married people. From singles, I heard about the higher cost and emotional toll of cooking and eating alone.

When it comes to food, we face three main choices: cook family-size portions, cook small portions, or buy prepared foods. Each of these involves different trade-offs. Cooking in general almost always provides the healthiest, most cost-effective way to eat. That's probably why so many singles do it despite the challenges.

Almost 150 of those I interviewed shared their eating habits with me. The vast majority—79 percent—ate food cooked in the home. Two-thirds of those who discussed food cooked for themselves. Only about one in six ate mostly prepared or restaurant meals. Men were more likely to do this, though plenty of them also cooked.[4]

Nearly all those who bought groceries reported a kind of "single tax," akin to the markup women often pay for things like pink razors. Buying food for one often costs more per meal and increases the risk of spoilage if you buy too much. Singles may also spend more time cooking because of how recipes scale. Sometimes singles even stop eating some of their culture's key foods.

Cooking big: the boring but economical option

Those who like to save time and money often buy and cook as if they had a family. I myself do this, as I can often eat for the week by only cooking twice. Singles who ate more meat than I do said they often bought family packs and froze several small portions. Cooking this way requires a refrigerator or freezer, however. In many parts of the world, people don't have this option.

Tanzanian Catholic Scholastica, 24, said she liked to eat pilau, a rice dish with origins in India. But her job as a development manager for a health-related NGO meant long hours. Like other young professionals I met, she probably had a long commute, too. Pilau takes a long time to cook. And like many people I interviewed, Scholastica lived without a refrigerator.

"Sometimes it's challenging to cook a big, big food when you are alone. You feel like 'How can I cook?'" Instead, Scholastica said, "You just take it simple. The food I eat alone is too simple, compared to when my friends come." Without a way to share her food or keep leftovers, Scholastica almost never made the dish she liked so much.

Even singles with a refrigerator often cook some larger dishes only if they can share it with several people. I've known many women who do a lot of their baking for coworkers or church potlucks. Even the best cake is usually too much for one person to eat!

When he lived alone, one Swiss Protestant man largely gave up bread for this reason. "It's usually a huge part of my culture," he said. But local bakeries only sold it in certain sizes. Each was too big for him. So until he took a roommate, "I didn't buy bread because it would always go bad."

Bread isn't the only thing that often comes in a family-size portion. People said items from mayonnaise to watermelon posed challenges for them. They were often surprised to learn they weren't alone.

Years ago, I bought a gallon of milk that went bad before the sell-by date. The store was just around the corner, so I took it back. (In the US, food shouldn't spoil before the sell-by date. If it does, stores usually replace it or give you a refund.) The store made it right, but only with some shaming. The man told me I had bought too much milk!

Cooking small: variety, but at some cost

Because of the limits with cooking big, many singles preferred to cook just one or two portions at a time. This takes more time per portion, but it has several advantages. You don't need a refrigerator. And you get a more varied diet.

On the downside, however, it's sometimes harder to make a single portion of some foods. Fr. Jerin and I laughed about the challenge of using just part of an onion to make a very small pot of dal, a lentil soup. Outside the United States, I saw many onions closer in size to an egg—much smaller than most sold here. But Fr. Jerin said he still divides his onion up for different uses.

Spices can be especially tricky. Scholastica's pilau probably used a small amount of cinnamon or cloves for a batch that could feed several people. How could you measure how little you'd need for just a one-person batch?

Challenges like this mean singles sometimes skip things altogether. "I stopped eating rice," said Filipina Catholic Chai, 36. In her culture, people may eat rice at almost every meal, but she didn't like to reheat it. Nor could she just cook less.

"A cup of cooked rice will generate enough for four people," Chai said. "You cannot cook rice, just a very thin layer of rice on the bottom. It needs to be shared." Eventually, Chai stopped making rice.

Buying prepared food: fast, but more expensive and less healthy

Given the challenges of cooking, plenty of people find other ways to eat. In some large cities, singles had many dining options. They seemed almost puzzled at the idea of cooking. And in places like Seoul, I heard that it's more and more common to find single-person seating at restaurants. Others didn't like to cook or had challenges doing so.

Tanzanian Catholic Nashon, 27, said he couldn't use his injured hand to cook. Ever since he was three months old, Nashon has lived with nerve damage. He said a botched injection might have caused it. The day we met, he walked out to the balcony attached to his employer's café but had trouble using his right side.

In many parts of the Majority World, disabilities like Nashon's could lead to living on the streets, begging, or being shut in most of the day. Fortunately, he's found work with Neema Crafts. The Anglican-run charity employs about 120 people with disabilities. Many of them work in Neema's large craft shop. Their trades range from carpentry to weaving and jewelry making. Neema also runs a guesthouse and popular café. As an employee, Nashon gets at least one meal a day there.[5] The rest of the time, he buys prepared meals.

To eat alone?

No matter how one eats, almost every person I talked to struggled with eating alone. A dinner I ate in Seoul helps explain this. One night, my married host described her shock the first time she ate with Westerners. "Everyone ordered their own food," she said. Once dishes started coming, things got stranger. People ate whenever their meal arrived. At the end, everyone paid for their own food!

In her mind, a shared meal means everyone eats the same food. They might even share the same plate or bowl. At this point, another guest explained that one of the Korean words for "family," sik-gu, combines the Chinese characters for "mouth" and "eat." In other words, those to whom you're most closely related are the people with whom you eat. Isn't that what Jennings said God wanted Peter to see?

Similarly, an Iñupiaq friend here in Anchorage told me that in his village, people often greet him by calling out, "Are you hungry?" If he says no, they'll answer, "You should eat something." In other villages, people who view him as family will call the same greeting, he said. Strangers won't.

These cultures recognize food's powerful role in relationship. As I heard in many interviews, we're meant to share food. In a fallen world, that's not always possible.

To cope with eating alone, singles sometimes invite people over for meals or share food with neighbors. Many watch TV; others read. A Norwegian Protestant artist admitted in a phone interview that he sometimes works while eating. But Asbjørn, 42, clearly disliked answering emails or paying bills while he ate. Because of him, I've made a particular point with this book to never write while I'm eating.

Some told me they even avoid eating alone in nice restaurants or on certain nights of the week. "Eating alone sucks," said a Brazilian Catholic, 42, who asked me to call her Angela. "Everybody looks at you with a pity face. 'Oh, poor girl, she doesn't have anybody.'"

One afternoon in Jerusalem, I couldn't avoid eating alone in a restaurant. But I felt too full of that day's events to munch silently. Spying another solo diner, I asked if we could share a table. In some cultures, this might have caused great offense or suggested sexual interest. Fortunately, the man seemed heartened by the chance to talk while he ate. I hope we both left the restaurant feeling refreshed.

How do you experience fallen eating? What does it feel like to eat alone? Whether you eat with others or mostly alone, are there ways you could enlarge your eating community?

Fasting's surprising fruit

Paradoxically, fasting provides one way for Christians to eat in communion, even if we do so alone. Of all three traditions, the Orthodox might fast the most. Those I interviewed said they spend about half the year abstaining from at least some foods. Each fast relates to a specific remembrance or preparation.

"The whole focus of Orthodoxy is identity in relation to God," said then-Archbishop David Mahaffey of Alaska.[6]

The Orthodox believe fasting helps people become more of who God intended them to be. "It's not so we can catch you when you don't fast," said Vladyka David, as he said I should call him. "It's because, if you really want to take control over your life and over your body, here we go. Can you refrain from entertainment, can you refrain from intimate relations, can you refrain from rich foods?"

It sounded like fasting almost serves as a form of exercise for Orthodox Christians. They fast weekly on Wednesdays and Fridays, as well as during four seasons. Two of these seasons they share with Protestants and Catholics: Nativity at the start of the church calendar and Great Lent in the early spring. The other two seasons I didn't recognize.[7]

Also like exercise, fasting involves both *when* and *what*. Some fasts change over the course of a season. For a certain stage, you give up meat but can still eat dairy products, like cheese. Eventually, though, you go fully vegan.[8]

Great Lent for the Orthodox starts with Cheesefare Sunday, the final day to eat dairy for a while. As Vladyka David explained, this fast before Easter has great relational importance. Cheesefare Sunday has a second name: Forgiveness Sunday. Similar to the Jewish fast of Yom Kippur, Forgiveness Sunday services include a time when all can extend forgiveness to each other.

"When you meet someone on this Forgiveness Sunday vespers, you say to them, 'Forgive me, a sinner,'" Vladyka David said. "The response isn't 'Okay, I forgive you.' It's 'I forgive and God forgives.

Forgive me, a sinner.' And then the first person replies, 'May God forgive us all.'"

Spouses do this too. "I've seen husbands and wives in tears with each other," he said. "Whatever animosity, whatever anger they've had throughout the year, it just melts away at that point."

It must be a powerful thing for singles to join this communal practice of peacemaking. On Forgiveness Sunday, *everyone* has relationships to mend. And even if you start drinking black coffee alone the next day, the bitter taste connects all Orthodox Christians to each other.

The communal nature of these fasts can complicate dating. One Romanian woman said fasts even cost her a relationship. Cătălina, 35, came back to the church in her twenties. As she got more involved, her growing faith caused tension with her boyfriend. When he objected to the church's stance on premarital sex, Cătălina gave in.

But even married couples abstain from sex during Orthodox fasts. According to Vladyka David, one should also abstain the day before attending liturgy. Cătălina faced a growing struggle with how to satisfy both God and her boyfriend. Eventually, he added her fasts to a growing list of ways he found her "too much."

For her, *that* proved too much. "The best luxury is to sleep with a clear conscience," Cătălina said. She decided that nothing good comes from rejecting church teaching.

"Whenever I'm doing what the priest recommends, it always turns out for the best," she said. Cătălina still doesn't know if she'll marry an Orthodox man, but for now, she continues to fast.

•   •   •

Fasting has shaped my own singleness too. For a few years during my thirties, I joined a virtual group of Christians who fasted and prayed each week about singleness. American Protestant Connally Gilliam said that she and her cofounder realized that "when God does break through, it often involves fasting and praying." She writes about singleness.

Through her group and other personal fasts since, God has challenged how I see the seeming gaps in my life. Singleness often appears a gaping hole. But what if fasts and singleness make space for God to bear fruit in me? Through fasting, God reminds me that He asks Christians to trust Him with our bodies in many ways.[9] It's not just with sex.

Orthodox Christians help me see that fasting can also connect us to our community. Protestant Christians often resist rituals as the trappings of "religion." Instead, the nondenominational churches I grew up in stressed relationship with Jesus. But relationship with Jesus radically changes the group of people to whom we belong. Done from a right heart, communal fasts can remind all Christians that we're part of God's family first.

The great feast: our foretaste of heaven

A study of food in the Bible leads inevitably to Jesus and all His dinner parties. At first I didn't know what to make of this. Was it a coincidence? Or might it, like Peter's vision, point to a deeper meaning? Vladyka David suggests the latter. "To me, God has given us food as a way of communion with him," he said.

That makes theological sense. Some I spoke to pointed out that sex and eating share a particular sensory pleasure. In fact, my former Arizona State University professor Don Benjamin once said they're the only two *fully human* activities we can experience. Only sex and eating involve all our senses. Viewed that way, God has given us two ways to bring our whole selves into communion with others. In the traditional church view, only the married should commune through sex. God gives eating to all of us.

Interestingly, we don't read of Adam and Eve's first meals. But sin entered the world in Genesis 3 when they shared food for the wrong reasons. They didn't eat to commune with God and each other. They ate in an effort to become *like* God.

How did God later have the Israelites claim and commemorate their salvation from slavery? By eating. Perhaps God did that to hint of His coming redemption. Someday, He would restore even eating.

Jesus took this further. First He told the crowds that true communion with Him required that they eat His flesh and drink His blood.[10] Then, hours before His death, Jesus served His disciples a meatless Passover. As they ate, He repeated that this was His body and blood, "poured out for many for the forgiveness of sins" (Matthew 26:28, ESV).

Ever since, Christians have shared some form of this meal. Depending on the circumstances, we may eat it monthly, weekly, or even daily. Each tradition sees the bread and wine (or juice, in some cases) differently. But the ritual remains so important in its mysteries that most churches limit who can partake.

As the apostle Paul wrote, "The cup of blessing that we bless, is it not a participation in the blood of Christ? The bread that we break, is it not a participation in the body of Christ? Because there is one bread, we who are many are one body, for we all partake of the one bread" (1 Corinthians 10:16-17, ESV). Each time we eat it, Christians affirm that relationship. But this side of heaven, we may never agree to *one* table.

How often Christians share communion varies a lot. Before this book, I attended a church with weekly communion. Other churches share it less often. While on the road, I often went weeks without communion. When I visited a church that had communion that Sunday, it sometimes felt like I was starving for it. I think that's why I wept the Sunday I couldn't take communion with the Orthodox. Thankfully, I could join their potluck lunch afterward, to which my host treated me.

However we share it, the Eucharist reminds us all that we belong to God's family. When we share our food, it declares anew that in Christ there is no male or female, Jew or Greek—or married person or single.

How often does your church eat communion? Is it often enough? I've heard some say that eating communion less often keeps it special. Is that how married couples approach sex? If Christians work harder at having consistent sex than regular communion, that suggests some skewed values. Is sex really more important to a marriage relationship than communion is to our relationship with God and the church?

Communion might be one of the only times singles in your church get to eat with others. It might be one of the only times some people can fully participate in the service. And don't we all need more of Jesus? If your church already shares communion often, how could you eat more meals with your spiritual family?

Gleaning: a signpost of redeemed eating

One of the Bible's most interesting stories about how food creates community is in the book of Ruth. When a foreigner follows her Jewish mother-in-law home, the two widows face a major crisis:

how to eat. Fortunately, a man in the community obeys the Old Testament command to leave some of the harvest uncollected. This lets people like Ruth come in afterward to gather food.

The early church expanded this practice. "There was not a needy person among them, for as many as were owners of lands or houses sold them and brought the proceeds of what was sold and laid it at the apostles' feet, and it was distributed to each as any had need" (Acts 4:34-35, ESV).

Yet only two chapters later, in Acts 6, unequal treatment of *Greek*-speaking Jewish widows led to the creation of the first deacon ministry. These volunteers usually take care of material needs. Between government welfare programs and continued ethnic tensions, the modern church still struggles with how to embody a unified family.

While in Lagos, I interviewed two divorced Christians from the Igbo tribe.[11] They attended a mainland Pentecostal church in one of Nigeria's largest denominations. Olabisi, 40, had been raising her three children alone for five years. The other, a man I'll call Sunday, worked as the church's chief security officer.

The pastor who translated for us wanted me to interview them because they were less literate. He knew if I only interviewed English speakers, I'd only get a wealthier, more privileged story of singleness. I'm not sure he fully recognized, though, the added struggles for women.

Sunday and Olabisi had some similarities, but differences emerged with food. Sunday said he didn't cook. Ever since the divorce, he'd eaten food from stands on the street. Olabisi had a more basic problem. Though she worked, school fees for her children sometimes ate up most of the money left over after rent.

Unlike in some countries, many Africans must pay to send

their children to school. These fees can cause hardship, especially for poorer families. When illness strikes or a crop fails, families often pull children out of school to free up money.

For Olabisi, school fees sometimes meant many days when she could only afford to buy biscuits and sachet water, a plastic-bagged option common in Nigeria. When I asked, she said she hadn't eaten at all that day.

At that point, I paused the interview to send someone for snacks and drinks. After we finished, I also asked my host to give Olabisi some of the groceries she'd just used my money to buy for us.

Months after our interview, the situation continues to trouble me. Why did her church do so little to help Olabisi? I also wondered about a simpler solution. Olabisi cooked but didn't have enough money. Sunday couldn't cook but had more money. Could they work out an arrangement that helped them both? I didn't know how to raise the question that day in Lagos, or if I should. When should culture dictate the shape of the church? Where and how does the Bible challenge cultural norms?

Since the end of my travels, I've spent more than three years living on the smallest income I've had since college. I couldn't work more and have time to write this book. This season has given me a new appreciation for gleaning.

In the past several months, God has provided hundreds of pounds of food. Much of it came from people who were moving out of Alaska. Some came from volunteer work for a produce company. There I sometimes literally gleaned from the compost box!

In both cases, I benefited from others' extra food. The more I shared it with others, the more God's floodgates seemed to open. If you don't currently glean, how could you start? Do you budget time and money to buy a few meals a month for people without homes? Could you help your church start a food pantry?

For most of my life, I attended churches where everyone else looked like me. We all seemed to have similar resources, too. This is not a coincidence. Sociologist Michael O. Emerson has found that churches where people look alike also have similar wealth or poverty. Only when churches are ethnically diverse do rich and poor worship together.[12]

No matter what your church looks like, gleaning can help us all share food with our ultimate family. Maybe you have a "gleaning Sunday," when people bring in the food they don't need for anyone to take. Maybe families bring some of their leftovers to share with widowers or other singles. Maybe singles share their extra milk with families!

If you're a wealthy church, maybe you partner with a poorer church in your city to help those brothers and sisters have enough to eat. If you're a family with a Costco membership, maybe you find some single folks who could help you use up that giant bag of flour, rice, or beans.

•   •   •

Though we eat yet at multiple tables, Jesus awaits us all at one. How we eat is one powerful, practical, daily way that we can each bring more of His Kingdom on earth as it is in heaven. As we close this chapter, take some time to reflect on food's role in your relationship with God and others.

What do you **grieve**? How do you experience fallen eating? Could fasting help you better grieve with others?

What do you **have**? Where do you experience redeemed eating? For what do you feast?

Is there something you need to **confess or repent of**?

What can you **give**? Might God have a larger place for gleaning in your life?

The Sourdough Starter That (Almost) Went 'round the World

ONE OF MY MOST FREQUENT PRAYER requests on the road involved finding the right people to interview. God proved incredibly creative in answering. One time I had to miss a flight. Sometimes I had to stay in Airbnbs.

For my Ghana interviews, He used my slightly obsessive sourdough smuggling. At first, I planned to visit each continent only once. But travel within Africa did not go as planned. A Ghanaian visa proved so hard to get that I eventually gave up plans to visit there.

Yet I couldn't shake the sense that I needed to travel to more than one West African country. Despite very thorough interviews there, I had a harder time in Nigeria than any other African country. Power cut out multiple times a day, for hours at a time. Roads were among the worst on that continent, and I had zero freedom of movement. The ATMs even charged me far worse rates than any others on my trip.

Everyone kept telling me Ghana was different. Just as I'd done in Eastern Europe, North and East Africa, and would do in large countries like South Africa, India, China, and Brazil, I wanted to look at more than one portrait of life.

For several months, it seemed I'd have to settle for having seen multiple parts of Lagos. Then I wound up returning to Europe for Christmas with my brother. A few days later, I joined a most providential London dinner party. As it turned out, that meal's bad news for my sourdough would finally pave the way to visiting Ghana.

By that point, I'd been smuggling my fermented dough for months. When my fellow diners in London warned me that it wouldn't survive Australia, my blood pressure surged. The injustice!

In my defense, I hadn't originally planned to smuggle sourdough with me. But after the arduous journey to start it, I'd become a rather obsessive dough mother. Obsessed enough that my cousin asked, "Do you think you'll take it on your trip?"

So then I had to.

Traveling with sourdough actually has a long history.[13] It even led to a nickname for California gold miners who came to Alaska.[14] (Perhaps that's why I succeeded so long.)

Despite many lengthy flights, the main things successful smuggling took were leak protection for the jar I stored the sourdough in and regular access to flour and water. (When sourdough goes too long outside a refrigerator, you have to replace most of it with fresh flour and water twice a day. Kept inside a fridge, it only needs these "feedings" every few days.)

Except for two days at an Airbnb in Chennai, something

always worked out. When my Kenyan hosts didn't have a fridge, their neighbor stored my sourdough in his. In Tanzania, a friend of my host stashed it in what must have been a fish freezer, to judge from the smell afterward.

So I kept explaining what sourdough was and sharing it with my hosts. When a home didn't have an oven, I made pancakes with chopped fruit. (Nutella works too.) In New Delhi, I introduced my hosts to homemade bread. They liked it so much, the wife kept some of my starter when I left.[15] Thus it continued, through nine months and three continents.

Then our grand journey stalled, that night in London. I'd hoped to conceal my jar until I cleared Australia's customs. But then I heard about the food-smelling dogs. And the TV show about how strictly Australia protects its pristine ecosystem. After learning about the fines they charge hapless passengers who keep airplane food to eat later, I'd heard enough.

I'd hoped to fly straight from Australia to South America. But clearly I couldn't take my sourdough—or several other pantry items—with me. Just this once, I decided to spend a bit extra. I'd leave my food in Singapore, while I spared myself an aneurysm, apoplexy, or worse. I'd just have to fly back there after Australia, and then fly west to South America.

And that's how I made it to Ghana. You see, that dinner party brought some good news too. That night I just "happened" to meet a Ghanaian woman with a well-connected father. When she heard about my disastrous efforts to visit her country, she assured me, "I can get you a visa."

She did. While I went down under, the sourdough sojourned in Singapore. Then a few weeks later, we finally made it to Ghana.

If not for that provision, I'd have missed meeting several people whose stories I share in these pages. I'd have left with a shallower experience of West Africa. And I'd have missed one of the trip's most moving spiritual experiences.

At the end of an interview in Kumasi, I reimbursed the woman for travel expenses and missed work (about twelve dollars). She burst into tears and held me a long time, saying, "Thank You, Jesus" over and over.

I felt so unworthy of that emotion . . . and grateful for whom she thanked. I have no idea why God chose *me* for this work. I'm sure I made far more mistakes than I'll ever know. But in God's immense kindness, He sometimes chose *my* hands and ears to help people receive His love anew.

Can you believe He even let me keep that sourdough in the bargain?

CHAPTER 7

SEXUALITY
AND THE BODY

God's Invitation to Wrestle

USUALLY I START THESE CHAPTERS WITH A STORY. But the enemy has caused such wreckage around our bodies and sexuality that I want to begin this topic differently. For us to hear what God might want to say through this chapter, we need to start with prayer.

Read and pray through part of Psalm 139. As you do, ponder: What does this show about God? What does it say about your body?

You created my inmost being;
    you knit me together in my mother's womb.
I praise you because I am fearfully and wonderfully made;
    your works are wonderful,
    I know that full well.
My frame was not hidden from you

when I was made in the secret place,
when I was woven together in the depths of the earth.
Your eyes saw my unformed body;
all the days ordained for me were written in your book
before one of them came to be.
How precious to me are your thoughts, God!
How vast is the sum of them!

PSALM 139:13-17

In the Bible's first reference to humans, we find a remarkable statement: "Then God said, 'Let us make mankind in our image, in our likeness'" (Genesis 1:26). In the very fiber of our physical bodies, we show something of the triune, relational God. One verse later, we learn that creating human beings in God's triune image took creating more than one: "So God created mankind in his own image, in the image of God he created them; male and female he created them."

As I started this chapter, I initially felt a sense of defeat. People go through so much pain around sex and embodiment. Carnage, even! To our shame, the church has played a big role in that. Far too often, we've attributed our own broken thinking to God.

To write about the body and sexuality felt like walking into the enemy's territory. But that's a lie. *God* invented human bodies. Sexuality helps show *God's* identity and nature. I think that's part of why the enemy wages such a fierce attack on this part of us. He'll do anything to keep us from seeing more of Who God is.

So let me set the record straight. In this chapter, we're on *holy* ground. Each human body contains an individual soul. But our bodies are also deeply communal. They reveal and start from the actions of others and the God who supplies our breath.

What kind of God *did* make us? Sexuality is one of the hardest parts of Christian singleness. In fact, some of you may have flipped to this chapter first to judge the rest of the book. Between how the church has handled sexuality and what the Bible says about it, many people think they have to choose between faith and sexuality.

I believe that's a false choice, yet *I* struggle with sexuality. This is the only topic in the book where I'm not sure how God meets singles' needs outside marriage. Obedience to His purpose for sex seems to restrict it to married life.[1] Must singles then live with unmet sexual needs?

If God is truly good, then so is God's plan and purpose for our bodies. If you, like me, struggle to believe that God's plan for our bodies is good, get ready for a wrestling match in this chapter.

It's going to take our full strength. We probably won't leave the same. But I think that's exciting. Imagine a God who's willing to let us wrestle Him! After Jacob did so, he left limping and probably humbled, but with a blessing and a new name.

The only way I ever get close to believing God's plan is good is when I draw close to Father, Son, and Holy Spirit. I have to feel God's love for me. To do that, I have to decrease, as John the Baptist said in John 3. Sometimes other people have to decrease a lot. God has to increase.

To help us with this, we're going to use the Lord's Prayer. The framework we'll follow draws closely on a study guide from the Canadian ministry Prayer Current.[2]

Think of the Lord's Prayer as seven related parts, each with its own theme.[3]

1. Our Father who art in heaven—*relationship*

2. Hallowed be Thy name—*worship*

3. Thy Kingdom come, Thy will be done—*God's good plan*

4. Give us this day our daily bread—*generosity and contentment*

5. Forgive us our trespasses, as we forgive those who trespass against us—*reconciliation*

6. Lead us not into temptation[4]—*the reality of battle*

7. Thine is the Kingdom, and the power, and the glory[5]—*surrender*

This approach to the Lord's Prayer has helped me many times over the years. Whenever I struggle to pray for a particular person or situation, I use these themes as a guide.

The Lord's Prayer can also help us avoid the sin of judgment as we discuss singleness and the body. As a journalist, my primary aim was to hear and report people's stories. I'm grateful for how honestly some of them shared about their lives.

At times, though, that may make it easier to see others' sin than our own. If that happens, Jesus shows us how to pray about it. He teaches us to focus on our part of the problem and where we need to change.

Relationship

Jesus' prayer teaches us that every conversation with God should start by declaring our relationship. If that's true, then it even applies to discussing sexuality with God. How, then, do we address God? *As Father.*

Human fathers vary greatly in how they relate to the children they sire. Perhaps because of this, Jesus gave several statements and pictures of God the Father. The one that's shaped me the most is His lengthy parable in Luke 15. I'm deeply indebted to my former pastor Tim Keller for helping me see it as a story of prodigal *sons*, plural.

Jesus' words in Matthew give us another picture of God as Father: "Which of you, if your son asks for bread, will give him a stone? Or if he asks for a fish, will give him a snake? If you, then, though you are evil, know how to give good gifts to your children, how much more will your Father in heaven give good gifts to those who ask him!" (Matthew 7:9-11).

Don, 34, a Korean Protestant, said this relationship helped reframe his understanding of sex. Don first went to church in high school but didn't have much of a relationship with God. "It was a really big roller coaster," he said. Don would live on his own as long as he could. He turned to God only in crisis. Whenever he felt more secure, he went back to "living like a non-Christian."

That changed a couple of years before our interview. Don's newfound relationship with God quickly changed what it meant to date and be single. "Before Jesus, it was about filling the insecurities of my identity, which needs to be filled with God, with recognition from other people.

"Now that I've recently come back to Christ, those are things that I'm struggling with—realizing how broken I was before and figuring out how I need to learn that in Christ before I get into a relationship," Don said. "The first stage of building my identity in God was breaking down all the false identities I'd built."

Before meeting Jesus, Don used dating relationships to feel okay about himself. After his conversion, Don saw this practice with new eyes. "When those false identities were all stripped off of me and it was entirely just me, I realized I was nobody," he said. "And that was really hard to accept. But I needed to accept that now to realize who I am in God. Through that process I realized, if you are God's child, if your identity is set in God, then money, work, sex—all these things become a blessing. But if you don't have that identity in God, then those things are just temporary gods that you try to fill that hole with."

Used in the wrong way, sex didn't satisfy him. "Sex is fun, but afterwards you feel that emptiness," Don said—the sense of a hole that you're trying to fill. "Once you have it, sex becomes nothing quickly. When you don't have it, you feel like it would be so great and amazing. Until you find God to fill that void, you keep on searching for that next thing."

No matter how long we've known God, we all struggle with that tendency.

Worship

The *First Nations Version* translates the second phrase of the Lord's Prayer as "Your name is sacred and holy" (Luke 11:2). How do we respond to what is sacred and holy? We treat it with reverence and care. Sometimes we bow. Often we devote extended time to it. God made human beings to worship . . . Him.

When we use our bodies to acknowledge God's supreme worth, we join all creation in praising our Maker. In Luke's account, Jesus enters Jerusalem before His death to a chorus of public praise. The Pharisees protest: "Teacher, rebuke your disciples!"

"'I tell you,' he replied, 'if they keep quiet, the stones will cry out'" (Luke 19:39-40). That's a pretty striking statement of how much God made creation to recognize its Maker's supreme worth.

But when it came to humans, God gave us free will. Ever since sin entered the world, humans have turned our instinct for worship away from God. In Romans 1, Paul says our misdirected worship often starts with sexuality. Note that I said *starts*. If you read the passage closely, it's clear that sexual immorality only starts a long list of great sins. Toward the end? Things like arrogance and gossip. We'll talk more about this passage in chapter 9.

The man who most clearly echoed Paul's words in my interviews was not the person I expected. Bohdan, 28, was a Ukrainian actor who'd been deeply hurt by the Orthodox Church. He was equally or perhaps even more cynical about his peers in the film industry, and the ways they often treated sex.

In one past job, Bohdan saw a director violate an actress in front of others to show her what he wanted on camera. Bohdan apparently didn't intervene, but afterward he told the woman that shouldn't have happened.

"People turn sex into a cult," he said. "I consider it an abomination of today's society."

Sex offers one of life's few ecstatic experiences, if it results in an orgasm. Perhaps that's why we so often risk everything to pursue it. Yet over and over again, people told me that treating sex as the ultimate thing left them dissatisfied.

Youssef, whom we met earlier, was in the process of divorce when we spoke. He'd spent years trying to make things work with a wife who had mental illness. Faithfulness to her meant spending a long time more like a single man than a married one.

Youssef turned to masturbation for sexual release but set limits for himself. "Pornography dehumanizes," he said, so he avoids it. "I'm participating in this process of making someone less human. That's sinful. I hate that. It's like you're thirsty and you drink salt water."

South African Pertunia, 22, said treating sex that way only increased her thirst. "I remember when *Fifty Shades of Grey* came out," she said. "One of my friends was like, 'Yo, there's a new book that came out that you have to read.'"

She lived in a township outside Pretoria—a poorer, majority Black community called Mamelodi. But thanks to the global economy, Pertunia and her friend tracked down an e-book version of the decade's bestselling book.[6] Once they did, she couldn't stop reading. "I didn't even sleep, going through that book every night," she said.

Both Youssef and Pertunia said they needed others' help to build healthier habits around sex. "I try to keep myself in check with one of my friends," Youssef said.

Pertunia had to change her approach to both dating and friendship. "Dating used to be a tool of escape, when I would not want to deal with my problems," she said. "I really felt unloved at home. I felt I was not given enough attention." Rather than try to work on things with her parents, she sought whatever love she could from a relationship. But each time Pertunia thought a new boyfriend would help, her problems got worse.

Through Christian community, Pertunia finally began to experience God in a different way. The day of our interview, she told me she didn't need anyone other than God. "It's literal to me that God is my fulfillment," she said. The woman who once thought it took a man to meet her deepest emotional needs had come a long way.

"Now I deal with challenges head on and deal with things as they are," she said. "I feel like I do not need to date to be fulfilled in any way. It feels refreshing."

God's good plan

Pertunia's struggle shows the oldest human failing: Time and again, we doubt God's plan is really best. The deeper the need, the harder it is to trust God. Very few needs feel as urgent as that to be loved. When God allows life to go differently than we think it should, it's incredibly hard to trust.

"I despise the fact that people sometimes refer to being gay as a decision," said Jonathan, 20, a Colombian Catholic. "Why would I want to choose a life where people judge me, marginalize me, or other men assume that because I get close to them, I want to have sex with them?" (A Spanish-speaking American priest helped translate for us.)

A fellow Catholic in Panama, who asked that I call her Lizondro,[7] raised similar questions. Until her early twenties, Lizondro, 43, could move like any other nondisabled person. Then it grew hard to walk. Eventually her family learned she'd been born with a virus that affects nerves and muscles in the legs. By the time of our 2019 interview, she'd used a wheelchair for more than a decade.

"I practiced abstinence for all my life, without even knowing that I was sick. I respected the commandments. I wanted to be a virgin when I got married," she said in Spanish.

Lizondro had met a man when she was 40. "I never thought that I was going to feel what I feel when I see him and when I talk to him." She knew the relationship didn't have a future. As she told me this, she started to cry.

"But he came when I was 40, in a wheelchair. Why did God put that in my path—for what? Why did He put that in my path? I don't understand."

She asked one of the hardest questions of faith. Why does God allow what sometimes feels so cruel? Is He really good?

Robin, a gay Catholic, whom we met in chapter 1, has faced similar questions. She had a surprising response. "Push into where it hurts," she said. "Like, obviously deal with trauma if there is trauma, but don't be afraid to push into tension and discomfort with God."

"Really, really work on understanding that you are a beloved creation of God. Once you can not only understand intellectually but you really understand emotionally that you are His beloved creation, that changes your entire experience," Robin said.

"I don't understand suffering to be a bad thing. I just don't." Robin wondered if that came from her Catholicism. I wonder if her work as a doula also shaped her perspective.

"Depending on the situation, suffering's an opportunity for growth," Robin said. "At the very least, it's an opportunity to grow closer to God. And I don't believe that God orchestrates suffering in order to get us to grow closer to Him. That view deeply maligns the character of God. Jesus suffered. The greatest thing that has ever happened for us came through deep, deep suffering. So I can't look at that and say, 'All suffering is bad and you need to avoid it at all costs.'"

In the deepest pain and confusion of my post-research season, I, too, have clung to the Cross. The whole of Scripture turns on what seemed like the worst thing: the death of God's promised-since-Eden Messiah. In the greatest paradox of all time, God brings the absolute best thing out of it: victory over death and sin's curse.

Generosity and contentment

Jesus offers a very practical way to trust God: ask Him to provide for *today's* needs. Whenever I start to really despair, I'm usually trying to face more than today. In fact, nothing's surer to trigger despair than trying to think what a whole life alone will be like.

But Jesus doesn't ask us to do that! On the contrary, *He forbids it*. Three times in Matthew 6, He says not to worry. The final time, He says, "Do not worry about tomorrow, for tomorrow will worry about itself. Each day has enough trouble of its own" (Matthew 6:34). Once I actually obey this, I almost always find that, indeed, I can handle being single today.

Other times, though, I go to God with *urgent* needs for today. I don't know how often that's happened with writing this book. So many weekends, I've gone for a prayer walk, sure that I won't complete that week's chapter. But as I continue, something changes. God provides an insight where a few minutes before, I had none.

I go home. Trusting that God will follow through, I open my laptop. I type in the password. And as I step forward in faith that God will provide, He gives me the words.

During my visit to the Community of St. Anselm, I met two celibate Catholics. They'd both left the Chemin Neuf Community in France for a time, to help with St. Anselm's. Like other consecrated people I interviewed, Joanna, 44, didn't see herself called to singleness. She said God called her to a *community*.

Through that shared religious life, she's bonded with people she didn't choose, the Polish woman said. "They are given to me. And I learn to love them." God provided for her needs. But it didn't always take the form she would have chosen.

Here's one practical way to love the people God's given you today: Look for ways to give and receive nonsexual touch. Some singles told me touch plays such an important role in their life that they ask for hugs. After going through COVID and losing my dad, I'm learning to do that too. No, I can't ever hug my dad again. Maybe I'll never embrace the man I love the way I want to. But God has given lots of father and brother figures whom I can ask for hugs.

Depending on your cultural context, affection might take another form. In Spain, it looks like kissing, a single Catholic man said. For them, the concept of family can include neighbors or other friends, he said. "You see these people as part of your family." So they greet like family would: with a kiss.

Two New Testament writers actually command such a familial greeting.[8] The Orthodox Church takes this seriously. Fr. Edward, 44, an American Orthodox priest in California, said clergy greet each other with three kisses on the cheek. "There is a great physical interaction in the Orthodox culture." When greeting the priest, parishioners kiss his hand. They also greet by kissing the other person's cheek.

Reconciliation

I'm not sure why Jesus prays about food before forgiveness. Perhaps He knew that it's harder to forgive when we're hungry. People shared some very deep wounds when we talked about their bodies.

"Sex outside marriage is very degrading to females," said an American single mother, 28, living in Delaware. Amora, as she asked me to call her, said she believed God intended sex for marriage. But living that out was hard. "I've had experiences where all men want is sex," she said. "Once they get sex, you don't really matter."

An American Protestant living in New York City experienced a similar pain. For Jenny, as she asked me to call her, it came from her disability.

"Guys find me attractive, but they're scared to go any further," said Jenny, 48. Like Lizondro, she needs a wheelchair. During her birth, the doctors used forceps to deliver her. This led to permanent brain damage, which affects use of her muscles. She graduated from college, but some of the brain damage also affects the way she speaks.

"I relate a lot to Gomer," Jenny said. In the book of Hosea, God tells the prophet to marry a woman in prostitution named Gomer.

"God created man to desire a Proverbs 31 woman who would take care of the household and the kids and all that." She can't do much of that. Jenny didn't blame men for struggling with her disability, but the fact remains. Few men know how to pursue a relationship, Jenny said.

"So I feel like Gomer—who in their right mind wants a prostitute as a wife?" Jenny said. "But God tells Hosea to go to Gomer. And I feel like God has to command a man. Not too long ago, I thought, *Who knows what God has planned?* There could have been a guy who God commanded, but through his disobedience, he didn't obey. I don't think I'll ever know. . . . It's all in God's plans."[9]

A third kind of pain goes back very early. Tatiana, 42, an American Orthodox woman, was sexually abused several times between five and ten years of age. Multiple men abused her, including a teacher, a relative, and a man who served in her church. Native American and Alaska Native women like her are much likelier to face sexual assault and violence than others.[10] Tatiana is Yup'ik.

"It was very hard because I was different, I was half," Tatiana said. (One parent is Yup'ik; one is not.) "I was 'pretty,' I was 'beautiful.' I didn't like it when those words would be said to me because then the bad things would happen to me. Sometimes I like to wear makeup, but I didn't want to stand out so much."

Tatiana said she thought the abuse was part of why she's still single. For years, anytime someone showed interest in her, she'd freak out. "That wall would go up," she said.

More recently, she's sought help. Like the Catholic Church, Orthodox Christians have a routine of formal confession. Tatiana said this ritual has helped her learn to share what happened to her. She also went through a community program called Beauty for Ashes, which helps people process and heal from various kinds of violence and trauma.

Remarkably, Tatiana said the abuse stopped at ten, when she made a conscious choice that she didn't want it to happen anymore. It sounds like she may have also wanted to spare her eight-year-old sister. "I still remember it," she said. "I was practicing my oboe in the basement, and he came down and was touching me inappropriately."

"After that, I would get very mean, or stern. I would talk back to that one individual. Start to stand my ground," she said. Not until she entered her teens would Tatiana dare to talk back to her mom. But something inside told her she had to do whatever it took to resist him.

I'm sure Tatiana has many hard questions about all that she went through. Rightfully so. Thankfully, the Bible gives us an entire book, Job, and dozens of psalms that model how to take our hardest questions to God. Some of the angriest psalms even go into detailed accounts of what harm the author wants for his enemy!

And yet. No matter what others might do to us, Jesus calls us to forgive them. It must be one of His hardest teachings. Who will bring justice if we stop holding that debt against those who've wronged us? But Jesus insists: He alone has the right to judge the world. And He bore all that judgment in a human body He *chose* to receive.

"In this is love," John says in his first epistle (4:10, ESV).

The reality of battle

If all this weren't hard enough, Jesus warned Christians to expect trouble. He even taught that we have an enemy who actively seeks our downfall. In John 8, Jesus says the devil "was a murderer from the beginning, not holding to the truth, for there is no truth in him. When he lies, he speaks his native language, for he is a liar and the father of lies" (John 8:44).

Think about that in light of what we discussed earlier. *Any* lie comes from the enemy! And who of us hasn't believed countless lies about our bodies and sexuality? In contrast, Jesus says, "If you hold to my teaching, you are really my disciples. Then you will know the truth, and the truth will set you free" (John 8:31-32).

For Annila, 35, an Indian Protestant, this sets up quite a battle in her thought life. The thoughts we fuel gain power, she said. "If you don't fuel that thought, then it just dies a natural death. It takes a lot of discipline."

Several others I talked to also stressed the importance of prayer—especially for sexual obedience. Francisco, the man who cared for his parents, said, "Life is a constant struggle. Work is a constant struggle. Sometimes you have to do things that you don't want to do—and you still have to do it." Echoing my father, years ago, he compared sexual desire to a wild horse that you have to tame.

Some, of course, object to that. As this chapter shows, people who call themselves Christians hold a range of views on sexuality. Some hold to the biblical teaching: (1) God intended sex for marriage between a man and a woman; (2) couples should remain married, if at all possible; and (3) Christians should generally not marry outside the faith.

Many I spoke to affirm this teaching but struggle to live it out. Others interpret the biblical passages behind these teachings differently or see them as not applicable.[11] For example, Angela, from chapter 6, thinks that her sexual ethic is compatible with her faith.

"I accept many things from the church," she said, "but this part about sexuality I just don't agree with."

For some Christians, her view amounts to classic (sexual) sin: rebellion against God. But Paul says, "All have sinned and fall short of the glory of God" (Romans 3:23). How do we Christians who think we've lived pretty good lives read that? The way some of us talk, you'd think Jesus reserved His most blistering remarks for the sinners of His world.

He didn't. He spent a lot of evenings going to their dinner parties. At least once, He even invited Himself over! Without exception, He showed gentleness and deep mercy to those who overtly broke God's commands. And He saved His sharpest rebukes for the seemingly righteous people who prided themselves on following God. Look at how Jesus describes the older son in Luke 15.

As Tim Keller points out, *it's not just "bad" deeds that fall short of God's glory.* "Good" deeds done for selfish reasons earn the wages of death too. It's easy to list overt sexual sins: rape, adultery, abuse. But a "bad heart," to use Bible translator Terry Wildman's phrase, poisons seemingly good deeds too.[12]

Kevin, the man with the rainbow fish pin, said he's come to

share Annila's concern with thoughts. During a lengthy phone interview, we talked about the role of nonsexual touch in his friendships—especially handholding.

Cultures view same-sex handholding very differently.[13] Yet many readers might struggle with Kevin's doing so as a celibate gay man. I include his perspective here because Christians do a very poor job of considering how self-giving love applies to physical relationships.[14] No one else addressed this as clearly as Kevin did.

"I've asked myself a number of times, 'Why do you want to hold this person's hand? What is the reason you want to do that?'" Kevin said. "I think the only honest way that I can answer is that I want to have a connection with this person."

To show self-giving love, he has to adjust. "I have to be very careful with different people because different people experience touch very differently," he said. With at least one friend, Kevin might cuddle during movies. "I've spoken to him about this—for him it's a friendship thing."

With others, he can't do that. "Some of my gay Christian friends have a very, very strong sex drive. And with them, I would be very, very careful to not get into a situation that might arouse them.

"I have to ask myself honestly, 'What am I trying to do here?' What I really want to do is, I want this person to feel valued by me, and therefore valued by God. I have to reset differently to each different person."

Wherever you're at, bring your bodily and sexual history to Jesus in prayer. Bring as much as you can right now. As Kevin said in chapter 4, "Jesus has taken my shame. Why would I want to hang on to it?"

If you need further encouragement, read what Paul says about his struggle in Romans 7:15–8:2. Ask God to guide you in paths of righteousness. Ask God to show you how your body and sexuality can make the world around you a better place.

Surrender

Jesus closes the Lord's Prayer with this reminder: God's is the Kingdom, the power, and the glory, forever and ever. Whenever we choose to follow Him, we take up a cross. And yet Jesus also promised: "Take my yoke upon you and learn from me, for I am gentle and humble in heart, and you will find rest for your souls. For my yoke is easy and my burden is light" (Matthew 11:29-30).

We can't use our bodies to bring God's Kingdom in the way *He wants* without first surrendering them to God. In closing, spend some time reflecting on what you have and haven't surrendered to God. What would it take to yield further?

• • •

What do you **grieve?** Where are you seeking control around your body and sexuality? Where are you seeking power or glory? Ask God to help you surrender.

What do you **have?** Ask how your body and sexuality can help bring God's Kingdom.

Is there something you need to **confess or repent of?**

What can you **give?** Ask how God wants to be glorified in your body and sexuality.

Of Unfinished Coats and Borrowed Machines

A Sewing Tale

UNTIL MY TRIP, I didn't understand why Jesus called clothing a source of worry. Pre-trip, I enjoyed a wardrobe of nearly four hundred pieces of clothing. (I once counted them all for a book review.)[15] Absent a boyfriend, I dressed solely to suit each day's mood and slate of activities.

Fieldwork changed that. I needed clothes that worked in a range of climates, cultures, and settings. They had to hold up to hard use, wash easily, and look okay without pressing. And to avoid offense in more conservative cultures, I needed to balance modesty with styles I could feel comfortable wearing over and over and over. (I didn't foresee the Nigerian church that thought I should cover my hair, but fortunately I'd packed a scarf-like Indian garment that worked.)

All this led to a very ambitious project list. Because of course I had to take a mostly hand-sewn wardrobe. I'd already made several garments that would work for the trip, but I wanted many more. Only a few reached completion.

I sewed the shoulder seams for my raincoat just hours before I boarded my departure flight from the US. When I wore it through security, one guard spotted the missing sleeves and raw edges. "Did you make that?" she asked.

Then, just five cities into the trip, I lost track of a favorite shirt in Bucharest. I forgot more clothes in Beirut: the now-finished raincoat and one of my only dresses, made from an especially costly knit.

I'd managed to replace the blouse, thanks to borrowed sewing machines in Germany and South Africa, and a Liberty of London bargain. The Beirut clothes were a different matter.

Thanks to longstanding hostilities between Lebanon and Israel, you can't travel or mail anything directly between them. You also have to time Israel visits carefully. Some Muslim countries won't admit you if you've visited Israel, even though that government doesn't stamp your passport.

In a great kindness, an American friend of my Beirut host agreed to take the clothes home to the States at Thanksgiving and mail them to my brother in Germany. (I reclaimed the clothes at Christmas.)

The worst still lay ahead. After a very stressful trip to the famous statue of Jesus in Rio de Janeiro, I checked the suitcase with my undergarments and warm-weather clothes for a short flight to São Paulo. I never saw it again.

Mercifully, my next few stops had cooler weather. And I had left all my cold-weather clothes in São Paulo. But now I had just two threadbare short-sleeved shirts with me. One had gotten so thin, I planned to stop wearing it.

By the time I reached Lima, Peru, clothes had grown to rival interviews among my worries. Before the trip, I'd wondered: *What sins will I battle?* Sin often shows up clearest in relationship. But fieldwork rendered me temporarily single-single. For seventeen months, I hardly saw anyone more than a few days. Most people didn't spend long enough with me for conflict.

To my surprise, the sin that emerged most clearly and often was distraction. But not until many months after the trip did I recognize how much I *worried* on the road too. As a self-funded traveler with a finite and shrinking savings account, money often ranked first in concern.

But I also worried frequently about interview contacts. This proved especially hard in South America, where I ran up against language barriers and the challenge of working with Catholics as an unknown Protestant writer.

Maybe the clothing loss was God's unsubtle reminder that He holds *all* my life, at home or abroad, in sickness and health, singleness or marriage.

Months before, I'd grappled with Jesus' poetic advice on worry (Matthew 6) when I had to eat unchilled leftovers for several days. Then, I'd learned how much more I trust in refrigerators than God for my food.

Now I faced the second half of that passage. Of course, I could have bought new clothes, as many people suggested. But those would increase a luggage weight that continued to push the airlines' limits.

And as it happened, I'd splurged on a few lightweight fabrics in South Africa and Singapore. If I sewed them up, I could refill my wardrobe without added luggage weight.

True, it would take more time to sew than shop. But the

difference in money and stress felt immense. I'd had a bad enough time buying new bras in Argentina. (Don't get me started on male shop clerks!)

So when I reached Panama City, I asked almost everyone I met if I could somehow borrow a sewing machine. The only woman who had one used it for work. But she very kindly bought me sewing pins and fabric scissors (also lost in the suitcase).

That night I pulled out my fabric and blouse patterns. Trusting that God would provide a way to sew, I cut out two blouses, kneeling on the bedroom's uneven floor.

The next day I had to change housing. On a whim, I asked my new host about a sewing machine. She found one. In God's kindness, He even provided all four of my interviews so quickly that I had time to sew.

And that's how I wound up making five shirts, most of a dress, and even a new purse in five days.

CHAPTER 8

PARENTING

Redeeming Relationships between Generations

INGRID WENT TO CHURCH to ask God's forgiveness. Things had gotten so bad that she planned to take her own life . . . and her daughters'. The Colombian single mother didn't think she could face homelessness again.

Motherhood brought one challenge after another for Ingrid, a Catholic woman I met in Bogotá. She first moved there while a teenager. By 19 she had had her first child. The father of Ingrid's first child abused her. "We moved in together, but he hit me when I was pregnant," she said. "I could not stand it. I bled so much that I almost lost the baby."

That relationship didn't last long. While Sofia was still young, Ingrid moved to Medellín. There she met another man. "Sometimes you think that you fix your life by finding someone else, but I was wrong," she said.

They, too, lived together. When Ingrid was 22, they welcomed her second daughter. Then Ingrid started taking a birth-control injection.

When she got pregnant anyway, things turned ugly. "He told me to have an abortion, but I could never do such a thing," Ingrid said. She kept the baby, and they eventually broke up.

Around this time, it sounds like Ingrid's mother took her in for a time. This, too, did not last.

"That was when my pain got aggravated," Ingrid said. "My mom rejected me, and so did my sisters. I suffered a lot, but I believe in the God of mercy. I hung on to Him. My mom denied me food and kicked me out of the house. I told her I would repay her for the help, but she never believed in me."

Seeing her situation, a male cousin who lived in Bogotá offered help. Ingrid and the girls moved there to share his apartment. A neighbor gave her a part-time job paying ten thousand pesos a day. In 2019, this was a little over three dollars. Ingrid found other jobs to supplement her meager wage.

Then disaster struck: Her cousin got married. "We couldn't continue living with him," Ingrid said. "We rented a small room, but my income was not enough."

It was not long before she found herself at church with plans of suicide.

•　•　•

Children have a complicated place in the lives of singles. According to a 2019 Pew Research Center analysis, a higher share of Christians live in single-parent homes than any other religion.[1] Women often head these households. Twenty-one of the thirty single parents I interviewed were women.

As Ingrid's story shows, many single mothers face acute financial hardships. Statistically, single mothers face more financial pressure than single fathers because of the wage gap and other challenges.

One African pastor told me he thought a single mother in his church sold her body to men to help feed her family. He personally helped a single man who appeared less needy, but not the mother. When I asked him if the church gave her any ongoing help, he said he didn't know of any.

Children raise other kinds of pain for singles too. When childless singles seek to know, teach, or support the young, parents sometimes push us away or question our motives. And singles who have children outside marriage too often face rejection and judgment from Christians rather than support and welcome. When singles choose to foster parent or adopt, they sometimes get mixed reactions. People may not respond as warmly as when a couple says they're expecting a baby.

For the church around the world to become a more integrated body, we have to rethink how children *and singles* fit into God's family. Over and over, the Bible describes God as Father to the fatherless, the God of orphans and widows. And Jesus said that when we receive a child in His name, we welcome Him (Matthew 18:2-5; Mark 9:36-37; and Luke 9:48).

None of these verses restrict care for children to those who are already parents. As we hear singles' stories of children and parenting, I encourage you to ponder the youngest humans' place in God's family. What role might singles have in forming the next generation?

Relearning

Children surface some of our most fundamental concerns. What does a virtuous life entail? What kind of people should we strive to be? Children also expose our beliefs about gender roles, especially for women. Who should play the biggest role in their training? And how much do we value that work?

Many forces shape our beliefs about children and parenting. Each does so imperfectly.

Rethinking who qualifies to train children

Several years ago, a Christian friend posed a parenting question on Facebook. Then he added: Childless friends, please don't comment. He did not explicitly ban single people, but it nonetheless represents an attitude many of us face.

Eunice, whom we met in chapter 3, has worked as a youth and children's pastor in Seoul. But she said people often think she can't understand kids because she's not a mother. One time she was about to join a children's ministry when the pastor asked if she was married. "She kind of dropped her face," Eunice recalled. "She said, 'Oh, I was praying for a really good mother who could understand the children more.' That really shocked me."

Eunice worked as a schoolteacher at the time. She put the question to God in prayer: Was she unqualified to serve as the children's pastor? The answer she seemed to hear was, "No, you can learn a father's heart, a mother's heart from Me directly."

"Who could teach me about a father's and mother's heart better than God?" Eunice asked. "I believe that God's heart is mom and dad's heart as well."

Tradition may influence this. Eunice and I are both Protestant. Unlike in the Catholic Church, pastors are usually married. They often also have children. This can reinforce the idea that leadership requires firsthand experience of marriage and parenting.

The Roman Catholic Church operates very differently. Priests cannot marry. For better or worse, celibate Catholics have long run church schools. That means roughly half the world's Christians attend churches that welcome or even require singleness of those who help teach children.

"You can't have every experience," said Alistair, 43, a married Protestant ministry leader living in Hong Kong. "You've got to counter or counterbalance the areas where you don't have as much experience by listening to other people."

Which is ultimately more important: experience or humility? Too often, Christians echo the secular view of sex, which also prizes experience. But isn't a teachable spirit more important?

Patricia, whom we met in chapter 1, never had children. A few years ago, she was asked to colead a young families' group with a married grandmother. The request surprised her, so she asked why they thought of her. "They said, 'You have a lovely presence with children. We'd like you to be part of the group.'"

The experience deepened Patricia's understanding of God's Kingdom. "It sort of helps me to reconfigure, 'What does family really mean?'" she said. "The link isn't necessarily by blood, but by spirit."

Redefining our worth when the church gets it wrong

The church should do a better job of teaching us how to relate to children. But here, too, we often get it wrong. Motherhood plays a key role in how some Christians understand womanhood. Where does that leave childless women? Finnish Protestant Johanna, 41, said women only had one role at a prior church: mother. "I felt like I was an outsider there," she said.

Perhaps because that church didn't seem to conceive what single Christian women could do, Johanna eventually left. The international church where I met her had a different tone. "Families and children don't dominate," she said. Though I learned of that church through friends who had a young family, Johanna found it easier to talk after services, whether with fellow singles or parents of young children.

For some women, 1 Timothy 2:15 even raises questions about their salvation. As a widely used English translation puts it, "women will be saved through childbearing."

Re-examining what our parents taught us

Perhaps the hardest messages to reconsider come from those who raised us. Whether or not we share our parents' or parent figures' beliefs and values, they profoundly shaped our views and attitudes toward children.

When I lived in that communal household with families, I was sometimes amazed at my instincts. I discovered strong views on whether we should leave kitchen cupboards unlocked for children to play in. Even if I had none of my own, I had all kinds of instincts for keeping children safe. Much of these I learned from my parents.

I have strong views on helping children learn, too. When a friend expressed concern about letting her preteen read all of the Bible, I couldn't stay silent. "That was one of the best things my parents let me do!" I *still* stand on the foundation laid from reading through the whole Bible as a child.

We also inherit much brokenness from our parents. "I don't want to be the mother I had," said a Peruvian Catholic who asked me to call her Kary. As a child, her mother abused her physically and psychologically. For years after the abuse, Kary struggled with fears, low self-esteem, and even an eating disorder.

Given the role her mother played, Kary, 41, said she could have easily become a teenage mother and never finished her education. "The person that I am now, I thank God. If God was not present in my life, what would I be now? God helped me a lot."

It doesn't sound like Kary knew her father much, if at all. She called a Christian uncle and her maternal grandfather her angels. Their love and support showed her a different way to live. Though her uncle has children of his own, he remains involved in Kary's life. Sometimes he even helps financially.

"He's my father," Kary said. "In my difficult moments, he supports me."

Abebe, from chapter 3, said the same of Italian Catholic Fulvio. "I'm his son."

Fulvio, 52, never expected that route to fatherhood. But during several years in Addis Ababa, he helped a series of Eritrean and Ethiopian men in crisis. He'd helped nine when I first met him and has continued to open his home since returning home to Italy.

At first, Fulvio saw himself as providing housing. Some men would have been homeless without his help. But some were refugees. One had been tortured. Another was bipolar. They needed more than a roof.

As a single man living in a large house, it seemed unchristian for Fulvio not to help them. But as one man led to more, he needed structure. So Fulvio came up with house rules. Twice a week, they all had to eat dinner together. And they had to work through conflict.

It was hard. They tended to see his place more as a hotel than a family. "I am very idealist, but then you have to fight the reality," Fulvio said.

The reality involved many challenges. Youthful testosterone.

Differences of culture, age, and power. And a complex history. His country once tried to colonize Ethiopia.

Still, Fulvio helped launch some of the men into adulthood. One became a music teacher at the Italian school in Addis Ababa. Others went to school in Italy, as Abebe does now.

And Fulvio learned he could father in a way he didn't expect to. "I never wanted to be a single," he said. "Most of all, I wanted to be a father. This situation in some way compensates for my lack, my emptiness," he said.

Obedience in the unexpected

When we let God reshape our thinking, He sometimes calls us to surprising actions.

Juliet didn't expect to become a foster parent, much less alone. "I've always felt and known I'm a mom; I just assumed I'd follow the plan," she said.

Then, in her late thirties, a women's group in her native South Africa discussed what purpose looks like for single, older women. Juliet, who has lived in five different countries, remembered that she had heard different prophecies over the years.

Several involved the phrase or idea of "mother to the nations." So one day, she went with a friend to meet a social worker.

The person said they needed safe adults kids could stay with while waiting for a permanent placement. "I said, 'Well, that I can do,'" Juliet recalled.

She had one clear limit: "I don't want to do anything permanent."

But after things reached discussion of several possible children, the process stalled. Juliet started to reconsider her limits. She eventually agreed to consider a long-term role.

Not long after, she got a call about a 20-month-old boy. Juliet asked people to pray, then agreed to meet the child. She hoped for some kind of sign if she was meant to take him. But Juliet had no reaction to the child.

With one day to decide, Juliet called her mom.

"What are you looking for, if not this?" her mom asked.

"I expected a bit more something."

Still unsure, Juliet asked God for a dream, which she doesn't usually get. That night, she woke up with a dream and two verses. But even then, she couldn't decide. The dream seemed unclear.

The next day, she called her pastor. As they talked, she realized the verses both seemed to say, "I love you." Maybe God was giving her a choice.

Clarity didn't come until she went to pick up her number for a marathon. "If I can run a marathon, I can raise a child," Juliet said. By the time we spoke, she'd had her foster son for a year.

"If you're choosing to be a single parent, it's not ideal. But I felt what I could offer him was better than being in a children's home," Juliet said. Thanks to several supportive friends, she knew she wasn't alone.

Support can take other forms. Around the same time Juliet's journey began, a family in my relatives' Protestant church started sharing about a similar need. Three of my cousins took notice.

"We are three single sisters that are stronger together than by ourselves," said Hope, 38.

Along with their youngest sister, then in her early twenties, the women live with their parents in rural Washington State. "We prefer to say our parents live with us," joked Joy, 40. Only their brother has married and moved out on his own.

After a year of discussion and prayer, all four women and their parents agreed to accept foster children. By 2022, they'd fostered nearly thirty children in six years. When infant triplets needed parents, they ended up caring for seven kids at once.

Placements have varied greatly. One stayed only an hour. A couple stayed just a night. Some have stayed longer. In 2019, Hope adopted two brothers they'd been fostering. Because the boys had been living with them so long by then, they mostly use her first name. "I wouldn't mind if they changed that, but I also don't want to force anything or insist on anything," she said.

In a way, this also simplifies things for the not-adopted kids in the home. Rather than call themselves "mom," the women trade off as "boss."[2] In addition to sharing parenting and housing, the sisters also all work in the family business on the same property. They divide up childcare in order to make sure they all can work an equal number of hours in the week.

"Big boss" runs things from 3:00 a.m. to 2:00 p.m., to account for when they have a baby in the house. "Afternoon boss" picks up from 2:00 p.m. to 4:00 p.m., followed by "dinner boss." At 5:00 p.m., they all help. Only when it's time for bed do they break into smaller groups. Then Hope reads with her boys. Her sisters each take a few others to say goodnight. Pearl, the youngest, usually takes care of any babies.

How have people responded to them? "They've been really supportive, at least to our face," Hope said. What they're doing challenges the nuclear-family norm. Yet Hope said most moms can see the benefits of how they parent together.

"Joy does things with the kids that I would never do," Hope

said. "I can't be all these people to these kids. They're so much richer because they have other adults around."

The parents I once lived with said similar things about our intentional community. They loved how many more interests and parts of life we housemates exposed their kids to.

Joy said it helps them, too. Getting to watch how others approach a tantrum or other challenge helps her grow. "I am such a much better parent and a more sanctified Christian because others can give feedback on how to handle something."

"What about father figures?" I asked. Their father has some involvement, but the state license only includes the women.

"I agree there are drawbacks. This is not the perfect setup," Hope said. They do what they can. If she needs to get counselors for the boys, she will.

Ultimately, though, this has seemed like the path of obedience.

"We have walked through each door as God has opened it," Hope said. If even one of the six adults in their home had objected, they wouldn't have moved forward. But everyone supported it. If God provided at the start, He will surely see things through to the end.

From hiding to healing

Obeying God often requires that we face some of our deepest pain. At no point does God say we're too broken for Him to heal us. But sometimes it takes a long time to even name some wounds.

When I made it part of my interviews to ask, "Do you have children?" I didn't think how some people would receive this. When I asked Robert, whom we met in chapter 3, he said no. Later, he admitted he wasn't sure.

Shortly before college, his girlfriend got pregnant. Robert wasn't a Christian then, but "I wanted to talk about other options," he said. She chose abortion. "Even though I had walked a few people through crisis pregnancies, when it was my turn, it was very different and moved very fast."

To this day, Robert doesn't know: Is he a father? Does he have a child waiting for him in heaven? "Part of me is so scared and part happy at the thought," he said. He wonders, "Am I dishonoring the life of that child by saying I don't have kids?"

Over the years, maybe half a dozen people have told me their abortion stories. Robert is one of three men to do so. Without exception, it shook them deeply. Yet because of the culture around abortion, it's hard to get healing. Secular discussion of abortion largely leaves men out, framing the choice as solely the woman's. In Christian circles, those who get pregnant outside marriage often face immense pressure.

A year after Robert faced his girlfriend's crisis pregnancy, a friend asked for his help with hers. Unlike him, she was a Christian. She and her boyfriend were very involved with their church. They, too, chose abortion.

Robert and the woman stayed friends. He said, "Years later, when I became a Christian and we talked about this, I said, 'Why did you come to me? I wasn't going to be able to pray for you or anything.' She said, 'The last place that I wanted to be was at church.'" From Christians, she knew she'd hear judgment and shame.

It was years before Robert started to process his own experience of abortion. When he started to open up about it, he was attending a very pro-life church. One day, he and some friends saw a TV report on protests at an abortion clinic. To his shock, he said,

"They were singing songs that I sing in church." He turned to a friend, who'd also had an abortion when she was younger. "I feel so dirty right now." Their simplistic approach to abortion deeply troubled him. Didn't being pro-life mean more than the program showed?

He called his pastors to discuss it. They encouraged Robert and others to start speaking about abortion differently and more openly.

Some of those who'd gone through abortions started talking to young-adult groups. They talked about how they viewed the decision now. "It didn't solve all the problems we were trying to take care of," Robert said.

They also met with the pastors. This led to a frank discussion of what it really means to be a pro-life church. The work doesn't stop at birth. That's when some of the most important work begins. How does a church support single moms who *did* choose life?

Robert said one pastor got very blunt. "Hey, can you guys babysit for her, so she doesn't regret her decision? How can we make her making that decision that we wanted a little bit easier?" He even went on to challenge men who might not consider dating a single mom.

So Robert's church kept talking to people. The more they did, the more abortions they learned of. "It broke my heart the number of people in my own church that had gone through abortions, and nobody knew," Robert said. "I remember one person, their spouse didn't even know."

When we hold our deepest pain and grief up to the light of God's love, He can do amazing things.

●　　●　　●

Ingrid lived to meet with me because she told someone about her great need. When she did, God showed Himself God of the orphan and the widow yet again.

The day she asked God to forgive her for the lives she planned to take, Ingrid met a priest. Perhaps he heard her confession that day. Whatever the case, he asked enough about her to learn of her crisis.

The priest sent her home with 300,000 pesos—the equivalent of a month's wages at her part-time job. Ingrid returned to the church with her girls. "We continued to come because he invited us to church," she said. "I told him that I wanted to work."

So the priest found work for her at the church. "That's why I say that he's a miracle because he didn't know me and gave me that opportunity," Ingrid said. Through him, God saved four lives.

Ingrid still worked for the church when I met her.

As we come to the end of this chapter, take some time for prayer and reflection. Whatever emotions it's stirred up, take them to God. Experience those feelings in His presence. Then ask what He wants to tell you.

●　　●　　●

What do you **grieve** about parenting—either what you received or your present situation?

What children do you **have** in your life? What parent figures do you have? What is your relationship with them like?

Is there something you need to **confess or repent of**?

What can you **give** to younger generations and those who may struggle to connect with them?

PART THREE

SPECIAL
SITUATIONS

CHAPTER 9

SEXUAL MINORITIES

The Struggle for Belonging

THE PILGRIM TURNED TOWARD HOME WITH A HEAVY HEART. He'd come all this way—for what? Rejection? Disappointment?

His friends and coworkers already puzzled at his interest. Why seek the God of another people? Abraham wasn't *their* ancestor. And why risk so much time and money to try to worship in *their* land?

God's followers were notoriously exclusive. They made foreigners worship separately. With skin like his, he didn't stand a chance of drawing near.

But in the end, he faced worse. It wasn't what they could see but what they couldn't that kept him out. They hadn't let him enter the space at all.

The strangest thing was how he had reacted. Inside him, one part began to weep and rage at the hopelessness of seeking a God who wouldn't let you draw near.

Yet another part still hoped. Against all evidence to the contrary, it whispered, *We're not done.*

Oh, cursed soul, to reject all the facts. Could he not hear the men's derisive tone as they shooed him away? Had he not seen the looks on their faces? All his senses seemed to attest to the futility of seeking God.

And yet. And yet somehow he had managed to find a new book of their Scriptures. He couldn't quite say why he bought it. Why add to his pain, when he already had so much?

And yet. No matter what all around seemed to scream, his heart couldn't accept it. Not wholly. If the spiritual realm existed, some part of him still believed that it beckoned.

As they pulled out onto the highway, he sighed and took up his new book: Isaiah. He could wrestle with fact and spirit once he got home to Ethiopia.[1]

•   •   •

The question at the heart of this book is this: How do we love people who are different from us and with whom we sometimes disagree? Each chapter has included people who don't agree with each other. (They probably doubt each other's Christianity, too.) Some won't even participate in communion together. That's why I have focused my reflections here on love. Jesus said that love alone would define His followers.

This chapter may prove the most challenging of all. When it comes to sexual minorities, Christians often rush to bring up verses on sexual sin. According to Scripture, God designed sex for marriage between a man and a woman.[2] Ideally, they share the same faith and never divorce.

For many people, the biblical sexual ethic ends there. As I've argued elsewhere, limiting the Christian sex ethic to boundaries doesn't do justice to God's character.[3] That view also makes it very hard to consider the people I interviewed for this chapter. Does the church have anything to offer people who are same-sex attracted, bisexual, or transgender and consider themselves Christian?

Singles in this situation face unique challenges. "My singleness is very much intertwined with my identity as a sexual minority," said a gay American Protestant[4] who asked me to call him Thomas.

For many of the gay Christians I've known or interviewed, coming to terms with their sexuality was traumatic. Thomas, 26, tried what's known as conversion therapy in an effort to change his attraction to men. It didn't work. Next, he tried celibacy for a time, but that led to a crisis. He continued to struggle, praying a lot. Eventually, he came to believe that having a sexual relationship with a man would be compatible with his belief in God.

All those I interviewed for this chapter described a similar struggle to process their sexual identity. The fourteen people I interviewed held a range of views about Christian ethics around sex.[5] All identified as followers of Jesus at the time.

If you haven't experienced this issue personally, it might be easy to see it as their problem. Not yours. But as we learned in chapter 1, we can't separate the health of the church from the health of its members. "God has placed the parts in the body, every one of them, just as he wanted them to be," Paul writes. "If one part suffers, every part suffers with it" (1 Corinthians 12:18, 26).

Too often, the church doesn't just fail to suffer with people like those we meet in this chapter. We often contribute to their suffering. An incomplete theology of sex plays a part in this.

I have a different struggle from those in this chapter. Yet I, too, have spent years wrestling with God over my sexuality. This often deeply painful journey has convinced me God is good. I've reached that conclusion by gaining a bigger picture of God's plan for sex. So in this chapter, we'll look at how worship, identity, and love fit into a biblical sex ethic too.

First, though, I need to explain my approach in this section. Up until now, this book has focused on concerns we all experience: friendship, shelter, eating, rest, and so on. In this and the next few chapters, however, we'll look at things only some Christian singles face firsthand. Most readers will come to these chapters as an *outside observer*—the same as I did. That requires an extra measure of empathy and humility.

For those of you who do relate firsthand to these three chapters, I hope they convey God's eagerness to embrace you.

In this chapter, the rest of us need to face our temptation to judge. If we don't, we'll struggle to really hear those who share their stories. For the global church to become a more integrated body, we have to rethink how sexual minorities fit into God's family.

As fellow members in Christ's body, *our fate is bound up with one another.* How we respond to sexual minorities profoundly shapes their experience of God. How well they fare affects the whole church.

Our temptation to judge

I began to memorize Romans a few years ago.[6] Even people who don't know much of the Bible have probably heard part of Romans 1, where Paul addresses same-sex intimacy in forceful terms. Memorizing that chapter profoundly surprised me and re-inforced the importance of reading Scripture in context.[7]

It also gave me a deeper appreciation for really meditating on God's Word. Christians often see the verses on "shameful lusts" (Romans 1:26) as the focus of the passage. But as I memorized, I came to realize that Paul speaks most forcefully about sins unrelated to sex. When I saw who received his most forceful words, it shocked me.

Whatever you think Romans 1 says, take a few minutes to read Romans 1:18–2:12 for yourself. If you can, read it several times. Try reading it aloud. Then note some observations. What does Paul talk the most about? How does he order things? Does he have a structure? What do Paul's choices show about how he views these various sins?

If I'm honest, I really struggle with Romans 2:1 and the verses that follow. I don't want to think Paul's talking about me. I read the sins in chapter 1, and I tend to think of other people. Not my sin! Yet starting in chapter 2, Paul says something very similar to what Jesus said in Matthew 7:

> "Why do you look at the speck of sawdust in your
> brother's eye and pay no attention to the plank in your
> own eye? How can you say to your brother, 'Let me take
> the speck out of your eye,' when all the time there is a
> plank in your own eye? You hypocrite, first take the plank
> out of your own eye, and then you will see clearly to
> remove the speck from your brother's eye."
>
> MATTHEW 7:3-5

The older I get, the more I struggle with this passage. It doesn't seem just. I feel like Jesus is getting it backward, until I realize what I'm assuming. When I judge, I think I'm seeing clearly. I think I'm seeing completely. In other words, I think I deserve to sit in God's place. No wonder Jesus and Paul take judgment so seriously!

What would happen if we took Jesus' words seriously here? If we wrestled with all that Paul says in Romans 1 and 2? How would our relationships with others change?

An invitation to worship

Paul makes a startling claim about our bodies in another key text on sexuality: "Do you not know that your bodies are temples of the Holy Spirit, who is in you, whom you have received from God? You are not your own; you were bought at a price. Therefore honor God with your bodies" (1 Corinthians 6:19-20).

Most teaching I've heard on this emphasizes our responsibility to God. And Paul certainly stresses that. But once again, we have to read the text in context. Paul makes an extraordinary statement about our bodies here. It speaks to the profound struggles with shame and self-hatred some in this chapter have faced.

After the Fall, people lost access to God. For a while, He showed up unexpectedly, only when He wanted to. Eventually He called for first the Tabernacle and then the Temple. These spaces provided more structured access to God. But the people still had to follow a very strict process. Only the high priest could enter the holiest place, and only once a year (Leviticus 16). Failure to obey brought death.

This went on for centuries until an astounding change. For the first time, the holy God came to earth as a *human being*. We could see Him, touch Him, smell Him. And then Jesus promised an even more amazing thing! After He ascended, He would send the Holy Spirit to His disciples. God, the third person, now lives in each of those who calls on the name of Jesus to be saved.

Ponder what this says about our bodies. The holy God thinks so highly of us that He wants relationship with us. He loves us so much that He wants to actually *dwell* in us all the time! And He loves us enough to forgive all the terrible sin that such close contact with the Holy Spirit reveals. He makes this invitation to everyone.

· · ·

Tony, as he asked me to call him, had long known he was attracted to men. But they were men at a distance. He only began to reckon with his sexuality when a Christian mentor encouraged him to keep silent about it.

Early in his twenties, Tony directed a play as an extracurricular activity during university studies. The day the cast rehearsed a scene addressing gay sex, one actor couldn't make it. The scene involved some intimacy at least one of the actors didn't want to do. Tony, who'd grown up Protestant, had to step in and help act it out.

When some Christian friends challenged him afterward, Tony got angry. "It had never occurred to me that as a Christian I shouldn't do the scene."

"I've always known that something was wrong," he said. Together, the scene and confrontation crystallized his sexuality. He felt attracted to women *and* men. "I felt like such a phony." Tony had been fairly involved with his church, but he abruptly withdrew from several activities.

A small-group leader followed up with him. Tony eventually explained why he'd pulled away. "That man helped me see that I can still be a Christian while afflicted with this," Tony said, referring to his sexual struggles. But the man couldn't show him *how* to be a Christian now. What did emotional honesty look like? How could he pray about it? Tony didn't have a vocabulary.

On the leader's advice, he told few people at church. As a result, only a few people could help Tony navigate how his faith and sexuality intersected.

They weren't well equipped to do so. But they didn't seem to realize that. Nor did they pursue the kind of learning and reflection they encouraged Tony to do. "I was really left to fumble in the dark on my own," he wrote to me after our interview.

Tony continued to process things, largely on his own. He talked to lots of people and read several books. "I thought I was so ready and prepared for the struggle," he said.

Then Tony met a man through a fashion show. Faced with opportunity, he said, it didn't take anything to cross the lines he'd drawn for himself. "So that was very disappointing."

Self-hatred soon set in. "For the first month after I ended that stupid one thing with that guy, I felt miserable all the time," Tony said. "I felt so pathetic."

One night he had a nightmare that he had died. "And then, in that moment of me still being in that intense state of fear, I realized that life apart from God is not going to change me, is not going to give me the strength to be anything different," Tony said. "At the end of the day, it's really God's love for me that is everything. That helped a lot."

The Holy Spirit in Tony had pointed him back to the truth. Even in his lowest moments, God still loved him. God still welcomed Tony's worship.

For Jonathan, whom we met in chapter 7, the shame involved

his family. "When I told my mom, I cried a lot," he said in Spanish. Jonathan, whose brother is also gay, said he asked his mom to forgive him.

"My family struggles with a lot of economic issues and family dysfunctions," he said. "I used to think that that was God punishing me for being gay."

Unlike Tony, Jonathan wasn't conflicted about having sexual relationships with men. But his church involvement set him apart from others in Bogotá's LGBT community. The day after our interview, the city had a Pride parade. Jonathan didn't plan to go. He liked the aim of promoting equality. But the actual celebration missed the point, he said. A lot of people would smoke pot and get drunk. The day's revelry might also encourage promiscuity.

Jonathan didn't agree with that approach to sex. "I feel a certain conflict," he said.

The Ignatian tradition puts a strong emphasis on accompaniment, which echoes Fr. Fred's idea about our need to share life deeply with others. That spiritual community has helped Jonathan with his struggles. "My cross is lighter when I seek accompaniment," he said.

He's also learned from the Jesuits about other ways to form deep community. "Obviously, I'd like to have a family," Jonathan said. He described the traditional form: marriage, kids, a house. Then he said, "I have come to believe that family is cultivating other people's seeds, which, when they grow and flourish, help that person be able to become a good person and put their best values into action."

He's thinking of adoption. Or maybe a different kind of service altogether. "I myself would like to be a Jesuit, being a testimony to many people," he said. "There's a lot of people who don't believe in God, but those people can come to believe in certain people, and through those people come to believe in God."

Given his youth, it makes sense that Jonathan was still considering his options. Yet how remarkable that he even included the Jesuits among them! They must have shown Jonathan that God's invitation could enlarge his life, not reduce it.

The gift of a new identity

In one conversation with a religious leader, Jesus famously said we must be born again to enter God's Kingdom (John 3:1-21). All who receive this birth also gain a new identity. No matter who we are or what we struggle with, those things don't define us. Only our relationship with Jesus does.

This offers incredible hope for singles. Our cultures, secular and Christian, can often define us by what we lack. But those who accept Jesus' invitation gain an identity that nothing can take away. We become co-heirs with Him (Romans 8:17)—beloved children of the King.

Over the past few years, God has repeatedly brought me back to this idea. Do I picture myself as an orphan or His beloved daughter? It makes a vast difference in how I handle hard situations.

Palak, 28, was born male but played more like a girl when around other Indian boys. A pastor who lived in the same part of New Delhi translated from Hindi to English for us. Here's a paraphrase of what Palak shared.

I grew up in a Protestant family. Because of how I played with other children, my parents worried the boys would rape me.

But how I played with girls concerned my parents too. My whole family—even my brother—beat me.

But violence didn't change my behavior.

A doctor took their money but gave them no solutions.

I finally left home at fourteen and went to Kolkata. There, I stayed with a kinnar community for several months. After returning home for a season, I eventually moved to New Delhi and joined a kinnar group there.

According to Palak and the pastor, *kinnar* usually refers to Indians who are born male and feel female. To go through castration, they have to receive a psychological test. Depending on age, they might also need parental approval for the surgery.

Kinnar often live in communities together and support themselves through work at Hindu events. People pay for their blessings at weddings and births. However, they're also seen as a possible source of curses. Outside sanctioned events, people often avoid kinnar and stop their children from talking to them.

Kinnar don't usually like Christians. But Palak continues to claim this minority faith. According to the most recent census data, Christians make up less than 3 percent of India's population.[8] The country has been listed as one of Open Doors's most difficult places to follow Jesus since 2019.[9]

Christian churches in India don't usually welcome kinnar either. Both Palak and the pastor said it would be very hard for kinnar to attend a Christian service. So it's remarkable that Palak continues to seek God, attending a Catholic mass about once a month.

Retelling Palak's story now, I'm reminded of African American theologian Howard Thurman's remarkable conversation with a Hindu man in India in 1935. As Thurman recounts, the man repeatedly raised Christians' three-hundred-year history of oppressing his enslaved ancestors.

The man concluded: "Here you are in my country, standing deep within the Christian faith and tradition. I do not wish to seem rude to you. But, sir, I think you are a traitor to all the darker peoples of the earth."[10]

I wonder if he'd say something similar to Palak. So I asked: "What has Jesus meant to you?"

"Whenever I have asked Jesus, He has provided," Palak said.

Many kinnar have major mental-health struggles. Sometimes they even commit suicide. But Palak said Jesus has helped with depression. "He satisfies me and gives me peace."

An identity rooted in Jesus makes a huge difference in how we handle life's trials. But too often, Christians reaffirm false identities. Kat, whom we met earlier, said she often calls her bisexuality "a twilight zone." People never seem to know what to do with her.

"Every single time I try to talk about it with others who are Catholic or Christian . . . they can't relate to the experience or it makes them uncomfortable to think about," Kat said. "Not only are people very frequently not compassionate toward my being bisexual and single, but they also don't know how to be."

When someone isn't straight, "there's crickets," Kat said. "There's not even an acknowledgment of how that person, of how I feel. It could be as simple as saying, 'Yeah, that does suck.' There's nothing."

People who affirm her sexuality do little better. "They often talk only about me dating other women or finding community in queer spaces," Kat said. "It's a lot of trying to squish me into being either straight or lesbian, which is really, really awkward and uncomfortable.

"When you deal with just being gay, it's not easy, but people tend to assume that *okay, you're not looking at the married life.* But when you're bisexual, you run into all the issues of being gay in the church."

Other Catholic singles have more options, she said. "Every single vocational path is open to them." This brings us to our last theme, which speaks to this crisis of purpose.

A call to love

All who enter God's Kingdom gain a new identity *and* a calling. Here, too, many of us need a bigger picture of God's plan. American culture has increasingly flattened the notion of love to romance and family.

Too often, Christians send the same message. When we do, it reinforces the lie that we can only experience love in certain types of relationships. Jesus radically upends that. He calls all His followers to self-giving love *even for our enemies.* Such a calling should reshape all our relationships *and* how we think about our purpose in life.

"The biggest challenge is really just dealing with the celibacy part," said Brock, 20, an American Protestant attracted to men. We spoke by phone.

Like Brock, several of the Protestants I interviewed for this chapter criticized the church's double standard around celibacy. Roman Catholics, of course, require celibacy for the priesthood. A few other types of consecrated life also exist.

Doula Robin called celibacy a call to God, among other things.

"Celibacy is *not* a call from something that God is trying to keep you from," she said. Yet that's exactly how many Protestants view celibacy.

In a 2019 blog post, ministry leader Pieter Valk argues, "Churches [should] teach that God first calls everyone to a period of abstinent singleness during which we discern whether we are called to a lifetime vocation of celibacy or a lifetime vocation of Christian marriage with someone of the opposite sex. . . . Every Christian has the same inherent capacity for both vocations and every Christian, gay or straight, should offer the question of celibacy or Christian marriage to God."[11]

Pieter, who helped found an ecumenically Christian monastery, chose celibacy. But like several others interviewed, he said, "I'm not celibate because I'm gay, I'm celibate because I'm called to it." His ministry, Equip, helps churches become "places where gay Christians thrive for a lifetime according to a historic sexual ethic."[12]

"I believe my singleness is a calling to labor and work for the sake of the Kingdom," Pieter said. His work involves helping churches. But he thinks celibacy can support secular work for the Kingdom too. What if someone devoted their life to teaching, therapy, the arts? What if someone God hadn't called to raise children poured that energy into addressing an issue like social justice? I didn't get to interview him, but Bryan Stevenson, founder and director of the Equal Justice Initiative, seems to exemplify this kind of singleness.

Kevin, whom we met earlier, said he wears his rainbow-colored Jesus fish partly because of his celibacy. He didn't grow up in a Christian family. Kevin came to faith around the time of his first sexual relationship with a man.

"I still, at that early age, was thinking about who Jesus was, and what that means," Kevin said. "I found myself in a cognitive dissonance of faith that said, 'You should abstain from this' versus my sexuality and desires that said, 'I want all of this.'"

After the relationship ended, Kevin felt relief. But then he left the church for a while. Kevin didn't return to regular worship until his early forties. It took another decade to come out to his pastor. Over his years of relationship and struggle with Jesus, he eventually committed to celibacy.

"We all need to surrender our lives. In order to follow Jesus, we need to surrender our lives, lay them down," Kevin said, echoing Jesus' description of discipleship in Matthew 16:24-25. To remind himself of that, he wears a rainbow fish.

Surrender to Jesus never comes easy. We have to choose every day whether to follow our own will or God's.

Even Jesus struggled to choose God's will. In Gethsemane, He actually asked God if He could avoid the Cross! The author of Hebrews says that Jesus endured *His* cross because of the "joy set before him" (Hebrews 12:2). I've never been able to yield myself without glimpsing more of the beauty of God's love and the joy He sets before *me*.

• • •

Several hours into his journey, the pilgrim reached an especially puzzling passage. Just then, he heard a voice. Surprised, he looked up. How had a stranger suddenly appeared in the middle of nowhere? He didn't even have transportation.

"Do you understand what you are reading?" the man asked. The question spoke so directly to his heart that he didn't pause to marvel at it. The pilgrim called to his driver, and they stopped to pick the man up.

He remembered their conversation the rest of his life. As their journey continued, the stranger began to explain how the book satisfied all the pilgrim's deepest questions—not with answers but with a person.

In Him merged past and future, fact and spirit. And the God whose word contained both prohibition and prophecy of welcome said, "Come."

The eunuch never grasped why God seemed to say such contradictory things of people like him. In the end, it didn't matter. When he couldn't go to God, the Lord came to him and dwelt within him.

•   •   •

As we close this chapter, take a few moments to reflect on the stories we've heard. Has God surprised or challenged you?

What do you **grieve**? If you related firsthand to this chapter, what pain did it stir up? If you come to these stories as an outsider, what pain have you experienced in this area?

What do you **have**? Sometimes this might not make sense, such as an inexplicable hope, but name it anyway.

Is there something you need to **confess or repent of**?

What can you **give**? If that's hard to answer, ask God about it. What does He invite you to give—either *as* someone who's a sexual minority or *to* the people God's brought into your life?

Of Parasites, Loss, and Armed Robbery

The Hard Parts

WHEN I TOLD MY DOCTOR WHERE I planned to go, she focused most on my African stops. My travel insurer had different concerns. *They* deemed the riskiest region closer to home: South America.

At first I didn't think much of this. In South Africa, everyone told me I shouldn't walk alone after dark. Ever. I followed their advice, and nothing happened to me.

I didn't get similar warnings in Brazil. It wasn't until my third city, Salvador, that I learned otherwise. My host was not a Christian, so my second night there, I googled churches. The closest one didn't have a website or service times. I decided to scout the location beforehand.

That's how I followed Google Maps's directions into what was probably a favela. As I walked through, I could tell it was a poorer neighborhood. Possibly that made it less safe for an obvious foreigner like me. But lots of people were going about their business. I didn't feel any sense of menace. So I kept walking briskly and hoped for the best.

Not until I climbed a hill and reached the church's address did I sense anything amiss. The church wasn't there. So, as I'd learned to do, I asked a passing woman for help in my limited Spanish. Fortunately the residents of Salvador seemed to understand this language fairly well. Later, the local police even complemented my "Portuguese"!

As I explained my search, the woman's husband came up. After learning I wanted a place to worship on Sunday, he offered to show me a different church.

He said *peligroso* many times before I finally learned that word for "danger." Apparently, it described the neighborhood through which I'd walked to his street and much of the surrounding area. That man ultimately spent at least half an hour helping me. First we found the second church. Then he walked me out to a street safe enough that he trusted I would get home in one piece.

But I still didn't fully understand the dangers. And I didn't think about how close my housing was to an area he'd called dangerous. So, from the spot where he left me, I walked a few more blocks to Walmart for groceries. Afterward, I walked home nearly a mile—now even more defenseless, thanks to my bags.

Not until I got "home" to the oceanfront apartments where I was staying did I realize I'd forgotten to buy flour for my sourdough. After the evening church service the next night, I took an Uber to Walmart. From there I walked down the same L-shaped route toward home. This time, I stopped partway to eat a late dinner. While I did, I read an e-book on my phone. It was such a short walk home that I didn't note the time or think to get an Uber. The street seemed brightly lit. I would even pass a statue of Jesus!

None of that protected me from the knife-bearing man who relieved me of all but the flour. None of my scant self-defense training helped. My only thought was, *Your stuff is not worth your life.* I didn't even scream until he'd run off. So much for reading all those detective novels with fearless female heroines.

For times when even your bladder betrays you, it helps if you can laugh. Right before I left for my walk to the thief, I'd been reading an uproarious Georgette Heyer novel. That helped me later, when my host used the robbery as an excuse to berate me to others in Portuguese. I asked myself, "How would Heyer have described this?" I'm not sure I've ever been quite so grateful for laughter.

God gave my soul more than humor. In between the bag loss and the robbery, I flew to Argentina. I'd just discovered I had parasites again. And I'd lost my longtime literary agent.[13] All the same day as the bag loss. The fluke death of a writer back home that morning only added to my grief.

I was still reeling when I interviewed Fr. John in Buenos Aires. He told me, "I have the conviction that nothing you give to the Lord and nothing you give up for the Lord is lost. On the contrary, you receive it—as He says—back a hundredfold."

As I wrote in my journal afterward, it was hard to believe. It was harder to believe once the thief took the bag with that journal and a Bible I'd carried for almost thirty years! The Bible never reappeared. But strangers found both my passports, some of my bank cards, and the trip journal, scattered on the beach.

I'll never know why God protected me in that favela Saturday night, but let me get robbed Sunday. Why did I lose the Bible, but recover the journal? I'll never know. But I do know He never left me.

After the police saw me safely through the apartment gates that night, I wound up in the night manager's office. He called a locksmith so I could get inside the condo. Then he asked what had happened. It was simple enough Portuguese that I understood. Seeing his computer, I asked in crude Spanish if I could use it. He nodded.

Pulling up Google Translate, I typed up a short account. For some reason, I included the loss of my Bible. After I finished, I went back to my chair.

The man read my translated words. Then he looked up. "God is in control," he said, in Portuguese even I could understand. Then, at last, I felt safe enough to cry. Despite all He'd let me lose that night, God provided what I needed most: Christian fellowship.

"Can we pray?" I asked in crude Spanish. Again he nodded. As we held hands and prayed in his office, each speaking in our own language, I knew I'd be all right no matter what happened.

CHAPTER 10

DISEASE, DISABILITY, AND DEATH

When Our Bodies and Minds Betray Us

AFTER JUDITH BROKE A SHOULDER, she and her husband decided they needed help around the house. So they drove to an Anchorage café known as a place to find day laborers. That's how they met Stewart. Over the next few years, Stewart became a fixture in the older couple's life. Though he hasn't had permanent housing for years—and spent one winter staying in a car—their Friday appointments have become almost sacred.

So when Judith's husband died seven years ago, she continued paying Stewart to help her.

"He's really kept me independent," said Judith, now 83. On a typical Friday, Stewart, now 57, calls Judith in the morning. He doesn't have a cell phone, so they agree where she'll pick him up. Another man, Alvin, 35, usually joins them.

Once the three meet up, Judith drives them all to the grocery store. The men push the cart or carry the basket while she shops. Then they carry it all out and put the bags in Judith's car. She drives them all to her home.

Stewart and Alvin then unload her groceries and put everything away. They also help take out her garbage. "Alvin is tall and able to reach things, so he's the garbage master," Judith said. Depending on the week, the men might help with other tasks too. Stewart once built a lamp for Judith and cut mats for her husband, an artist. "Anything we asked, he can figure out how to do."

Over the years, the men have become more than paid helpers. "I consider him a friend," Judith often says of Stewart. She saves him the crossword puzzle. And she's served as a point of contact for him.

When Stewart's wallet fell into other hands, someone turned it in to the Alaska Native corporation listed on his ID. Like Alvin, Stewart is Iñupiaq, a tribe indigenous to the Arctic region. Because Stewart kept Judith's number inside his wallet, the corporation contacted her to return it.

At the time of our interview, Stewart was staying in a temporary shelter near Anchorage's downtown. When he doesn't have a place like the shelter, he sleeps outside.

Whichever of them dies first, I hope God provides a way for the other to learn the news.

•   •   •

No one wants to face the reality of aging and illness. But the body betrays each one of us. We can't control when or how that happens. These betrayals take many forms. Some I interviewed went through it at a young age or only for a season, at least so far. Others deal with lifelong illness or disability. And, like Judith, many older people face the ongoing losses that age brings.

Disability and chronic illness increase the challenges of singleness. As Stewart and Judith show, relationship takes creativity, trust, and endurance. Others' weaknesses give Christians some of the greatest tests of our love. When they can't repay us, will we treat them as if they were Jesus Himself? Will we treat fellow believers as the family Jesus made them to be? Or like the strangers most cultures would deem unrelated others? The life and health of Jesus' body, the church, is deeply bound up in how we handle the physical needs of one another.

In this chapter, we need to face our temptation to avoid the weak. For the global church to become a more integrated body, we have to rethink how physical and mental brokenness fit into God's family. To do that, we'll look at the importance of care, attention, and treating others as if they were Jesus. Lastly, we'll consider what legacy looks like for singles.

Our temptation to avoid the weak

In one of Jesus' most famous stories, He tells how three people respond to a man in great need (Luke 10:25-37). Two out of three go out of their way to avoid the injured man. Such rejection and refusal to help remains common throughout the world. I saw people with disabilities begging on the street in many places.

Only some countries try to ensure people with disabilities can get around. Cities like New Delhi now have some sidewalks and train-station elevators. But they're not in every part of the city. And even in high-tech Hong Kong, I heard about problems with the transit service intended to help disabled people.

In some ways, my country does better than most. The Americans with Disabilities Act has done a great deal to prevent discrimination and ensure access. But we still love to separate based on ability. Schools often have three groups of students: accelerated (or gifted), regular, and special ed. And as people age, families often send them off to nursing homes. Whatever you call it, they're all forms of segregation.

Christians should do better, but often don't. Of the dozens of churches I visited, I remember only three with disabled people. At one of those churches, a pastor told me people with disabilities and their families are more unchurched than almost any other group.[1] His church includes such people because they make a point to. Still, some members have struggled with the cost of it. The pastor said some complain about people who "disrupt" the service.

We, too, seem to prefer a segregated body. That's not the way of God's Kingdom, but I'm part of why it still is.

Any attempt at breadth sacrifices depth. You may see that most clearly in this chapter. I found it hardest to find and include people with nonphysical disabilities. Some disabilities prevent consent.

To remind us what we're aiming for, let's revisit our text from chapter 1:

God has placed the parts in the body, every one of them, just as he wanted them to be. . . .
    The eye cannot say to the hand, "I don't need you!" And the head cannot say to the feet, "I don't need you!"
    . . . God has put the body together, giving greater honor to the parts that lacked it, so that there should be no division in the body, but that its parts should have equal

concern for each other. If one part suffers, every part suffers with it; if one part is honored, every part rejoices with it.

1 CORINTHIANS 12:18, 21, 24-26

If we want to better embody Jesus in the world, the church must do better at integrating and honoring our weakest members. As Jesus shows in Luke 10, this starts by meeting the people God puts in our path rather than avoiding them.

Jesus' miracles suggest that engagement with the sick does more than show love. It's also a vital part of healing. Genesis 1–2 shows God's very words have the power to create out of nothing. Jesus' healings from afar show He has the same power to heal. Why, then, do these miracles involve so much drama?

Modern medicine tends to treat bodies like a machine.[2] Thus, illness becomes a breakdown or malfunction. Fixing things might take some new parts or a new formula. This mindset leaves out the spiritual.

What researchers call the placebo effect exposes more intangible aspects of healing. In one review of several studies, Harvard researcher Ted Kaptchuk concludes, "The more elaborate the ritual, the higher the placebo effects."[3] As the *New York Times Magazine* summarized his thinking: "The placebo effect is a biological response to an act of caring . . . the more intense and focused [the caring act] is, the more healing it evokes."[4]

You can't measure how a mother's care helps her child heal. But I think Kaptchuk's findings show part of the social and spiritual nature of healing. Jesus doesn't need to use a ritual *at all*. Yet even in His distance healings, the sick person gets to see another person's care for them. They see the parent (or even boss!) depart on their behalf. They become well and then hear how the person who cares for them met with Jesus.

Much more often, the sick experience Jesus' care for them in person. Sometimes, He goes to surprising lengths. In one case, Jesus asks a man lying next to a pool known for its healing powers if he really wants to get well (John 5:1-15). In another case, Jesus heals a blind man in phases. In between, He asks what the man can now see (Mark 8:22-26). When the woman with years of hemorrhaging tries to receive healing without Jesus' notice, He declares her healing in public (Mark 5:24-34).

Many healings proved as unique as the person healed. Maybe that's the point. Healing has as much to do with relationship as it does with restoration. The bleeding woman spent twelve years hearing others call her unclean. Maybe she needed both the physical healing and to hear someone declare her *clean*.

Maybe the man with the multistage healing had spent years having his complaints dismissed. Maybe he needed both to be able to see and to be heard. Maybe he needed a healer to validate his report. And maybe the man at the pool had lapsed into cynicism and despair. Maybe he needed to face, once for all, what he really wanted from life.

"I was sick and you looked after me. . . . Whatever you did for one of the least of these brothers of mine, you did for me," says Jesus in Matthew 25:36-40. The care we show to our weaker siblings is one of the most important ways that Christians love Jesus. When we obey that call, we meet Jesus in unique ways.

Singles face a particular vulnerability in weakness. As Solomon put it, "Two are better than one. . . . If either of them falls down, one can help the other up. But pity anyone who falls and has no one to help them up" (Ecclesiastes 4:9-10). Facing the body's betrayals alone can lead to isolation, exclusion, and greater vulnerability. Health in Christ's body requires us to give and receive care, attention, and support with our weakest members.

The power of care

Others' care when we get sick can have a powerful role in our healing. Lily, 31, a Kenyan Pentecostal, was visiting family in Nairobi when we finally met for an interview. Over a pizza, she described a recent trip with a cousin. To make the almost four-hour trip to Kitui, they took a matatu, a commonly used informal bus.

Whatever they had eaten for lunch made Lily quite sick. "My tummy just flipped on me. I had the worst time on the drive there," she said. "Somewhere along the way, I just felt really, really unwell."

As Lily fought what was probably food poisoning, she felt profound gratitude she wasn't alone. "I thought, 'What would I have done without my cousin?'" she said. "Having someone there was such a comfort."

Kim, 38, an American Protestant I interviewed in Moscow, *had* been sick, alone. A few months before our interview, she spent four days in the hospital. "It was one of the most depressing times of my life," she said. "I felt really alone."

She had a good church community but seemed to get few visitors. Instead, Kim talked to her mom by phone a lot. "But someday my mom won't be there," she said.

Many others shared Kim's concern about growing old alone. "It's scary, especially the aging thing," said Joanna, 48, a Messianic Israeli woman. "Who's going to take care of me?"

A few months earlier, Joanna had started to face a more serious health situation. "I received the phone call, and my first thought was [that] I was alone," she said. "But I'm so not alone." Each time she needed help—whether rides to the hospital or someone to go to appointments with her—God provided.

One woman in particular has been especially faithful. "It's been six months, and she has gone with me to every appointment," Joanna said. "Without her, I would probably still be at my first meeting."

The gift of attention

When communities plan only for the well and nondisabled, we leave out the weak and disabled. Tony, a Protestant Jewish man, said his growing weakness made it harder to attend services. He was 80 when we met. "I can't easily get to fellowship," he said. "Sometimes I just cannot get on the bus. The step is too high."

His home in Jerusalem also lacked safeguards, like extra railings. It had several trip hazards. Other Christians connected me to Tony, but it wasn't clear how often they visited him.

A widowed and childless Nigerian Protestant, 80, said she had lost income as she aged. Before, she farmed cassava and maize and raised beef for slaughter. But when we spoke, she only had the strength to "sit down and sell" from a one-room shop outside her house. She couldn't afford to buy much to sell, however.

Fortunately, her younger sister let her share her house. Even working together, though, the sisters struggled with things like wet laundry. Neither could hang it on a line. Instead, they spread it out on the floor to dry. It sounded like they also had to use their clothes carefully, given the difficulties with washing them or buying new garments.

During our interview, their pastor came to visit the widowed sisters. It wasn't clear whether Christians in their church or culture would think to come help with a task like laundry. Only the younger sister had children. The child who bought the house lived in England.

To support others as if they were Jesus

For many singles, the ultimate fear is dying alone. "One of the saddest things about living alone is people die and it says, 'They were found,'" said Chris, the Australian we met earlier. The Japanese even have a word for this: kodokushi.[5]

Chris suspects he, too, will be found. It happened to an older aunt of his. At the end of her life, she fell down the stairs, could not get up, and died there. Someone found her a few days later.

Growing old "used to trouble my mind," said Grace, the woman who chose singleness over a high dowry. "That is the time when you need support. You need somebody to be with you." India doesn't offer much help for the elderly, however. Hiring such help takes money.

Grace said God has reassured her, however: "'Even in your old age, I will care for you'" (see Isaiah 46:4).

Jenny, who compared herself to Gomer, lives in New York. She should get more government support as she ages. But no program can replace genuine care.

"I think about the church a lot," Jenny said. "God gave us the church as a family. We're supposed to come around people." Still, she seemed to hesitate. Would people *really* care for her in her old age? Would Christians *really* come be with her in her last days?

"It's hard," Jenny said. "God has a plan, but I just have to trust in that. God always provides, whether I worry or not. That's who He is, and so why worry?"

Colin, from chapter 2, helped another Christian single face death. A close friend and former colleague had just gone to work for herself when she got a cancer diagnosis. She had barely entered her fifties.

At first, aggressive treatment seemed to cure her cancer. But the next year, it came back and spread to other organs. Deirdre still worked as a freelance photographer. It's not clear what kind of health insurance she had. She also had a mortgage. So Colin moved into the house she shared with another woman. Giving her the rental income was a practical way to show love. But he also knew that in time she might need help with more than just errands.

He was right. In her final spring, Deirdre went to a relative's wedding several hundred miles away. But while she was there, her health got so bad that a sister had to fly home with her.

Colin picked them up from the airport and drove straight to the hospital. They admitted Deirdre one week before Maundy Thursday, but eventually released her. "When she came home for hospice, I realized how much I had feared she wouldn't come home," Colin said in a phone interview.

A steady flow of friends filled their home. Deirdre had loved having people over. "The Wednesday night of Holy Week felt like any of her other parties," Colin said. But a priest came the following day to give her final communion. Another priest came in the afternoon. Since so many friends had missed mass to be there, he served them all communion and gave a short homily.

"It just all seemed so right, is the best way that I can put it," Colin said. "She loved God, and she got to be united so closely in

Christ's passion and resurrection—to live through Easter Sunday." She died the following Thursday.

"To be loved so much by someone that she would entrust her last days to you, that's an incredible gift," Colin said. "Regardless of our state in life, to be able to be there, and to help out to the extent possible, and to remain by her side until the end, is what we're called to as disciples."

Leaving a good legacy

Facing death doesn't come easily, and for good reason. Death came *after* the Fall. But until Jesus' return, every person must face it. Some of us will face a long, slow retreat toward death. Others won't see it coming. We all face some choice of whether to plan for it, however.

Many singles said they struggle with this. Should they plan for old age and death as if they'll never marry? Or wait and hope God will still provide a spouse?

Tatiana, whom we met in chapter 7, was one of the only younger people I met who'd started planning. "Especially now that I'm getting older, I've started to think about who will be my beneficiary," she said.

In our state, Alaska, I learned that it's easy to make a simple will. But every place has different rules. If you *don't* have a will, the government often decides what to do with your property.

I may have been the last in my immediate family to make a will. I'm the oldest child, but I never joined the military like my siblings did. Two of them deployed to the Middle East. At least my sister drafted a will because of that.

But I wasn't ready. Like buying condoms while unmarried,

drafting a will in my youth seemed to hasten events I didn't want to reshape my singleness. Staying unprepared seemed protective, in a strange way.[6] Then my father died. For a brief time afterward, I wasn't sure *he* had left a will to take care of Mom. His cancer progressed too rapidly to focus on much besides trying to fight it.

Fortunately, they had a basic will. Still, I put off writing my own. A few things helped me finally put the plan on paper. First and most important: refocusing from the thought of death to legacy.

If I were to die before using up all my resources, what people or causes would I want to support? That question helped me a lot. I hope to have many years left. But every week brings more news stories of fatal car accidents on local roads. If God should allow me that fate, a will spells out whom I'd want to bless at the end in what small way I could. As we heard earlier, Lili benefited greatly from her single housemate's last kindness. Whom could I do that for?

More recently, a fellow single woman raised harder questions: What would I want for my funeral? Who would I want to be notified when I die? Like Judith, we probably all have people in our lives whose importance few others know.

While working on this chapter, I learned of two deaths. One I had interviewed for this book. I knew the other person from Bible study. In God's kindness, I learned of Karen's death two days before her service.

The year of our shared Zoom Bible study brought some of my lowest points on the road to this book. At times, I questioned my calling as a writer altogether. Had I failed at life and adulthood? I had spent almost three years barely working, for the sake of a book that might not ever get published.

Karen did not know me outside our nine-month Bible study.

But she had married a fine-art painter. She didn't question my choices. She encouraged my faith in God's plan for this book at a time when I greatly needed it.

So it mattered a great deal to me to attend her service and tell her family how much her words had helped me. No one had any idea because of how brief and limited our contact had been. I'm not very connected to our few mutual friends, so I had to find her obituary online.

I still struggle with writing a list of people to notify when I die. But the deaths I learned of last week underscore the importance of some public announcement. And, ultimately, Karen's service helped me get closer to drafting some basic plans for my funeral. I still hope I'll get to plan a wedding first, but a funeral's the only service I can count on.

Karen's seemed to have more worship than many other funerals I've been to. Hers opened with two beloved songs I'd not sung in a while. One by Keith Green, "There Is a Redeemer," went back to my childhood.[7] As we sang, I wept so hard that I could barely gasp some notes. More of my resistance to planning melted.

Yes, I thought. *Yes. I want that song sung at my funeral. I want plenty of worship.* I can't give that final gift (as I hope it proves!) to my loved ones if no one knows I want that. And if I write it down, I won't have to remember. That will leave me freer to enjoy whatever God *does* have left for me.

•   •   •

As we close this chapter, take a few moments to reflect on what we've heard. Has God surprised or challenged you?

What do you **grieve**? Where have you or a loved one lost physical or intellectual ability? What's hard about that?

What do you **have**? If this is hard to name, possibly walk through the senses: sight, smell, hearing, touch, taste.

Is there something you need to **confess or repent of**?

What can you **give**? How can you help and support those facing greater weakness than you? Would you be willing to walk all the way to death with someone who's not related to you? If you died soon, whom would you want your final gifts to bless?

Worship in Other Languages

TWO DAYS BEFORE THIS WRITING, I joined my church's weekly tradition: mass choir. After we finished singing three or four verses in English, one woman sang the hymn's chorus in what I think was Iñupiaq.[8]

As she sang, I felt deep gratitude. After all my travels, God has brought me to a church that shares something with my experience of worship on the road. I spent many Sundays in services that I understood only partly or hardly at all.[9]

Despite that, it's surprising how many times I *did* understand part of the service. While in Cairo, I went to an Arabic Anglican service mostly attended by Sudanese refugees. I recognized at least one melody, even if I couldn't name it. And thanks to a paper liturgy with some sections translated into three languages, I recognized one part of the service.

In another part of Africa, where only foreigners could legally attend church, I missed the English service. So I went to the Mandarin one. This surprised some of the friends I later made in the church courtyard. Why attend a service I couldn't understand?!

It's the same Holy Spirit, I told them. Even if I couldn't understand a word, I'd be in God's presence. In kindness, the Spirit granted me a bit more than that. At one point, I was pretty sure they were reciting the Lord's Prayer. And when the sermon came, a small miracle occurred.

The woman sitting in front of me opened a large Bible. She flipped to a passage a little past the halfway point of the book. At the top of the page, I could see the chapter number, but the book name was all in Chinese characters.

I looked back down at the two columns of text on the right-hand page. Most of the characters ran in typical paragraph blocks. But in one place, the lines were set differently, as if poetry. Then the chapter continued in prose again.

Pulling out my own English Bible, I flipped through until a similar distance past the middle. Not one of the Minor Prophets; they're nearly all set as poetry. But voila! A passage of poetry in between paragraphs. The chapter number matched too. He was preaching on Matthew's Beatitudes, a fact an English speaker later confirmed.

Another time, a Brazilian pastor preached on a single verse. Matching the Portuguese reference to English, I found it: Isaiah 41:6. From the very little I could gather, the sermon seemed to praise brotherly encouragement.

Since I couldn't understand, I read more of the chapter in my Bible. To my surprise, I realized the service's text did not describe God's followers. No, the brotherly encouragement was among those rebelling against God! The pastor may have had a good theme. But he chose a poor text to support it.

This discovery did not help my mood. That church service happened almost twelve months into my research and just a few days before the first of my May 2019 disasters. Looking back, I think I was experiencing strong spiritual attack then. Thing after thing went wrong. I felt so drained and heavy. Many times since, I've had a similar weighed-down feeling vanish after listening prayer.

That night, I turned back to Isaiah. Then suddenly, one section jumped out at me.

"The poor and needy search for water,
 but there is none;
 their tongues are parched with thirst.
But I the LORD will answer them;
 I, the God of Israel, will not forsake them.
I will make rivers flow on barren heights,
 and springs within the valleys.
I will turn the desert into pools of water,
 and the parched ground into springs.
I will put in the desert
 the cedar and the acacia, the myrtle and the olive.
I will set junipers in the wasteland,
 the fir and the cypress together,
so that people may see and know,
 may consider and understand,
that the hand of the LORD has done this,
 that the Holy One of Israel has created it."

ISAIAH 41:17-20

Tears came. Several times over the years, God has shown up through His Word in remarkable ways. The first occurred during a barren time in college. One day when I felt more like calling my mom, I tried God first. The Scripture reading that day did not augur well: It was Paul's closing greetings in 2 Timothy 4. Then I got to the line where he says, "Only Luke is with me." I started crying. *God knew.* In the midst of a loneliness I couldn't even articulate, He understood. And He met me that day in that passage.

Several years later, I got bad news about a man I had once hoped to marry. That night, I felt so low, I almost skipped a midweek Bible class on Deuteronomy. But partway through the discussion, a woman asked the pastor about God's jealousy. A lively discussion ensued.

At first, none of it moved me. Then I thought of the unrequited love I've felt throughout so much of my adult life. I nearly bent double. *God knew.* God knew the anguish of longing to love someone who doesn't love you back. And He met me in my pain that night in one of the most unlikely books of the Bible: Deuteronomy. When I finally spoke up to suggest unrequited love was connected to God's jealousy, my voice shook with all the tears I had to hold back.

So of course, in the midst of an especially barren place, God met me through a sermon I couldn't follow and a text taken out of context. "I am convinced that neither death nor life, neither angels nor demons, neither the present nor the future, nor any powers, neither height nor depth, nor anything else in all creation, will be able to separate us from the love of God that is in Christ Jesus our Lord," Paul wrote (Romans 8:38-39).

If anything, I experienced God's love more deeply because of worshiping in so many different contexts.

CHAPTER 11

SINGLES IN MINISTRY

Work the Body of Christ Struggles to Understand

FR. MICHAEL, AS HE ASKED ME TO CALL HIM, didn't expect to become an Orthodox priest so soon. He lacked a seminary education. He wanted to wait until his wife and he had raised their three young children.

Then one day, he came home from his full-time, secular job to a phone call. The rural Canadian parish where he'd grown up had urgent need of a priest. The latest candidate had withdrawn. Would he, already a deacon, become a priest? The chancellor gave him two weeks to decide.

Eventually, Fr. Michael said yes. The parish schedule could not support a full-time priest. So, like other priests in Canada, he took the role on top of his full-time job.

In addition to his duties at work, church, and home, he soon added education. "It was baptism by fire," Fr. Michael told me by phone.

Soon insomnia started. He most reliably fell asleep with a TV on in the background. But his wife of more than a decade didn't want one in their bedroom.

He started sleeping on the couch so he could use the TV in the living room. Then one day, Fr. Michael came home to news from his wife that blindsided him. She was leaving. She no longer loved him. She planned a new life with a man he once considered a friend.

"I didn't see it coming at all," Fr. Michael said. Less than two years into the priesthood, he found himself a single father at 43. (They would ultimately split custody equally.)

Because of how the Orthodox handle the priesthood, he had no hope of remarriage. He must either remain celibate until death or give up the priesthood forever. "I'm handcuffed. I can't get a second chance at a relationship," Fr. Michael said.

"I never used to question, 'Why me?' I used to say to my ex-wife, 'We are very blessed.' But after this happened, I asked the question 'Why? Why did this happen to me and my family—why, God? I was a faithful servant. Why did this tragedy befall me?'"

He tried praying. But in the Orthodox view, he said, "you don't ask for favors from God. We're taught to pray for others first."

Fr. Michael told me his story little more than two years after his wife left him. Their divorce had gone through just weeks before. "As I pray now, I don't even ask for help anymore," he said. "Now the question I ask: 'Where does He want me to go from here?' I'm just in burnout."

•   •   •

Singles in ministry face unique challenges. One of these: serving people with very different lives from theirs. According to the

Pew Religious Landscape Study, about half of all US Christians are married.[1] A separate Pew analysis of census data around the world shows that most Christians live with children or a spouse.[2] This parallels what I saw during fieldwork. Parishes and congregations often skew toward married people and their children. Urban churches often have more singles. However, I visited many churches whose pastors or priests initially struggled to think of *any* single parishioners.

All this means that singles in ministry serve many people who may not understand their lives very well. For many Christians, marriage gives life its primary narrative arc. Across cultures, our world tends to see life as a progression from childhood to adulthood. Marriage leads to parenthood, and then eventual retirement and decline.

I suspect this contributes to a lack of understanding for singles in ministry, whether Catholic, Protestant, or Orthodox. We struggle to conceive the alternate storyline into which a single pastor or priest's life might fit.

Singles in ministry *can* have more bandwidth for relationship. However, sometimes their singleness leads to relational deficits. Many priests and pastors live alone. And across all three traditions, singles in ministry face acute demands on their time and energy.

The seeming nobility of the task only makes it harder. They're doing important work. No less than Paul said singleness allows them greater devotion to God than a married person. How could they possibly set boundaries?

Not all singles in ministry end up being celibate for life. But whether they choose to stay single, leave the ministry, or eventually marry, Christians in these roles need several things to thrive.

In this chapter, we'll look at single ministers' need for community, boundaries, and purpose. Each of us can play a role in providing those things for the single ministers in our lives. First, though, we need to face our temptation here: idolatry.

Our temptation to idolize marriage

Across traditions, single ministers told me that Christians tend to deem marriage better than singleness. In every country I visited, Christians treated marriage as the normative and better relational state. Even singles who cited Jesus and Paul as examples often said they'd like to marry. Of the 196 never-married people who told me how they felt about their single state, almost two-thirds wanted marriage.[3]

In addition to single laity, I also interviewed dozens of singles in ministry.[4] Only about half of them were unmarried by choice. That creates all kinds of difficulties for priests and single pastors. For a large part of the church, leadership requires a state—singleness—commonly seen as inferior.

Three traditions, three views of leadership

For most of the Catholic Church, only celibate men can serve as priests.[5] Orthodox Christians also ordain only men, but allow both the married and single to serve as priests. Once ordained, however, you cannot marry if single, or remarry if your wife dies or divorces you. Starting with subdeacons, unmarried clergy must remain celibate.[6] Both the Orthodox and Eastern Catholic Churches also require celibacy of bishops.[7]

Both Catholics and Orthodox Christians also have celibate monastic communities of monks and nuns. However, only monastic men can ascend to higher-level roles. Protestant and charismatic traditions are much more diverse.

The handful of Protestant monastic communities vary greatly. Some include men and women, married and single people.[8] Others, like the French Diaconesses de Reuilly and Cameroonian Sisterhood of Emmanuel, gather celibate women.[9]

Protestants are also the only branch of the church to ordain women as pastors. Only some denominations do this. A handful of Protestant movements, like the Shakers, valorized celibacy. But the Shakers didn't require it only for leaders; their whole community chose it. Today, they've all but died out. As Pieter Valk has noted, Protestants most often bring up celibacy in the case of same-sex attraction.

How our idolatry hurts single ministers

Because the traditions view leadership so differently, single leaders encounter idolatry of marriage in different forms. For Protestants and Orthodox Christians, professional bios often include family details.

"It's very much part of how we summarize people in the church," said Rosina, a Protestant pastor we met earlier. She said academic journals often list one's marriage and number of kids in author bios. Not being able to specify that has "a part of shame connected to it."

In the Orthodox Church, many languages have a special word for the priest's wife.[10] The Orthodox Church in America website lists the spouse of every married priest. After Fr. Michael's wife left him, one of the first things he had to do was get that line removed from his online listing.

Catholics can encounter the idolatry of marriage as soon as

they announce their ministry plans. "There is always that rejection when you mention that you want to join the seminary—either from your family or from your community," said Fr. Francis, 35. I met the Kenyan priest during his graduate studies in Rome.

Unlike the priest whose story opens this book, Fr. Francis's parents supported him. But others challenged them. "They got a lot of pressure from their community," Fr. Francis said. "They were asking them, 'How can you allow a young man to manipulate you? You should stop him. How come you are not able to tell him no?'"

One man in the community stopped greeting him, he said. "Even now, when he sees me, he is not interested. But that is not a big issue because it is a personal choice, and I like being a priest." Still, Fr. Francis said, some people always reject him for his choice—many of them Christians.

Some American priests also said loved ones didn't understand their choice. I suspect it has a lot to do with how people believe sex relates to humanity and especially masculinity.[11] As the elder pointed out in chapter 1, people suspect men who show both too much and too little interest in women. To value something more than sex itself seems well-nigh heretical.

In North America, according to Protestant pastor Mark, 51, some churches actually discriminate against single ministers. Within a denomination, for example, churches seeking a pastor can share whether they prefer married or single candidates, or don't care. "That would be illegal anywhere else," he said.[12]

Mark once applied to an international church that was very interested in him. But the congregation couldn't get past his singleness. "They could not extend a call or go further with me because the congregation would never accept a single pastor," he said. "If they did, it would be too strong a reach for them" given all their other challenges. The church hired someone else.

Urban churches tend to understand single pastors more than suburban ones, Mark said. We met in Vancouver, Canada. Even there, he said, "people were constantly trying to hook me up. I got tired of telling people no. I would have to explain to them, 'No, I'm committed to being single. Please stop trying to connect me to your friends.'"

One Swiss pastor, 48, had it better than most single Protestant leaders I interviewed. People didn't seem to question his ability to do the job. But sometimes they've thought he's gay, he said. That's less of an issue now.

Some single leaders themselves thought they could minister better with a spouse. "Getting married is really paramount for my work," said John, 31, a Ghanaian Protestant associate pastor. "The person you get married to can be your second person. She steps in when you are down, when you are weak. She encourages you. She's your helper," he said. "Getting married will help my ministry."

In addition to helping with household chores, John hoped a wife could provide significant prayer support. "If I don't get married, I will struggle a bit," he said.[13]

The Bible offers a more ambiguous account of our relational options. On the one hand, the book starts and ends with weddings. But on the other hand, Jesus Himself never married. God instituted marriage before the Fall. Yet Jesus said we won't marry in the afterlife (Matthew 22:30).

God clearly values *both* states. Of the two Old Testament figures who met Jesus during the Transfiguration, Moses had married. But it's assumed Elijah lived his whole life single. And while

Paul preferred singleness, he called both states a gift of God: "I wish that all of you were as I am. But each of you has your own gift from God; one has this gift, another has that" (1 Corinthians 7:7).

Focusing on the yes instead of the no

Across all major traditions, however, Christians clearly—and strongly—favor marriage. I understand that view, as I still want marriage myself. However, I can't help thinking Christians' general discomfort with celibacy shows something about our discipleship. It's as if we don't want following God to cost us this much. We'd prefer to maintain and grow the church through procreation rather than proclamation.[14]

I'm guilty of this. One early goal for this book was to counter a view of Christian singleness that assumes God intends the unmarried for the mission field. I resented the lack of alternate examples and narratives of singleness. Must failure to marry qualify one for other kinds of suffering as well? It didn't seem fair—on God's part, or the church's.

Such a view focuses on the no of celibacy: no sex, no children, no marriage. But every no has an implicit yes. In fact, no often starts from yes. I say no to sex as a single woman because I only want to share my body as part of my whole life. If I give my body to a man I'm not married to, I'm holding back my money, my house plants . . . all kinds of things. I'm giving him only part of myself. And I'm using him. If I take his body without commitment, I can leave when he gets sick or enters old age. I'm taking only the parts of him I like, for as long as I like. I'm not receiving *all* of him.

When I say yes to a man, I want it to mean something. To protect that yes, I have to say no to anything that would divide my life and my body, or his. To give myself as wholly as I can, I say no to what would separate the sexual from the emotional, intellectual, or spiritual. To give myself in love means giving *and receiving* all of each other: both the beautiful parts and the broken, the lovable parts and those that need God's love the most.

Why is it so hard to see what celibacy says yes to? I think it's partly related to death and procreation. Having children is the oldest and most basic way a person can prepare for old age. Despite the initial cost to rear them, people around the world have long seen children as a way to increase household wealth and ensure some support in old age. That might sound cynical or utilitarian, but the bonds of filial obligation are some of the hardest to break.

On a deep level, nearly all of us recognize the immense sacrifice our parents made to care for and sustain us at our most vulnerable. When we could not even feed ourselves or move, they cared for us. Most people honor the debt we owe our parents by providing increased care when their strength fails.

Perhaps that's why so many people struggle to conceive how or why one could choose to go through life without any help for life's end. Who would choose to grow weak alone? Who would actively forego the biggest and most reliable sources of help when our bodies give out?

The Dominican priest I interviewed in Buenos Aires put parenting in a different light. "God's the Father," he said. "But Jesus says in heaven we won't be married. One way to cooperate with God is to marry and bear children, but God is the source of life, and He's actually the Father of children. So there are other ways of associating with God in this giving of life. I think that's a key issue there: discovering that we are all called to bear fruit in some way."

Fr. James Martin, the American Jesuit writer, echoed that. "I see chastity as a way of loving many people deeply and also freely," he said. "It's a different way of living—it's not better or worse. I always remind people that Jesus was a single man. He can be a model, and yet no one would say He didn't receive love or give love."

As we continue through this chapter, try to use that framework for thinking about ministry. Not all of us get to become biological parents. But Jesus said all who abide in Him will bear fruit. And He said *love*, not children, would identify His followers to the world.

Living in love

Celibacy was most common among the Catholic leaders I interviewed. Yet the priests and two others consecrated as part of the Chemin Neuf Community all insisted they weren't "single." Each stressed that they'd pledged themselves to a community. It might not be a community formed by marriage and the blood ties of parenthood, but it was still a committed group.

"You are not alone," said Fr. Bassols, whom we met at the start of this book. He mentioned a 1981 encyclical by Pope John Paul II that covers single life. "You are part of the family because there is self-giving, there is service, and there is love. You love the service you are doing, and you have given yourself fully to it."

Fr. John said his Dominican vows of poverty, chastity, and obedience all involved promises to his community. "The giving of yourself is central," he said. "It's the core of my calling, my way of engaging with Christ, with God, and with others. And that's very fulfilling. There's more happiness in giving than receiving."

Joanna, the consecrated woman we met in chapter 7, echoed

this. "Obedience, chastity, and poverty is the way for me to find God," she said. "It's for me, but not only for me. It's to bring more God for my brothers and sisters."

Her Chemin Neuf Community in France gave Joanna a very clear and specific sense of community. Fr. John in Buenos Aires had something similar.

Other celibate Christian leaders have more challenges. As we saw in chapter 6, Fr. Jerin became rather isolated during his years away as a student. Single Protestant pastors can also face significant challenges, on top of the usual struggle for community outside church.

"Community is kind of automatic, but the problem—the other side of that two-edged sword—is you can't have the church be your only community," Mark, the Protestant pastor, said. "You need people who you can process your job with. I've made that mistake. I made that mistake in spades."

Unlike the other single Protestant pastors I interviewed, Mark was committed to celibacy. But as a Protestant, almost no formal structures exist to support that choice. "Celibacy is very difficult," he said. "You need a community that's backing you."

Fortunately for Fr. Michael, he did find that in his darkest hours. "I had never contemplated committing suicide in my life," Fr. Michael told me. "But at that time, I was very vulnerable. Some days I would really just like to end everything."

His parishioners' tangible love and support helped him keep going. "The body of Christ, the family of Christ gave me the strength," he said. "For that, I am very grateful, because I love my children and I wanted to be there for them as well. But at the same time, I felt like escaping. I feel like where I am is a prison."

The archdiocese didn't have the resources to deal with a crisis like his. "It was the parishioners who supported me," he said. "They gave me the strength to endure."

Fruitfulness when overwork seems to hurt only you

Two summers ago, a friend of mine planted carrots and beets in her yard. Like all good gardeners, she planted many seeds. But when they sprouted, she couldn't bring herself to thin them. When the frost came, almost none of her many beets and carrots had grown even as big as a finger.

Part of thriving requires saying no. This can prove especially hard for singles in ministry. A 2021 literature review found study after study that showed frequent burnout among priests.[15] Many of the priests lived alone, and often near the church. This increased loneliness and made it harder to set work-life boundaries.

Like its Orthodox sister, the Catholic Church also faces a shortage of priests. This increases their workload. "During our formation time, we are always told we are a priest for twenty-four hours," Fr. Jerin said. "There's no point in life when you are not a priest. We are not supposed to say no to anyone."

Protestant and Orthodox clergy struggle too. Fr. Michael said poor boundaries may have contributed to his divorce. "Anything that anybody asked of me, I did it," he said. "That was one of the problems that my wife had with me—that I was a yes person."

Jesus summarizes the second most important commandment this way: "Love your neighbor as yourself" (Mark 12:31). Many Christians seem instead to hear, "Love your neighbor *better than* yourself." Saying no to someone's request can seem unloving or selfish.

No becomes easier when we really know and value what we're

saying yes to. As we saw in chapter 3, God calls each of us to rest.
In Psalm 127:2 (ESV), Solomon says,

> It is in vain that you rise up early
>> and go late to rest,
> eating the bread of anxious toil;
>> for he gives to his beloved sleep.

Healthy boundaries start with a yes to the God of rest. Healthy
boundaries also accept our human limits. The Bible tells at least
two different stories of someone setting boundaries in the face of
overwork and burnout. In Exodus 18, we find Moses serving his
community "from morning till evening." When his father-in-law
Jethro sees this, he challenges Moses: "What you are doing is not
good. You and the people with you will certainly wear yourselves
out, for the thing is too heavy for you. You are not able to do it
alone" (Exodus 18:17-18, ESV).

He has Moses set up a whole structure of people to handle the
job. Not only does this relieve him, it also helps the people. Before,
they all had to wait their turn for Moses. Under Jethro's system,
people got help much faster.

Where might this principle apply in your life? Are there people
you could better serve if you referred them to someone else? What
about leaders in your church—do you respect their boundaries
and humanity? Or do you call or text at all hours? How could you
help honor their human limits?

The next story comes in 1 Kings 19. After an immense spiritual
battle on Mount Carmel, Elijah has a breakdown in response to
a death threat. He flees into the wilderness and asks God to end
his life. After sleep and two meals provided by an angel, Elijah

then makes a longer journey to Horeb. There, God asks what he's doing, and Elijah complains that he's the only one left serving Him. That's not actually true, as God points out a few verses later.

But God hears his complaint. Elijah clearly feels alone. He seems to find his call too much to carry. So God charges him to anoint two new kings and a successor as prophet. Though Elijah's story continues a few chapters more, we hear little of him from then on.

That fact has always puzzled me when reading the Transfiguration accounts. Why was Elijah so revered when he had only one really big moment: Mount Carmel? I may never learn the answer to that. But for the purposes of this chapter, let me point something out. Both figures Jesus met in the Transfiguration had set boundaries around their workload. Was that why He met with them? Of course not. Some say Moses and Elijah represent the Law and the Prophets in that moment. Others that they were the two greatest leaders or voices in Israel prior to Jesus.

Whatever their meeting with Jesus meant, it entailed a high honor. They had set workload boundaries that maybe you struggle to consider for yourself, *and they still received that high honor.* Would you ponder that if you struggle to say no to others?

Yes, Jesus said that greatness in the Kingdom requires becoming a servant. But even servants deserve rest! (Ahem: See the Sabbath laws.) Do you believe in God's love for you enough to receive His gift of rest?

Single clergy's superpower

Having a sense of meaningful work helps combat burnout. The research shows this, as does my own experience. I reached

Argentina the day after losing half my travel wardrobe. I'd had a long, hard month in Brazil, with little to show for it. As an English-speaking woman at a Protestant church recognized, I was struggling with some burnout myself.

But every time I saw signs of God's work, my spirits revived. I came back from my interview with Fr. John, the Dominican, so encouraged. He expressed a vision of Christian celibacy that really moved me. The thought of getting to share his and others' stories with you helped keep me going. The same thing has happened during the writing process. Time and again, I've seen God again in rereading notes from my interviews. Every time, this fresh evidence that we serve a living God rekindles my energy.

Those I interviewed shared a similar experience. "I am celibate for something," said an Indian Catholic priest, 35. "It is a means for an end."

"I don't have children, but I do experience some of God's fatherhood in His children," Fr. John said. "A lot of my life is kind of being in the shop, or the office. I'm not the carpenter, and I'm not the wood, but I'm there, and it's fascinating. It's not your fruit, it's His fruit, but you share in that in some way. And sometimes in a very, very high and a full way.

"As a priest, you are an instrument in very intimate and important moments of people's lives. You strive to be as much His as possible, so that what He is shines forth and my shortcomings don't impede that. Yet I'm still myself, and He wants that. He's chosen me to give what I am."

Fr. Edward, whom we met in chapter 7, said part of what he gives *is* his single life. Lots of the new converts he meets in his San Francisco Bay Area parish are single young men. "A lot of young men are struggling with pornography addiction," he said. "That's the biggest issue that so many face."

Like me, Fr. Edward first went online as a teenager. When we began to navigate what the internet meant for sexual and relational desires, we were in high school. Younger singles faced that much earlier, Fr. Edward said. He's worked with some young men who've been looking at porn since they were six or seven.

To share their struggles with a *single* priest helps a lot. "I think they feel a camaraderie," he said. As a celibate priest, Fr. Edward can cosuffer with those who find it hard to abstain from sex outside marriage. He can say he's struggling with it too. "I think that can be the advantage of a celibate priest who's serious about it."

Mark, the Protestant pastor, described a similar response. In one of his early sermons, he talked about singleness. "People still talk about it, just because I was so brazen," he said.

Another time, he met with a group of singles near Washington, DC, while a candidate with a church there. After his talk about singleness, many were "openly weeping," he said. "I remember how salty those tears are—they really are."

For both groups, it was probably the first time people heard a *single* pastor address the topic. "How you address the question of loneliness is a key question to addressing how you have a happy and flourishing life as a single Christian," Mark said. He speaks to that differently than a married pastor would because he faces that challenge himself.

His sense of purpose makes a vital difference. "A large part of the loneliness is connected to the hard feelings of bitterness, being left behind by your friends," he said. "That begins to go away as you begin to accept singleness not as a vocational call or a temporary call, but as a spiritual call on your life that has legitimacy."

• • •

Researching this book exposed a lot of idols I'd long smuggled into my faith. I'd follow Jesus as long as I lived in comfort. As long as I had stable electricity and drinkable water. As long as I could keep food in a refrigerator. In theory, of course, I was ready to take up whatever cross Jesus asked me to bear. But in practice, I clutched many things I didn't think Jesus should ask me to sacrifice.

My fieldwork revealed a lot of those idols. God also showed me, firsthand, that sometimes His work requires single-minded devotion. I couldn't have done my research with a boyfriend, much less a husband and children.

My time zone changed often. I sometimes didn't figure out my housing for the night until a few hours beforehand. I rarely had more than a week to adjust to a city, contact a local church, and set up and complete interviews. In the first seven months on the road, I visited *twenty-five countries*. I had almost no emotional or spiritual bandwidth for anything else.

I also couldn't have worked as nimbly and flexibly, were I more tied down to others. I set out thinking I'd finish the fieldwork in twelve months. It took seventeen. I hadn't wanted to give up my beloved living situation, but in hindsight, I had to.

All this leads to an uncomfortable thought. Maybe this book is part of why God kept me single into my forties. (He could still intend more than that, but we'll see.) I first got the idea for this book around 2012. But I wasn't ready financially, professionally, or spiritually. I still carried student loans. My savings was much smaller. A painful but important season of professional refinement didn't start until 2014. And God didn't start dealing with my racism and ignorance of race-based injustice until 2014 either.

What if I had married in my twenties or thirties, as I once hoped? I would never have been willing to put my husband and family through a project like this. I couldn't have. Further, I doubt interviews would have gone the same, had I been married. I don't believe anthropology or journalism requires insider status. Indeed, you often need an outsider's perspective. But knowing singleness firsthand, and at length, took the interviews in a different direction.

God had perfect timing.[16]

Sometimes I look at my aging body and wonder if God will yet give me marriage and motherhood. Whatever He does, I'll have less sex than I once hoped to enjoy. Sometimes that's hard to think about. At such times, I try to remember the wonderful final stanza of Dana Gioia's poem "Summer Storm."

And memory insists on pining
For places it never went,
As if life would be happier
Just by being different.[17]

Who am I to say God's plan for me needed more sex to improve it? Am I God?

For most of my life, I've longed to see Jesus at work firsthand. This book gave me that. I experienced God's incredible provision for and during this trip. And God also entrusted me with an incredible number of stories about His work in the world. I've gotten to see the global church as very few people get to. I've gotten to experience the triune God in a remarkable way. Can anything really top that?

Many years ago, I began to start each day asking God to help me seek first His Kingdom and His righteousness. I'm incredibly privileged in how much of Father, Son, and Holy Spirit I've experienced. Who am I—and who is anyone—to dictate which parts of the Kingdom God gives us?

Each day, we *all* choose anew which Lord we'll serve: ourselves or God. If God truly rules us, then He gets to oversee *all* of our lives—including whether we marry or have sex. He wants *all* of it. He deserves all of it. He is the potter and we the clay, God the maker and we the creation.

• • •

As we come to the end of this chapter, take some time to think about God's call on your life.

What do you **grieve**? What's hard about your present work? Are there dreams you've sacrificed?

What do you **have**? What's good about your primary occupation, paid or not? Where do you see God working?

Is there something you need to **confess or repent of**?

What can you **give**? How can your work help bring God's Kingdom? And if you know singles in ministry, how could you better support them?

TOWARD MEANING AND COMMITMENT

WHEN WAŊGARR'S SECOND HUSBAND LEFT HER, she struggled with whether to stay in her homeland of Elcho Island, Arnhem Land, or leave. She had only to go to the nearest city to drink away her pain. How she longed to escape her grief and the anguish of betrayal.

But Waŋgarr kept coming back to her unfinished work on a Bible translation. Years before, the Indigenous Australian woman had been living "in a comfortable outstation, going hunting all the time." Then one night, she had a dream with Mount Everest in it. A group of people asked for her help.

When she woke up, Waŋgarr said to herself, *Ah! It's only a dream*. But then she got a phone call. Would she help with back translation of the Bible?[1] Her people could not yet read the Bible in their language. Would she help?

"God called me from that place back to Galiwin'ku, Elcho Island," Waŋgarr told me. When she reached the project office at Galiwin'ku, one of the first things she saw was a poster. It read, "I lift up my eyes to the mountains—where does my help come from?" (Psalm 121:1).

Suddenly Waŋgarr remembered her dream about Mount Everest and people in need. It seemed like God's confirmation that He wanted her there. She joined the translation team.

Waŋgarr had no idea how much that sense of God's call would later matter. But when her marriage collapsed, that call anchored her.

"When my husband left me, I was thinking of those two things: that dream and that poster," she told me. In them, she seemed to hear God's encouragement: *Doesn't matter, Waŋgarr; I will be there, helping you.* Then she thought of the work remaining. Who else could carry it to completion?

Waŋgarr stayed. The translation took another five years to finish. By the time we spoke, she was nearly 60. For a few weeks each year, she left Galiwin'ku to work at the Indigenous Bible college in Darwin, where I met her. There she continued her studies and taught, serving as one of the only Indigenous instructors.

"I'm always thinking that I don't have to worry about everything, even my husband," Waŋgarr said. "I'm busy with other things, especially doing God's work."

•   •   •

As we've seen throughout this book, many Christians deal with what Malin Lindroth calls "unchosen singleness." And of course, even Christians who find love and marriage may face unchosen chronic illness, unchosen disability, and many other hardships.

Christian painter and author Makoto Fujimura often uses the Japanese practice of kintsugi as a metaphor for Christian life. In kintsugi, one uses gold to mend the cracks in chipped or broken pottery. This both restores things' usefulness and renders them more beautiful than before.

Paul uses a similar metaphor for the Christian life:

> For God . . . made His light shine in our hearts to give us the light of the knowledge of God's glory displayed in the face of Christ.
>
> But we have this treasure in jars of clay to show that this all-surpassing power is from God and not from us. We are hard pressed on every side, but not crushed; perplexed, but not in despair; persecuted, but not abandoned; struck down, but not destroyed. We always carry around in our body the death of Jesus, so that the life of Jesus may also be revealed in our body.
>
> 2 CORINTHIANS 4:6-10

In some mysterious way, the life of Jesus within us enables Christians to endure hardship in a way that displays His glory and power. What allows us to endure without being crushed, in despair, or destroyed? I believe it's the ongoing experience of Jesus' love as tangibly displayed through the church. For singles, I believe it's the specific expression of Jesus' love shown through a better narrative, meaningful work, and committed community.

What do we mean by *church*, anyway?

By now, I hope you have a good idea what I mean by *church*. But let me get more specific as I talk about what I hope you take from this book. *Church* can mean a lot of things.

When I was a child, church meant the multistory building in Seattle where my family worshiped each Sunday. Church meant an event, a weekly ritual. When I accidentally pulled the organ bench over on myself, church marked me for life.

The Holy Week of my eighth year, a woman at church invited me to go shopping with her and her daughter. To my amazement, she bought me something too. In those days, my family drank powdered milk and rationed our juice. I had never had a brand-new dress for Easter. That year, I wore a sleeveless pink dress with a white yoke.

Mrs. Clifton's kindness gave me my first real taste of God's family. She's dead now, but I still remember the raspy warmth of her laugh: as if it came from someplace deep inside.

When we moved to Phoenix the summer I turned eleven, our family joined the first church that felt more like a community. Their logo even depicted that. They used the drawing on everything from bulletins to gray T-shirts. In it, people formed a human pyramid that was shaped like a church building—steeple and all.

As a homeschooled kid, I didn't fit in well with the youth group. But our family made some lifelong friends there. I still keep in touch with one woman, whom I met when she was a young mom and I a precocious preteen. (We bonded over knitting.)

When my family moved to Singapore two weeks after I graduated from high school, I lost my home. So a family from church let me stay with them until I left for college. The following summer, another family from that Phoenix church let me live with them.

It wasn't just that church. Years later, when I found myself unemployed and struggling in New York City, my church helped again. That congregation had far more attendees and a much bigger budget. They assigned me a deacon to help with my journey toward financial stability. For a couple of months, the church paid my rent and my cell phone bill and gave me gift cards for groceries.

My Bible study helped too. I probably shared my financial needs first as a prayer request. But the group soon realized I needed more than prayer. One week they collected a donation for me. Another week, I shared that I needed more social contact while writing but couldn't afford to visit coffee shops. The group's host had a giant glass bowl of change on the counter. So, at someone's suggestion, they counted it out and gave it to me. It was more than thirty dollars in all.

It's probably no coincidence that this group also had lots of diversity. We had two married couples and several singles. Age-wise, we ran from late twenties to thirties and forties. We were men and women, of various ethnicities and professions. I was probably the poorest one.

Like many New York communities, that group eventually scattered all over the country. So when I came through Atlanta for my fieldwork, a couple from that long-ago study hosted me. When you start treating people the way you would a loved one, it seeds love for them. Something changed the night that Bible study decided to help me tangibly. In some ways, that was the first night we all began to see ourselves as community, as family.

That's the heart of what I've meant when I say *church* in this book. Yes, sometimes I mean the sum of Christians all over the world. Other times I mean all the Christians of a certain tradition, like Catholicism. More often, I've meant individual congregations or parishes.

But where a church really comes together as Christ's body is on the small scale of a Bible study or care group. It's probably no coincidence that Jesus chose *twelve* disciples. A group that size can accommodate both similarities and differences. It's small enough for everyone to know each other. You can eat together. But it's also big enough that you can do significant things for each other or your community.

Now maybe at this point you're still a bit skeptical. I've shared from my own experience, after all. Many others feel deeply betrayed by the church.

Robin, whom we met earlier, was one of the strongest advocates I met for persisting with the church.[2] She came to those views in a very surprising way.

At 16, Robin was just preparing to come out as a gay woman when a youth pastor at her church did the same. When that woman got engaged to another woman, she lost her job. Robin left that church soon after. At the time she thought, "There's too much going on, and I don't feel safe."

But after a six-month relationship ended, she felt called to go back. "Why would You call me back to a place that's so painful?" she asked God. The sense of call persisted. Eventually she returned. From then until her departure for a year abroad, she cried every Sunday.

"I just sort of had to trust that there was a reason why I felt called there," Robin said. After her year away, she returned home. "That call to this particular community deepened," she said.

Robin obeyed. And when she sensed God's call to celibacy, she obeyed that, too. Almost a year before our interview, she took her vows in a ceremony that roughly forty friends attended.

"It was so sacred and holy and surprising," she said. "I'm really glad that we treated it like a wedding."

"I was already living into singleness before then," she told me, "but it felt significantly different after the ceremony, and I didn't expect it to." Afterward, she went on a retreat as a kind of honeymoon with God.

"Over and over, I sat in this deep satisfaction that I'd never really felt before," she said. "It's just like a deep sense of peace and satisfaction that, like, no matter what else is happening in my life, I'm in the right place. I'm in the right significant relationship. Having God as my number one, it is correct."[3]

If we, too, would follow God, we *must* put Him first. Following God also means accepting His plan for the church. God doesn't provide an alternative community. When we accept Jesus, the Spirit connects us to all the others God's called to join His family.

As we said before, God doesn't build the church from natural friends. God chooses natural enemies to form this community. That's why Jesus said, "By this all people will know that you are my disciples, if you have love for one another" (John 13:35, ESV). It's a miracle! It's a miracle that we can love each other. And it's a miracle when we keep showing up for even a deeply broken community.

"Just because you have a bad experience with a particular community doesn't mean that that's it," Robin said. "But it's not necessarily a bad thing to go through a season where you don't feel safe in the community. It's not necessarily forever."

Nor is it necessarily the same community. Palak, whom we met in chapter 9, faced terrible resistance at some churches. In the end, it took leaving the Protestant tradition to join regular worship with the body of Christ.

If Palak could persist like that, how could you give the church a chance?

A better narrative

Throughout human history and cultures, people tend to tie their legacies to their children. Perhaps that's because procreation seems like one of the most godlike acts we perform. Thus, as I said earlier, we try to fit most lives into the narrative arc of childhood-adulthood-marriage-parenthood-old age.

The Bible resists that storyline. Yes, Genesis tells the origin story of God's chosen people. But the story defies our efforts to frame it as success through procreation. Many key figures wait decades before becoming parents. Jacob, who sires the most children, fathers the most dysfunctional family of all. (Read Genesis 34–35 and 37–38 for more detail.)

A paean to procreation Genesis isn't. Its leading figures tend to follow one mistake with another. That's part of why I love it. The humans all screw up terribly. Some prove so broken, it's amazing one could put them to *any* use. Yet each patriarch proves a vessel through whose story God pours out hope for the next generation.

And that's why, time and again, I come back to Genesis when I despair of God's plan for my life. If I hold my life up to the procreation narrative, it's unclear what kind of story I'm in. A good one? A sad one? A tale of hope deferred until death? But when I compare my life to Genesis, I find good and ample company. *Oh, we all have a hard time trusting God. Oh, God often asks His beloved ones to wait on Him.* Eventually my perspective and my questions change.

When I try to judge God by where I fear my life's headed, I start to doubt and despair. Genesis shows me how badly things go awry when people distrust God. Instead, the book points me back to the present. How does God ask me to trust Him *today*? What does obedience look like *today*? Am I waiting on God to fulfill a promise? Do I need to give up something I've put more of my hope in than Him? Am I called to work with integrity in a role I didn't choose? Can I trust that God can bring good from *any*thing?

In the previous chapter, Protestant pastor Mark said accepting singleness as a spiritual and legitimate call can help bring people more peace. Then he said, "In order for people to embrace that, the church has to teach it." *All* of us choose what kind of stories we tell ourselves and others about life. However, pastors and priests have a particularly significant role in shaping the common narratives.

If that's you, please prayerfully ponder how you can teach a more biblical tale of the Christian life. If Anna the prophetess (Luke 2:36-38) went to your church, would she feel encouraged in her journey to faithfully serve God and not remarry? Or would she hear those who marry and have children be constantly valorized?

If Elijah the prophet joined your parish, would he gain strength to continue his unconventional journey of following God? Or would he feel judged in his seemingly unstable, unproductive life?

If the Ethiopian eunuch tried to worship with you, would he feel welcome? Would he hear that God offers him a "monument and a name better than sons and daughters"? Or would he leave lamenting, "I am a dry tree" (Isaiah 56:3, 5, ESV)?

We also need a more biblical story about how the church endures and grows. Too often, Christians put our hope in procreation. Yet study after study shows that each generation of Americans has less interest in church than the previous one.

That shouldn't surprise us. The same pattern runs throughout the Old Testament. Read through Judges and the accounts of the kings if you need a reminder of how well "cradle faith" endures.

Parents can't count on transmitting the faith to their children. We too often forget. And maybe it's easiest to forget when we haven't personally experienced God's grace and forgiveness. As Jesus constantly taught the Pharisees, we can't experience God's mercy unless we recognize that we're sinners. When you grow up with religion, it's all too easy to think yourself too good to need real salvation.

Thankfully, the Bible offers an antidote: proclamation of some very good news. It starts with bad news: We all have sinned and fall short of the glory of God (Romans 3:23). He considers our best works filthy rags (Isaiah 64:6). But if we ask God, He won't judge us by our "good" or bad deeds. He'll judge us by Jesus' work instead (1 John 1–3).

When we let Him take charge of our lives, He begins the work of binding our shards into a vessel that can showcase God's glory to the world. He can use *any* life to do that. Yes, even your life can pour out the hope of a living God who yet works to make all things new.

Telling *that* good news caused the early church to grow as fast as it did despite the growing danger of following Jesus. What would change if you told your life's story like it were part of the Bible? What would change if you told other people's stories that way?

Meaningful work

Embracing this story of the church has great importance. When we persist in insisting the church grow mostly through procreation, it leaves out the barren and we shirk our call to proclaim Jesus' message of hope and salvation.

But when we remember the Bible's account of church growth through proclamation, it enlists us all. Old or young, disabled or not, female or male, single or married: We *all* have a part in God's work. And God invites us to keep on joining His work, no matter how else our lives change.

When Ethiopian Protestant Almaz Tarekegn lost her husband, she faced a choice. If she believed her life's meaning came through procreation, she could grieve in peace. She and her husband had two children before he died. Almaz, then in her forties, could easily throw herself into living through their daughters. She could find most of her life's meaning in that biological legacy.

Or Almaz could continue to embrace the call she and her husband shared, even in this new season of singleness. Shortly before his death, the couple had started work to develop a school in Sendafa-Beke, northeast of Addis Ababa. After her husband's death, Almaz closed the office for two months and mourned him.

Then she resumed work: renting a building and hiring nannies, teachers, and guards for protection. The first year the school opened, it served seventy-five children. The second year, enrollment grew, and they added a meal.

"The children are from the poorest of the poor families," Almaz said. "They eat one time, whether breakfast or dinner or lunch. They fall on the ground because of lack of food. They can't follow the education. They can't learn properly."

Over the next few years, the program continued to grow. Then the fourth year, the landlord tried to double the rent. Almaz refused him, though it meant moving to their third building in four years.

At year's end, the government provided land but no funds to build. Almaz had no money to pay for a building. Or did she? Outside her work with the school, Almaz had begun to look for land to build herself a new house. It would replace a home she and her husband had shared in Bole.

"No one in Ethiopia sells their home," her friend Solomon told me when he first mentioned Almaz. Other Ethiopians agreed, saying mortgages barely exist and land is expensive.[4] Many people can never afford a home. Those who manage to save enough for one often live there for years. It sounded like homes can also serve as a kind of retirement.

But Almaz soon came to see her housing change as an opportunity. She asked her daughters: How would they feel if she sold the house and used the funds for the school? They approved. So Almaz decided to pay for the building after all. "It was sacred for me. I didn't want to tell anybody," she said. "I gave the money for the ministry for only God. That was the sacred reason."

An act so at odds with her culture couldn't stay a secret for long, however. Perhaps that helped propel the school's growth. By the time of our interview, the school had close to three hundred children. Their website lists more developments since then, including economic ventures to help provide more support for the community.[5]

Almaz invested in the school because she sensed it was the right thing to do. But over time, it blessed her, too. The work has transformed her singleness. "When I see other widows, they cry," she said. "They have no satisfaction, they have no happiness."

"My life is not the same because I am Christian," Almaz told me. "I have work to serve the needy. That is my satisfaction." Even though she lost her husband after barely two decades together, she has found meaning and purpose in her work for God's Kingdom. "I got my grace from the Lord," she said. "I have a happy life and satisfaction in my work."

When we seek God first, He offers a meaningful role for *all* of us. Few Christians seem to have a missional view of their work, however. When I attended Redeemer Presbyterian Church in New York City, they had a whole ministry devoted to helping people think about faith and work. I've not encountered a program since that equals their Center for Faith and Work. Redeemer, of course, had more resources. But that's not an excuse.

Churches around the world have a huge opportunity to help attendees think about how our work can honor God. How can we glorify God in our job or main occupation? How does He affect how we treat people? How does faith affect how we *do* our work? Do we build or teach or buy or sell differently because we follow Jesus?

The laity may have to take more leadership in such discussions. We probably understand our own work better than a full-time pastor or priest would. Whatever the form and leadership, such discussion could greatly enrich and expand the work of *all* of the church, single and married alike. My research and my own experience suggest this could also bring much more fulfillment and joy to singles who may never marry or feel called to full-time ministry.

Commitment

For most of my first three decades in the church, I thought good teaching was the most important thing for a strong relationship with God. I was wrong. That humble, faithful Brooklyn Bible study was where I first glimpsed how much God forms us through community.

Formation takes commitment. It takes me staying committed to my community, even when I don't like it. Sometimes that discomfort comes from ways that others wound us, as Robin talked about. Other times, it's the pain when they help us recognize our weaknesses or sin. Either way, growth often requires my commitment to those relationships.

It also takes commitment on the part of my community. The most life-changing confrontation often comes in committed relationship. But singles rarely have access to such relationships. We need people who know us well enough to observe the patterns we can't see in ourselves. And we need people who love us deeply enough to help us work on changing. We need people who'll keep on loving us despite the things we can never fully, or ever, change. That takes commitment.

Keith Watts, 30, an American Protestant who asked that I use his full name, came out as gay in college. At the time, he believed celibacy was the only way he could live as a faithful gay Christian. One night during his senior year, Keith broke down while talking to one of his closest Christian friends.

"I can't do life alone," he told Johnny. "It's monotonous, it's sad—the idea of waking up, going to work alone, coming home alone, eating alone, sleeping alone." Johnny cried with him.

And then the next morning, life carried on. Johnny continued preparing for marriage to a woman named Ellis. Keith kept counting down the days until he left for a final semester in Spain.

The school year ended, and the friends went their separate ways. Spain brought a host of new experiences. But even as he got to know new people and a new city, Keith stayed in touch with loved ones back home. To some, he sent postcards.

One day, Johnny and Ellis wrote back. They sent not a postcard but that rarest and most precious kind of mail: a handwritten letter. Toward the end, they turned to the future. "You would be welcome to stay with us, whether for a season or for life," they wrote.

You would be welcome . . . to stay. Keith said it took a while to grasp their words' full import. "I think that came about more from reflecting on God than reflecting on them. 'I have a physical community that has God's spirit.'"

When they finally talked, Keith told them, "This really meant a lot to me. The idea of really being part of your family really shows me a lot of the nature of God."

He first shared this story with me six years ago, when he was on staff at our church. His story has stayed with me ever since. At 24, as he was then, Johnny and Ellis's commitment played a big role in Keith's faith that he could trust God with being gay.

The meaning of that commitment has evolved. Today, Johnny and Ellis live at least an eight-hour drive from Keith. They've become parents to two girls. When he comes to visit, as he did recently, they call him "Uncle Keith." For his part, Keith understands faith and sexuality a bit differently now. He's open to marrying a man. But he told me recently, "There's not a day that goes by that I don't think about their commitment."

In a recent phone interview, Keith called his bond with Johnny and Ellis a "spiritual friendship," alluding to a book by celibate Episcopal priest Wesley Hill. But Keith also expressed discomfort with Hill's model.[6] "Is it the only way to be single in a world that is not for single people? My world is not for single people. Is spiritual friendship the only way to thriving?" he asked. "What does the commitment say of the two parties? That's something I will always wrestle with."

We discussed the erosion of commitment. "Are single people relegated to being the child?" Keith asked. "I don't find that worldview to be liberated or empowering for single people. It keeps us wanting more, when we are enough."

After we hung up, I thought back to the Yooper Christmas cards, and the friendship they entail. How will that evolve? I think of the pumpkin-carving tradition I once shared with the St. Clair family. We managed one virtual edition during COVID. But the thousands of miles between us make it much harder.

No Christian community or commitment ever goes perfectly. Even the best bonds give way to death. But ultimately we try to love and commit to others as a crude picture of how God treats us. *We*, the church, constitute Jesus' body now.

I was deep in a crisis of faith the first time I really longed for someone else to meet Jesus. My own relationship with Him felt deeply inconvenient at the time. But as I looked at my friend's life, I thought of the Jesus described in the Gospels. *Oh, if she could just encounter that Jesus.* More recently, I've anguished for another friend, often weeping. *Lord Jesus, he needs to meet You!* I've implored.

As Teresa of Ávila once wrote, "Christ has no body now but yours. No hands, no feet on earth, but yours. Yours are the eyes with which He sees, yours are the feet with which He walks. Yours are the hands with which He blesses all the world. Yours are the hands." (The Porter's Gate sings a wonderful setting of this.)

Will we, the church, accept that charge? If we truly serve a living God, our bodies will display this, as Paul said.

•   •   •

As we come to the end of this chapter—and this book—I encourage you to take a longer time of reflection. Proverbs 10:19 says, "Where many words are spoken, sin is not absent" (NCB). May God forgive my failings and blow away all the chaff in what I've said.

If some wheat does remain, what might God be calling you to do?

What do you **grieve**?

What do you **have**?

What do you need to **confess or repent of**?

What can you **give?** And who can you love as if they were Jesus in disguise?

METHODOLOGY

THIS BOOK DRAWS PRIMARILY ON original research I completed during seventeen months of self-funded, in-person fieldwork across six continents.[1] During that trip, I conducted long-form, semistructured interviews with 261 people, most of whom were unmarried at the time.[2] All but nine people I spoke to in person. I spoke to another sixty-four people in eight groups of varying sizes. Some of these groups included married people. In each of the sixty cities where I did research, I also tried to interview at least one pastor or priest for broader context.[3]

After my last research stop, Los Angeles, I interviewed fourteen more people by phone and four more in person. The book also includes, with their permission, two men's stories I learned through friendship rather than interviews. *Solo Planet* thus draws on conversations with 345 people from forty-eight countries:

(*on the road*: 252 in person + 9 by phone + 64 in groups) +
(*post-trip*: 14 by phone + 4 in person + 2 friends).

Because I mostly stayed with families or singles, and worshiped in local churches as often as possible, the book also includes some ethnographic observations.

For a number of practical reasons, including safety, internet access, and ease of transportation, I conducted nearly all the interviews in major cities. This book primarily reflects the reality of single, urban Christians' lives around the world.[4] Because I usually interviewed English speakers, it also reflects the lives of more educated Christians.

Fifteen percent of the conversations occurred in a language other than English.[5] For most of these, a translator helped us. I began and ended the stint outside the United States with interviews in German and Spanish, respectively. I am fluent only in English, so I recorded these interviews. Early in the writing stage, native speakers helped me fill in my notes of those interviews, since I understand less than I can say in German and Spanish.[6]

I interviewed most people (224) one-on-one. However, in some cases, it made sense to interview small groups. The research also included fourteen interviews with two people, three with three, three groups of four, and one group of six priests. I also took notes on eight group conversations for which I couldn't track comments by name. Translators helped with some of these, including three larger groups in Dar es Salaam, Tanzania.

To get a good cultural and geographic balance, I divided my time among six continents: all except Antarctica. For each region, I tried to get a good mix. According to an annual analysis, eleven of the countries I visited had high to extreme persecution of Christians at the time.[7]

In Europe I visited eleven cities in Switzerland, Romania, Ukraine, Russia, Finland, Sweden, England, Spain, and Italy. I spent roughly three months in that region, split between two visits.[8]

In Africa I visited fourteen cities or towns in Nigeria, Ethiopia,

South Africa, Kenya, Tanzania, Egypt, Ghana, and one place not named to protect sources. I spent more than three months there, split between two visits.

In the Middle East I visited three cities in Lebanon, Israel, and Palestine, spending almost a month in that region.

In Asia I visited nine cities in China, South Korea, Japan, India, the Philippines, and Singapore. During a stopover in the Asian part of Istanbul, Turkey, I also did an interview with someone temporarily working there. I spent almost three months in this region, over two visits.

In Australia I visited two cities.

In Latin America, I visited eleven cities in Brazil, Argentina, Peru, Colombia, Panama, Cuba, and Mexico. Because of the holdup in Salvador, Brazil, I did interviews in only ten of the Latin American cities. I spent a little over four months in this region.

In North America, I visited ten cities: San Antonio, Nashville, Atlanta, Dover (Delaware), New York City, Des Moines, Anchorage, and Los Angeles in the United States. In Canada, I visited Toronto and Vancouver. I did about ten weeks of interviews in this region.

A handful of stops included family visits, but I never had a full break from research. Either I continued arranging travel and interviews for future stops, or I had to take care of things like computer upkeep, wardrobe repairs, or medical visits to deal with some of the parasites I got on the road.

I recruited most people by contacting a local church. To the extent possible, I spoke to the most common type of Christian in each country. My interviews reflect a somewhat better balance than the stories I share here.[9] As a Protestant, I struggled to make connections in countries that were majority Catholic or Orthodox. Early on, someone connected me to a translator at the

Vatican. "Do you know any Catholic singles I could interview?" I asked. She said no. In many cases, I probably should have tried harder to find Orthodox or Catholic Christians.

Because of my views on the local church, I always tried to respect the local authorities in place. Whenever possible, I first approached a church's pastor or priest to get their blessing and help. Sometimes I met a parishioner first, and that person started thinking of friends or contacts. I met a handful of people through other means.[10]

In each place, I aimed to interview about five people: two men, two women, and a pastor or priest. I made a particular point to ask for people who were older, disabled, or of a sexual minority.[11]

Because my interviews draw more on the tradition of journalism than sociology, I asked most sources if they wanted me to use their full name, their first name, or a different name. My editor and I ultimately decided to use only first names for all but those who were already public figures. I later reconfirmed in writing with most people what I planned to use from our interview. Where people asked for a different first name, I have noted that.

I did not pay sources for their participation. However, in some cases I reimbursed them for travel costs and/or lost work time. In an interview with two older Nigerian women, the pastor who translated for us told me I should offer them a gift. They offered one in return at the end of the interview. In a handful of other cases, the person interviewed mentioned a financial need that I felt moved to help with. I quote some but not all those people.

To my surprise, a number of people I interviewed treated me to a meal, if we spoke while eating. One Australian man, who has since died, also made a very generous contribution to my travel expenses. A few of the people I interviewed also hosted me in their homes during my stay.

As time went on, I settled into a typical structure for most interviews. However, I began nearly all interviews with a prayer. I didn't know what parts of that person's story I most needed to hear. So each time, I asked God to guide our conversation and help me honor the other person's story. When I could, I prayed in their language, however crudely.

ACKNOWLEDGMENTS

HUNDREDS OF PEOPLE made this book possible. Among the most enduring supporters are the dozens who have formed my prayer team—before, during, and after the fieldwork. I'm no Moses, but thank you so much for taking up Aaron's and Hur's work on my behalf. May God richly repay your faithful intercession for this work.

Makoto Fujimura helped with contacts in my earliest work on this. (Perhaps fittingly, he also painted the small illuminated letter I carried with me throughout the trip and shared with all my hosts.)[1] Kate Shellnutt shaped the two-part 2013 series for *Christianity Today* that helped develop some of my earliest thinking for this book.[2] May God honor both of you in your efforts to develop others' gifts.

Almost a year after those articles, Soong-Chan Rah and Kathy Khang challenged my thinking about race and racism. Their words helped launch a protracted and by-no-means-finished reckoning. I now look back and see how greatly I needed to spend that particular season in reflection and repentance before attempting this book. May God continue to encourage you both in the work He's called you to.[3]

Once God brought this book idea back to me, in fall 2017,

Gina Zurlo and Jason Bruner provided valuable academic input on my approach.[4] I'm indebted to Gina for pushing me to go beyond the Protestant Christianity I know best. This book is immeasurably richer because of that. Jason helped me expand my Asian stops, which also improved the book. Thank you both for making time for a researcher neither in school nor (presently) attached to either of your institutions. May God continue to bless your generosity toward other scholars, especially those outside academia.

Then came the practical concerns: logistics and housing. Countless friends and strangers provided contacts, housing, and other help. I regret that I can't name you all. May God richly repay your help and hospitality to me. I hope your connection to this book has somehow encouraged you.

Most importantly, I owe a great debt to the 345 people who shared their lives with me, and the many pastors and priests who helped enable those conversations. Thanks especially to my translators on the road:[5] Pastor Yemi, Sisbow Asrat, Erick Oguta, William Saidi, HyeJin Oh, Sangeeta Verma, Devender Verma, Lynette Wilson, John Wiafe, Camila Peixoto Souza, and Fr. Brad Mills. May God honor your willingness to invest in this project, and may it bear good fruit from your stewardship.

Thanks also to scholars who shared some of their research with me. Nokuthula Mazibuko explained aspects of ilobolo to me. Meredith Lake provided background on Christianity in Australia. May God bless both of you in your ongoing research.[6]

As I headed toward the North American phase of fieldwork, Jason Shelton and Billy Honor Jr. gave insight on some of the unique ways singleness plays out in the Black church.[7] Mark Charles and Ray Aldred provided input on how to sensitively include Native Christians.[8] At the time, I didn't realize how many such requests for help you four might get from people like me. I wasn't thinking enough about reciprocity. May God honor and reward your willingness to help me nonetheless, and help me show the same generosity to others.

Karen Swallow Prior and Amy Julia Becker provided vital help with finding an agent for this book. They pointed me to the indefatigable Chris Park, who has been an answer to many prayers. Chris, thank you for such continued wise counsel, and your tireless faith in this book. May God honor your dogged persistence. Thank you, all three, for helping this book in its journey to print.

Sociologists Michael O. Emerson and Orestes P. Hastings also provided input on data analysis.[9] May God bless your research and generosity to researchers like me.

During the search for a publisher, both my agent and Ed Gilbreath provided very important feedback on my approach to the book. Thank you both. Your editorial direction played a key role in clarifying how I handle stories in this book. May God continue to bless your counsel and show His delight in your faithful exercise of these gifts.

I'm deeply grateful to Dave Zimmerman and NavPress for ultimately acquiring this book. May God bear great fruit in churches and individuals because of your willingness to bring this book to print.

Once I started writing, a team of mostly Anchorage-based native speakers of Spanish and German helped me translate interviews. Huge thanks to Sylvia Guzmán de Sánchez, Fiorella Isla-Gálvez, Gaby Shelton, Lucía García, Mikela Broach Cervantes, and Sara Huber. May God bless you for your participation in this project.

Turning two hundred–plus transcript files into topically organized material took hours of patient data entry. Thank you to Mary Ting, Lucas Moore, and Gladys Ignacio. May God honor your investment in this extremely important, behind-the-scenes work. I don't know how I would have drafted my chapters without you.

Deborah Sáenz Gonzalez and Elizabeth Schroll have been better editors than I dreamed of and such an answer to prayer. Deb, thank you for all those phone calls and pre-draft reviews. Those helped me immensely. Your edits pushed me in all the right ways; this book is so much stronger because you edited it. And Elizabeth, your attention to detail amazes me. I know this project really put your fact-checking through the paces. Thanks especially for catching all those details of math and geography! Thanks also to Michael Ray Smith for providing such a thorough review of all things journalism. I'm deeply grateful for all your input on quotes. May God pour as much loving care into the details of your lives as you three have invested in this book.

Even a book full of words needs some visuals. Thank you, Brian Adams and Eva Winters, for your patient work with me on the headshot and cover, respectively. I know my requests may have challenged and surprised you, but I'm so grateful for your willingness to work with me. May God honor the risks you both took with me.

Thanks also to Olivia Eldredge, Robin Bermel, and the Tyndale marketing team. I'm so grateful to have your support in this. May God use your efforts to bless the church.

Last, but certainly not least, thanks to Anthony Adams for your patient help with both video and tallying all the people I quote. I never imagined how much would result from following Google Maps's guidance past the church that day, but I'm so grateful, for God directed my route. May Creator pour out His love on you.

To all those I couldn't name, thank you, gracias, danke, xièxiè, āmeseginalehu, quyana. May God generously repay what you invested in this book.

DISCUSSION QUESTIONS

Introduction: Why Another Book on Singleness?

1. What role has the church played in your life during single seasons? Has it disappointed you? Helped you? Surprised you?

2. How have you seen the demographics problem play out in Christian community? Where do you find it challenging? Where do you see opportunities in this?

3. Have you seen churches or Christians handle singleness well? What did that look like?

4. Anna describes four theological problems that contribute to the marginalization of single people in the church. Which have you seen or experienced the most?

5. In which areas of your life do you tend to focus on what you *have*? Where do you focus on what you *lack*? How does this change your perspective and experience? How could you help others focus on what they have?

6. What are your hopes, fears, or expectations for reading this book?

Chapter 1 | Community: How the Gospel Redefines Family

1. Which of these three concepts do you resonate with the most: integrated diversity, interdependence, or shared welfare? Which is hardest for you to accept?

2. How have you been hurt by people different from you? Now think of a time you might have hurt someone else because they weren't like you. What were you thinking or feeling when you treated them that way?

3. When have you experienced integrated community? What did you learn from it?

4. Who usually initiates plans in your circle of friends? What do you usually do when you gather? How do you feel about that? Have you ever talked about how well this approach works for everyone?

5. Have you ever let a friend help you with daily routines? Has a friend let you into theirs? What did it feel like? How did it affect your relationship?

6. Have you experienced friendship with someone richer or poorer than you? What was that like? What would it take to go deeper with someone of different means?

Chapter 2 | Celebrations: Rethinking Communal Gratitude

1. How much of the church calendar do you currently celebrate? Do you celebrate any holidays with people you're not related to? Why or why not?

2. What do you long for during the Advent season? How could you long with others?

3. During the Christmas season, where do you invest the most time and energy? How could your Christmas celebrations make room for others?

4. What place does lament have in your life? Do you ever let other people grieve and weep with you? Are there other people whose pain God wants you to help grieve?

5. How do you relate to baptism? Have you ever celebrated someone's baptism or spiritual birthday? What would it look like to do so?

6. Which events get the biggest celebrations in your life? Why do you think that is?

7. How could you rejoice in more of God's gifts, either to you or to your friends and family? Are there small moments or milestones that deserve more celebration?

Chapter 3 | Leisure: What We Need to Really Rest

1. What relationship do you have with the earth? Have you ever thought about how it connects with your spirituality? What are some ways you could connect more with God through creation?

2. What surprised you about Kevin's friendship with his married friends?

3. Is there a single person (or two) in your life whom you could integrate into your leisure habits or travel plans? If not, what would have to change for this to happen?

4. Have you experienced inequalities in your church or family when it comes to getting together? How could you address

this? If you haven't ever discussed it, you might start by asking each other how you feel about it. Where is it hard? How is it good? Could you change anything so that you all feel better about getting together?

5. What are some ways you could offer the land on which your church building sits to your community? Could you build an orchard that anyone can pick from? Plant a flower garden?

Chapter 4 | Emotional Health: How God Transforms Our Pain

1. Have you ever thought a change in circumstances would "solve" problems or take away hard emotions? Did that belief help or hurt your ability to handle the present? What would you say to a friend who's thinking this way?

2. What do you think about asking God questions, as Anna describes doing in listening prayer? Have you ever prayed like that before? Have you heard others pray like that?

3. What do you think about bringing pain to God? Did that idea surprise you? What role might fellow Christians have in helping each other bring our pain to God?

4. How have you experienced loneliness, shame, or powerlessness? If you've been married *and* single, did either state change these emotions at all? Why or why not?

5. How could you encourage someone who's dealing with hard emotions?

Chapter 5 | Housing: How Shelter Shapes Our Character

1. What do you think about the idea that sharing a roof is sacred? What feelings does this stir up?

2. With whom do you share or have you shared housing? For how long? Under what circumstances? How does God fit into your practices and posture toward housing?

3. As Joke showed us, helping each other doesn't have to stop at the front door. Do you currently share chores with anyone or help others with the day-to-day? What would it look like to do more of that?

4. What do you think of your culture's views of sharing and maturity? Is there something you could learn from another culture?

5. When have you needed more care? What was that like? Who in your life needs more care or more support in caring for someone else?

Chapter 6 | Food: How Meals Connect Us to God and Each Other

1. Where have you experienced a broken relationship to food? Have you ever connected this to your spiritual life?

2. Have you ever fasted? If so, what was the reason? If you've only ever fasted for secular reasons, what would it look like to explore fasting with God?

3. How did you react to the statement that eating alone is harder than sleeping alone? If you mostly eat alone, what is

it like for you? Do you wish to change that? If you mostly eat with others, is there anyone you could invite to join you?

4. When you have extra food, what do you do with it? How could you let others glean from it? When you need food, where or how do you get it? What would it look like for you to glean?

5. How often does your church take communion? How often do you share other meals as a body? What would it look like to eat together more often?

Chapter 7 | Sexuality and the Body: God's Invitation to Wrestle

1. What kind of parent do you think God is? Do you picture God as your Father who gives good gifts to His children? Where have you believed lies about the Father, Son, and Holy Spirit? Ask God to help you understand how His loving character impacts your identity as His child, including how you view your body and sexuality.

2. What does worship look like in your life? Where has it become confused? Ask God how your body and sexuality can help you become a better worshiper of your creator. Describe what you love best about God's design for sexuality and your body.

3. Where have you doubted or resisted God's will for your body and sexuality? Ask for help in your doubt. Ask for help trusting God's goodness.

4. Where do you question or even resent God's provision for your body and sexuality? Ask to see God's provision more

clearly. What about your body and sexuality are you grateful for? Thank God for those things. Ask God to help you grow in contentment and generosity with your body and sexuality.

5. Jesus put forgiveness toward the end of the Lord's Prayer. Why do you think He did that? Which is harder for you—to receive God's forgiveness, or to forgive others? Why do you think Jesus said to seek God's forgiveness before we forgive others? Ask Jesus to help you apply this prayer to your body and sexuality.

Chapter 8 | Parenting: Redeeming Relationships between Generations

1. Where do you struggle with what your culture says about how you should relate to children? Where do you struggle with what the Bible shows?

2. Whether you have biological children or not, think of the times when you feel a deep sense of worth. Then think of when you *least* feel a sense of worth. Does anything surprise you about your answers? What would you *like* your worth to come from? How could you help others who struggle with their sense of worth?

3. What parental figures has God given you? What did they teach you—good and bad? Are there things you've had to relearn or things you would teach children to do differently?

4. Where has God called you to obedient faith in a child's life? How could you support someone else called to foster or adopt?

5. Have you had any experiences related to parenthood that you struggle to name or discuss? Would you consider letting God

or others into your pain? If you have already done this, what gave you the courage to do so? Could you help provide that for others?

Chapter 9 | Sexual Minorities: The Struggle for Belonging

1. What surprised you or stood out to you about the stories in this chapter?

2. Why do you think Jesus said love would identify His followers? Where do you struggle with this? Have others ever shown costly love to you?

3. Do you personally know people who struggle with their sexual identity or are same-sex attracted? Have you heard their stories? How have you responded to the struggles they've shared with you?

4. Have you ever been in a context where you felt out of place or not sure where you belong? Were you treated kindly by anyone? How did others' treatment affect your experience?

5. What does surrender look like in your life? If you have given up something significant for Jesus, what motivated you?

6. How could you show God's love to someone who doesn't feel like they belong in the church because of their sexual identity?

Chapter 10 | Disease, Disability, and Death: When Our Bodies and Minds Betray Us

1. What do you think about framing disease and disability as "betrayals" of the body and mind? Have you experienced this? How would you want to be treated in such situations?

2. Why do you think the first two men in Jesus' story avoided the injured man? Do you ever struggle to approach people in need? What do you think the Samaritan received from the wounded man?

3. Have you ever needed help you couldn't repay? Whom did you think you could ask for such help? Now think about times others needed your help. Did they share your criteria for receiving help? What did it feel like to help them?

4. How do you relate to the vulnerable people in your church or neighborhood? What's hard about these situations? Where do you think Jesus is in these situations? If you're vulnerable yourself, what would you like others to know?

5. When you relate to people weaker or more vulnerable than yourself, do you expect to give or receive? Now imagine yourself in their place: Do you expect to give or receive? What would it look like to have a more mutual relationship?

6. What is your posture toward death and legacy? Whether you are single or married, have kids or not, how can you approach these questions in a way that honors your life and God?

Chapter 11 | Singles in Ministry: Work the Body of Christ Struggles to Understand

1. How did this chapter shift your thinking about single ministers' needs for community, boundaries, and purpose?

2. Has someone ever rejected your help or advice because you lacked experience? What did that feel like? Have you

ever received helpful advice from someone who hadn't experienced your situation?

3. How do we give and receive love from the people around us? How do we bear fruit in the circumstances God appoints for us? How do we help others bear fruit?

4. Where is it easy for you to say no? Where is it hard? What do you think of the idea that saying no to something means saying yes to something else?

5. Are there any places where you struggle to respect the boundaries and limits of others? What happens when you primarily turn to one person for help? What happens when you have multiple people you can turn to for help?

6. Could the single leaders and ministers in *your* life count on support from you, even in times of crisis?

Conclusion: Toward Meaning and Commitment

1. How do you define church? Did anything about Anna's definition surprise or challenge you? What narrative tends to define your life? Has that narrative ever let you down? What would change if you told your life story as a journey with Jesus?

2. What things do you most easily encourage others to try—foods? Products? Habits or techniques? How do you feel about telling others about Jesus? Has He been good news for your life? Why or why not?

3. What would change if you and your church focused more on proclaiming God's Kingdom than on procreation? Which is easier to do? For whom?

4. What forms of commitment do you have access to? Are there commitments you want to work on? What's good about commitment? What's hard?

5. What would it take for your church to feel more like a family? What would depend on you? What would depend on others?

NOTES

INTRODUCTION | WHY ANOTHER BOOK ON SINGLENESS?

1. US Department of State, "2020 Report on International Religious Freedom: Kenya," accessed March 2, 2022, https://www.state.gov/reports/2020-report-on-international-religious-freedom/kenya.

2. Given the white supremacy and cultural assimilation that has too often accompanied missions, I should be clear that I reference this as a call to grow the church more through evangelism than procreation and to become the multiethnic community God intends. In any case, Jesus first commissioned Jews, not European Gentiles.

3. From 2018 to 2020, the survey found that 30 percent of never-married Americans said they never attend religious services. When resurveyed in 2022, 44 percent of the same group said they never attend religious services. Lindsey Witt-Swanson, Jennifer Benz, and Daniel A. Cox, "Faith after the Pandemic: How COVID-19 Changed American Religion," January 5, 2023, https://www.americansurvey center.org/research/faith-after-the-pandemic-how-covid-19-changed-american-religion.

4. I used this term on the recommendation of the National Center on Disability and Journalism, but I struggle with it. Fundamental to handling the many differences this book addresses, I try to describe people in terms of what they are rather than what they're not. Thus, single and married, female and male, gay and straight, old and young, and so on. Whenever possible, I try to avoid labels altogether and give specifics (e.g, "is attracted to both men and women," "has Down syndrome," and so on). Sometimes, however, I couldn't avoid speaking of groups who share something in common. These cases almost always present pitfalls on either side. *Sexual minorities* leaves room for the list to change down the road. Some, however, object to this term as stigmatizing. The term's meaning will likely change over time and in unpredictable ways. When it comes to disability, I recognize that moving away from *abled* probably seeks to address the hurt and stigmatization felt by many people with disabilities. But it seems strange to me to treat disability

as the norm, as use of *nondisabled* implies. I worship a God who spent much of His earthly ministry healing people's bodies. The Bible clearly portrays this as a foretaste of God's Kingdom. Yes, the resurrected Jesus had scars, but His wounds had healed.

5. Pew-Templeton Global Religious Futures Project, data filtered by Christians, male and female, 2010 and 2020, each of the fifteen-year age cohorts: 0–14, 15–29, 30–44, and so on. To avoid including minors or those who might rethink their faith upon adulthood, I considered only Pew's 2010 estimates of Christians 30 and older: 577,890,000 women and 492,140,000 men, a difference of 85,750,000. For 2020, Pew estimates put the gap at almost 90 million more women. This figure takes the Pew-Templeton Global Religious Futures Project estimate of US Christians in 2020 (252,870,000) and applies the Pew Religious Landscape Study's demographic data on the ratio of women to men in the US church (55 percent female to 45 percent male). See http://globalreligious futures.org/explorer#/?subtopic=15&chartType=map&year=2010&data_type =number&religious_affiliation=51&destination=to&countries=Worldwide&age _group=all&gender=all&pdfMode=false; http://www.globalreligiousfutures.org /csv/51463/preview; and https://www.pewforum.org/religious-landscape-study /christians/christian/#demographic-information.

6. Vicky Walker, *Relatable: Exploring God, Love, and Connection in the Age of Choice* (Milton Keynes: Malcolm Down, 2019), 125–127.

7. I say *Christians* here because the view owes more to secular cultures than the Bible. First Corinthians 7 in particular takes a very different view of marriage and singleness.

8. As Pieter Valk writes, "Churches never teach about lifetime singleness, there are no models in their church for doing this well, and they don't invite straight people to consider celibacy. It begs the question: if we aren't offering celibacy to straight people, do we really believe it is good?" Pieter Valk, "The Gay Teen Test," Equip, March 13, 2019, https://equipyourcommunity.org/blog/2019/3/13 /the-gay-teen-test.

9. As one example, Gospel Coalition blogger Kevin DeYoung published a response to the Supreme Court ruling on *Bostock v. Clayton County*, and in it he urged Christians to "hav[e] more children than you think you can handle": "The future belongs to the fecund. It's time for happy warriors who seek to 'renew the city' and 'win the culture war' by investing in their local church, focusing on the family, and bringing the kingdom to bear on the world, one baby at a time." Kevin DeYoung, "It's Time for a New Culture War Strategy," June 17, 2020, https:// www.thegospelcoalition.org/blogs/kevin-deyoung/its-time-for-a-new-culture -war-strategy.

10. I visited forty-one countries, including the United States. Due to stopovers and a small amount of personal travel, I did interviews in sixty cities across thirty-seven countries. Given a combination of people interviewed by phone and/or outside their country, I interviewed people from slightly more cities and

countries than I visited. The trip began May 21, 2018. I left my final research stop October 23, 2019—seventeen months later. On my website, I describe the trip as eighteen months because I didn't finish the road trip to Alaska until November 24, 2019. I did a few more interviews between Los Angeles and Anchorage. See the methodology for more details.

11. For more on this, see Anna Broadway, "Confessing My Racism," *Christianity Today*, August 8, 2014, http://www.christianitytoday.com/amyjuliabecker/2014 /august/confessing-my-racism.html.

12. Except for German and one interview in Colombia, I used a native speaker from the same country as the interview (e.g., a Cuban translated my interviews from Havana, and a Peruvian translated those from Lima).

CHAPTER 1 | COMMUNITY: HOW THE GOSPEL REDEFINES FAMILY

1. Several years ago, I committed to praying for a block in my Brooklyn neighborhood each time I walked through it. The walk only took a few minutes. For several weeks, the prayers seemed almost powerless. But eventually, a pastor and his family moved into the block. As a result, a neighbor started going to church with them. See more in Anna Broadway, "The Praying Pedestrian: A Lenten Discipline," *Christianity Today*, April 7, 2011, https:// www.christianitytoday.com/ct/2011/aprilweb-only/praying-pedestrian-lenten-discipline.html.

2. I use more than one translation of the Bible in *Solo Planet*. One reason: readability. As an editor, I learned that the lower an English text's grade level, the easier it is to read—for anyone. I don't want language to keep some Christians from reading this book. Where possible, therefore, I've chosen easier-to-read translations. The variety also reflects my efforts to include all of the church.

3. Duane Elmer, *Cross-Cultural Servanthood: Serving the World in Christlike Humility* (Downers Grove, IL: InterVarsity Press, 2006), 47. I'm indebted to my aunt Ruth, a former missionary, for suggesting this book to me before my trip.

4. Katelyn Beaty, "Joshua Harris and the Sexual Prosperity Gospel," Religion News Service, July 26, 2019, https://religionnews.com/2019/07/26/joshua-harris-and -the-sexual-prosperity-gospel.

5. Figure based on my analysis of data at IndexMundi.com for thirty-five of the countries I visited. IndexMundi pulls its population estimates from the CIA World Factbook, https://www.cia.gov/the-world-factbook. I found it easier to pull demographic snapshots from the secondary rather than the primary source.

6. He's not alone. Here in Anchorage, I invited a widowed friend over for both Thanksgiving and Christmas because he had no other plans. He's been part of the same church for decades.

7. The economics of marriage also kept people single. Men from another Tanzanian church said they were too poor to support a wife, even though some of them had become fathers.

NOTES

CHAPTER 2 | CELEBRATIONS: RETHINKING COMMUNAL GRATITUDE

1. We need to look beyond milestones, as I argued in an earlier version of this chapter. See "It's the Summer of Weddings. Here Are Other Milestones We Can Celebrate," *Christianity Today*, June 14, 2021, https://www.christianitytoday.com /ct/2021/june-web-only/its-summer-of-weddings-celebrate-spiritual-milestones .html.

2. Most US newspapers and the style guide used for this book capitalize geographic regions of Africa, Asia, and Europe. I find this problematic, given that South Africa is a country and the American continents already have south and north in their names. Moreover, some people think of Africa as a country rather than a continent. (See, for example, the book *Africa Is Not a Country: Breaking Stereotypes of Modern Africa* by Dipo Faloyin.) However, at least some English newspapers in Africa also capitalize references to regions of their continent. I have therefore followed this practice here.

3. Psalm 126:5, WEB.

4. Kelsey Kramer McGinnis, "150 Weeks of Composing Psalms Reaches Its Finale," *Christianity Today*, November 8, 2022, https://www.christianitytoday .com/ct/2022/november-web-only/poor-bishop-hooper-everypsalm-psalm-150 -songs-psalter-proje.html.

5. Michael Card, *A Sacred Sorrow: Reaching Out to God in the Lost Language of Lament* (Colorado Springs: NavPress, 2005), 29.

6. It took me a long time to realize I could learn ballet as an adult, too. My family couldn't afford lessons, so I tried to learn as a child using library books. All of them showed only children learning. When my self-instruction failed, I assumed I'd missed my chance to learn ballet. Not until moving to Alaska did I realize I could still learn it as an adult.

7. This graduation happened after she completed medical school and residency. According to the American College of Surgeons, residencies can last three to seven years. They focus on the doctor's chosen specialty. See "How Many Years of Postgraduate Training Do Surgical Residents Undergo?," American College of Surgeons website, accessed February 20, 2023, https://www.facs.org/for-medical-professionals/education/online-guide-to-choosing-a-surgical-residency /guide-to-choosing-a-surgical-residency-for-medical-students/faqs/training.

8. "My World Cup game in Siberia" is how I came to tell the story. No Russian ever corrected me. However, I've since learned that Ekaterinburg is more like halfway between Moscow and Siberia. Oops. Perhaps, to outsiders, it's a bit like how New Yorkers view the rest of the state. Anything north of the Bronx? Basically upstate. When you don't have a good sense of Russia's scale, anything a long journey east of Moscow must surely be in Siberia.

CHAPTER 3 | LEISURE: WHAT WE NEED TO REALLY REST

1. Even this was a privilege. During one drive through Lagos, a Nigerian told me that people in his country often don't address car problems. Instead, they wait until it becomes a crisis. Most people don't have the extra money for preventive maintenance. When you're struggling to feed yourself and your family today, planning for the future is a luxury.

2. See, for example, Ope, "Black Tax: When You Are Your Family's ATM," January 14, 2019, https://cowrywise.com/blog/black-tax.

3. The name changed to Puducherry in 2006. With several Indian places that changed names, my sources tended to use the older name in our interviews. I see a similar pattern in Alaska. Though several cities and at least one mountain have changed their names back to those Alaska Natives used, many people continue to use the previous name.

4. See, for example, "Odds of Dying," US National Safety Council, accessed February 15, 2023, https://injuryfacts.nsc.org/all-injuries/preventable-death -overview/odds-of-dying.

5. The Ethiopian Airlines plane was the second Boeing 737 MAX to crash in a relatively short span of time. The second crash drew scrutiny of the design. Eventually some major problems were revealed, which Boeing had to fix on all the 737 MAX planes.

CHAPTER 4 | EMOTIONAL HEALTH: HOW GOD TRANSFORMS OUR PAIN

1. Timothy Keller, "The Wounded Spirit," December 4, 2004. Available online at https://www.youtube.com/watch?v=pkL3R27ZV1o. An unofficial transcript also appears online at https://www.monergism.com/wounded-spirit-proverbs-1225 -transcript. These five factors include the physical, the relational, the moral, the existential, and the faith aspect.

CHAPTER 5 | HOUSING: HOW SHELTER SHAPES OUR CHARACTER

1. "As they were walking along the road, a man said to him, 'I will follow you wherever you go.' Jesus replied, 'Foxes have dens and birds have nests, but the Son of Man has no place to lay his head'" (Luke 9:57-58).

2. Unlike many of Jesus' stories, this one has more dialogue than action: "Then the Chief will say to the sheep on his right, 'The blessing of my Father rests upon you. Come into the Land of Creator's good road that has been prepared for you from the beginning of the world. For I was thirsty and you gave me drink. I was hungry and you fed me. I was a stranger and you gave me lodging. When I needed clothes, you gave me something to wear. When I was sick, you took care of me, and when I was in prison, you visited me.'

"'When did we do all these things for you?' the good-hearted ones asked.

"'I speak from my heart,' he answered them, 'whatever you did for the

least important of my fellow human beings who needed help, you did for me'"
(Matthew 25:34-40, FNV).

3. Figures reflect slight rounding. Those who lived alone: 82 (38.68%); with
family: 86 (40.57%); with others: 37 (17.45%); in community: 5 (2.36%). Two
didn't have housing (0.94%).

4. Lim Tin Seng, "Land from Sand: Singapore's Reclamation Story," *BiblioAsia*,
April 4, 2017, https://biblioasia.nlb.gov.sg/vol-13/issue-1/apr-jun-2017/land
-from-sand.

5. Singapore Housing and Development Board, guide to buying a flat, "Singles,"
accessed June 8, 2022, https://www.hdb.gov.sg/cs/infoweb/residential
/buying-a-flat/understanding-your-eligibility-and-housing-loan-options
/flat-and-grant-eligibility/singles.

6. "Residential Units Constructed and Sold by Housing and Development Board,"
Department of Statistics Singapore, last updated April 26, 2022, https://table
builder.singstat.gov.sg/table/TS/M400151.

7. Kate Julian, "Why Are Young People Having So Little Sex?" *The Atlantic*,
December 2018, accessed June 8, 2022, https://www.theatlantic.com
/magazine/archive/2018/12/the-sex-recession/573949.

8. The Chinese Christians I spoke to sometimes used terms like this for fellow
believers.

9. Jaime L. Natoli et al., "Prenatal Diagnosis of Down Syndrome: A Systematic
Review of Termination Rates (1995–2011)," *Prenatal Diagnosis* 32, no. 2
(February 2012): 142–53, https://doi.org/10.1002/pd.2910.

10. Learn more at https://www.familyofbrothers.org.

11. Pieter Valk, "The Gay Teen Test," March 13, 2019, https://equipyourcommunity
.org/blog/2019/3/13/the-gay-teen-test.

CHAPTER 6 | FOOD: HOW MEALS CONNECT US TO GOD AND EACH OTHER

1. In Genesis 1, God provides work first, then food. (Genesis 1 compresses the
creation of man and woman as one event.) Genesis 2 mentions plants' food value
first, but suggests God gave Adam his work, then food and companionship.

2. Willie James Jennings, *Acts*, BELIEF: A Theological Commentary on the Bible
(Louisville, KY: Westminster John Knox Press, 2017), 106.

3. Jennings, *Acts*, 107. Emphasis mine.

4. Forty percent of the 146 people who described what they ate were men. But
60 percent of the twenty-five people who mostly ate out were men. Cooking
seemed somewhat more gendered in some African countries, but not all.

5. According to a February 19, 2023, email from Neema's codirector, Ben Ray,
employees contribute 5,000 Tanzanian shillings per month toward meals (about
two dollars at the time). Neema subsidizes the remaining cost. Employees get
about twenty-three meals a month.

6. David Mahaffey served as the church's top leader in Alaska until his death in 2020.

7. Vladyka David also mentioned Dormition and Saints Peter and Paul.

8. In some monasteries, they may not even eat cooked food during fasts. Instead, they might eat dried fruit and nuts.

9. For more on this, see my chapter "How to Trust God with Your Body," in *Venus and Virtue: Celebrating Sex and Seeking Sanctification*, ed. Jerry L. Walls, Jeremy Neill, and David Baggett (Eugene, OR: Cascade Books, 2018), 79–91.

10. I'm indebted to Vladyka David for pointing out the significance of this speech in John 6. So many of even Jesus' "disciples" leave that He asks the Twelve if they plan to go too.

11. By many accounts, the Igbo suffered genocide during the Nigerian civil war that ended in 1970. But not until 2014 did the *Journal of Genocide Research* devote a special issue to the war and "the question of genocide." The opening article noted, "Many defeated Igbo claimed that their genocidal experience was denied during the war." The church Sunday and Olabisi attended also had many Yoruba Christians, including the pastor who translated for us. I didn't know enough of this at the time to ask how their church handled the two tribes' complicated history. Lasse Heerten and A. Dirk Moses, "The Nigeria–Biafra War: Postcolonial Conflict and the Question of Genocide," *Journal of Genocide Research* 16, nos. 2–3 (2014): 169–203, https://doi.org/10.1080/14623528.2014 .936700. See also Nobel Prize–winner Wole Soyinka's comments in YouNews, "Wole Soyinka Speaks on Achebe's Costly Mistakes, Ojukwu & Biafra," May 19, 2013, http://www.younewsng.com/2013/05/19/wole-soyinka-speaks -on-achebes-costly-mistakes-ojukwu-biafra; and World Directory of Minorities and Indigenous Peoples, "Igbo," accessed February 20, 2023, https://minority rights.org/minorities/igbo.

12. For more on this, see Michael O. Emerson, *People of the Dream: Multiracial Congregations in the United States* (Princeton: Princeton University Press, 2006), 51–52.

13. Emily Russell, "AK: Bringing Sourdough Home for the Holidays," Alaska Public Media, December 23, 2016, https://alaskapublic.org/2016/12/23/ak-bringing -sourdough-home-for-the-holidays.

14. See, for instance, Bailey Berg, "Why Longtime Alaska Residents Are Called 'Sourdoughs,'" *Atlas Obscura*, January 15, 2021, https://www.atlasobscura.com /articles/what-is-sourdough-alaska.

15. I also left starter "children" in Switzerland, Kenya, and Egypt.

CHAPTER 7 | SEXUALITY AND THE BODY: GOD'S INVITATION TO WRESTLE

1. We'll talk more about a biblical sex ethic in chapter 9. Christians often summarize the Bible as teaching that God reserves sex for marriage between a man and woman who ideally share the same faith and never divorce. In fact,

I believe God gives us more than just boundaries for sex. And only sometimes does He use explicit commands to teach us. Other times He uses stories and examples to teach His purpose for sex. I believe God does this to invite us into deeper relationship and ongoing dialogue with Him and with Scripture.

2. John F. Smed and Justine Hwang, *Prayer for the City: Bootcamp for Urban Mission*, 3rd rev. (Vancouver: Prayer Current, 2019).

3. Because of its importance in oral tradition, I am using a version that Catholic and Orthodox priests reported using and that my own Lutheran church uses as well. Considering that the three traditions often read different versions of the Bible, I was moved to learn that our English versions of this prayer are so close.

4. Some churches say "Save us from the time of trial" here.

5. Not all churches recite this line. Some translations also note that this line doesn't appear in the earliest manuscripts.

6. Calvin Reid, "BookScan Reports 'Fifty Shades of Grey' Is Bestselling Book of the Decade," December 18, 2019, *Publishers Weekly*, https://www.publishersweekly .com/pw/by-topic/industry-news/bookselling/article/82019-bookscan-reports -fifty-shades-of-grey-is-bestselling-book-of-the-decade.html.

7. Lizondro and I discussed the masculine ending of this name. She confirmed that's the name I should use for her.

8. Paul commands it in 1 Corinthians 16:20, a striking counterpoint to the book's frequent focus on sexual sin in that church. Peter also calls for greeting each other with a kiss in 1 Peter 5:14.

9. In the end, God's plan did include a husband. Jenny married in 2022.

10. According to a 2016 report, 84.3 percent of Native women have experienced violence and 56.1 percent have experienced sexual violence. André B. Rosay, "Violence against American Indian and Alaska Native Women and Men: 2010 Findings from the National Intimate Partner and Sexual Violence Survey," National Institute of Justice Research Report, May 2016, https://www.ojp.gov /pdffiles1/nij/249736.pdf. An older report showed that Native women experienced rape and sexual assault 2.5 times more often than women of all other races. Steven W. Perry, "American Indians and Crime, a BJS Statistical Profile, 1992-2002," US Department of Justice, 2004: 5, https://bjs.ojp.gov /content/pub/pdf/aic02.pdf. In a 2019 letter to the Inter-American Commission on Human Rights, the Indian Law Resource Center wrote, "Current federal data and statistics on disappearances and murders of Native women in the United States are deficient. What little is available is limited, dated, and generally of poor quality." Available at https://indianlaw.org/sites/default/files /Supplemental%20Response%20to%20Questions%20from%20Thematic%20 Hearing%20October%202018%20(final).pdf.

11. God's work to refine people extends throughout our whole lives. Many people told me how their views had changed throughout their journey of trying to follow Him. As a project of journalism and, to some extent, sociology, this book focuses on how people live. The Bible is, of course, the final authority on how

God calls us to live. And the Bible itself includes many things God condemns. No less than David, often called "a man after God's own heart," gets a painfully honest portrayal. The Bible's authors trust us to distinguish honest reporting from endorsement of conduct. Such candor about God's people underscores the depth of God's love in that He still pursues and saves us. And it makes clear that only God deserves the glory; we could never earn our standing with Him.

12. Wildman led work on the *First Nations Version* of the New Testament. See more on his use of "bad heart" in that translation's glossary.

13. I wrote more about this in "Americans, It's Time to Get Comfortable with Platonic Touch," *New York Times*, May 22, 2021, https://www.nytimes.com/2021/05/22/opinion/friends-holding-hands-touch.html.

14. For more on this, see Anna Broadway, "Practicing Trust: The Self-Giving Ethos of Biblical Sexuality," *Books and Culture*, January/February 2012, available online at https://www.annabroadway.com/news/2012/2/1/practicing-trust-the-self-giving-ethos-of-biblical-sexuality.

15. Anna Broadway, review of *Overdressed: The Shockingly High Cost of Cheap Fashion* by Elizabeth L. Cline, *Paste Magazine*, July 10, 2012, https://www.pastemagazine.com/books/elizabeth-l-cline-overdressed-the-shockingly-high.

CHAPTER 8 | PARENTING: REDEEMING RELATIONSHIPS BETWEEN GENERATIONS

1. Stephanie Kramer, "Key Findings: How Living Arrangements Vary by Religious Affiliation around the World," Pew Research Center, December 13, 2019, https://www.pewresearch.org/fact-tank/2019/12/13/key-findings-how-living-arrangements-vary-by-religious-affiliation-around-the-world.

2. This mainly means the adult who's in charge. Foster parents have strict accountability for kids' health and safety.

CHAPTER 9 | SEXUAL MINORITIES: THE STRUGGLE FOR BELONGING

1. Assuming the man was a eunuch vocationally and physically *and* that temple guards or gatekeepers recognized this, they likely would have barred him because of Deuteronomy 23:1. It reads, "No one who has been emasculated by crushing or cutting may enter the assembly of the LORD." See, for instance, Bob Deffinbaugh, "The Ethiopian Eunuch (Acts 8:26-40)," Bible.org, accessed February 16, 2023, https://bible.org/seriespage/13-ethiopian-eunuch-acts-826-40.

I'm not a Bible scholar, but the idea that "eunuch" referred only to the man's job seems strange. The story already shows God's dramatic pursuit and welcome of him as a Gentile. And Jesus welcomed sexual outsiders. In fact, Matthew's genealogy goes out of its way to name several of the outsiders in *Jesus'* lineage.

If anything, it seems more likely the man *was* an ethnic and sexual outsider.

After all, Luke says he was reading Isaiah just a few chapters before the prophecy of welcome for both ethnic and sexual outsiders (Isaiah 56:3-7). Remarkably, a single verse extends God's welcome to both foreigners and eunuchs! I find it very hard to believe the eunuch of Acts 8 only *appeared* to meet both these conditions.

2. Not all the Bible's teaching on sex comes in the form of explicit rules, such as the Ten Commandments. We also learn from stories. In other places, the Bible lets us draw conclusions from what happens (for example, when a man has multiple wives). As a whole, however, the church—Catholic, Protestant, and Orthodox—has historically accepted this view of the Bible's teaching on marriage and sex. I discussed my own convictions on this in *Sexless in the City* (New York: WaterBrook, 2008). Following what I believe God asks of me may cost me the chance to bear children and even to marry.

3. Anna Broadway, "Practicing Trust: The Self-Giving Ethos of Biblical Sexuality," *Books and Culture*, January/February 2012, https://www.annabroadway.com /news/2012/2/1/practicing-trust-the-self-giving-ethos-of-biblical-sexuality. Notably, such a narrow reading of the Bible leaves out love entirely! And it does not say anything about the motives and intentions Jesus highlighted in Matthew 5–6.

4. This book includes all three major traditions, and many readers will dispute whether some I talked to are truly Christian. For simplicity, I relied on people's self-identification as Christian. This includes some who were baptized as a child. Publishing partner Tyndale sees affirming the Bible as inspired by God and authoritative as a defining characteristic of being a Christian.

5. Though I tried to get a balanced group, those I talked to skewed young and male. Of the fourteen I talked to, eight were men, five were women, and one was transgender. Eight were in their twenties, four were in their thirties, and two were in their fifties.

6. This may prove a lifelong project. I've only made it partway through chapter 2 . . . so far. I hope to resume at some point.

7. Note that when Satan tempts Jesus, he quotes Scripture out of context. The temptation in Genesis 3 also involves distortion of God's word. We have to be very careful to read the Bible closely and deeply.

8. "India Religion Population Data," accessed July 23, 2022, https://www.census 2011.co.in/religion.php.

9. Open Doors, "World Watch List," accessed January 27, 2023, https://www .opendoors.org.au/world-watch-list. India was listed as the tenth most dangerous country to be a Christian from 2019 to 2022 and eleventh in 2023.

10. Howard Thurman, *Jesus and the Disinherited* (Boston: Beacon Press, 1976), 5.

11. Pieter Valk, "The Gay Teen Test," Equip, March 13, 2019, https://equipyour community.org/blog/2019/3/13/the-gay-teen-test.

12. Ministry purpose taken from "About," Equip, accessed February 20, 2023, https://equipyourcommunity.org/about.

CHAPTER 10 | DISEASE, DISABILITY, AND DEATH: WHEN OUR BODIES AND MINDS BETRAY US

1. The reality is much more complex. In a 2022 research review, scholar Erik W. Carter writes, "In nearly every study, half or more of individuals with disabilities were reported to attend services. Such findings contrast with oft-made claims that people with disabilities and their families are largely 'unchurched.'" That said, these studies do show less frequent attendance compared to "similar-age individuals without disabilities." He also cites a study that found only a fraction of adults with intellectual disabilities who lived in group homes attended religious education classes.

   As Carter summarizes: "Many young people with disabilities are participating in Sunday school classes, youth programs, Bible studies, and other contexts for learning about their faith. Whether and how that participation is supported is less clear. . . . The inclusion of adults with disabilities in religious education seems more limited." Erik W. Carter, "Research on Disability and Congregational Inclusion: What We Know and Where We Might Go," *Journal of Disability and Religion* 27, no. 2, 179–209, February 8, 2022, https://doi.org/10.1080/23312521 .2022.2035297.

2. For a fascinating contrast, see the book *God's Hotel* by physician Victoria Sweet (New York: Riverhead Books, 2012). In it, she describes her research on mystic Hildegard of Bingen, who saw the body more as a garden.

3. Ted J. Kaptchuk, "Placebo Effects in Acupuncture," *Medical Acupuncture* 32, no. 6, December 16, 2020, https://www.liebertpub.com/doi/full/10.1089 /acu.2020.1483.

4. In a study comparing three placebo responses to people with irritable bowel syndrome, "both treatment groups improved more than the no-treatment group." The group that received the "more elaborate doctor-patient interaction . . . did best of all." Gary Greenberg, "What If the Placebo Effect Isn't a Trick?" *New York Times Magazine*, November 7, 2018, https://www.nytimes.com/2018/11/07 /magazine/placebo-effect-medicine.html.

5. I'm indebted to Mitali Perkins for pointing this out in her book *Steeped in Stories: Timeless Children's Novels to Refresh Our Tired Souls* (Minneapolis: Broadleaf Books, 2021), 70. The *Japan Times* even has an article for its stories of "lonely death": https://www.japantimes.co.jp/tag/kodokushi, accessed October 19, 2022.

6. In the case of sex, I know too many single Christians end up pregnant because they didn't prepare for that to happen. And because of religious pressures, too many such pregnancies end in abortion. So far, I've felt like *having* birth control on hand would make it easier for me to compromise my standards. God has kindly protected me from rape, for reasons I may never know.

7. This song was written by Melody Green and popularized by Keith Green. "There Is a Redeemer," track 6 on *Songs for the Shepherd*, Sparrow Records, 1982.

8. Sometimes people at church also sing hymns in Yup'ik.

9. I attended services in Russian, Swahili, Arabic, Korean, Japanese (in a bilingual service), Portuguese, Italian, Tagalog, Mandarin, and Spanish. A handful of times, I missed attending church on a Sunday. Everywhere else, either I attended an international church or my hosts' congregation spoke English.

CHAPTER 11 | SINGLES IN MINISTRY: WORK THE BODY OF CHRIST STRUGGLES TO UNDERSTAND

1. Based on analysis of Pew's data for Catholic, evangelical Protestant, historically Black Protestant, mainline Protestant, and Orthodox Christians. "Religious Landscape Study: Marital Status," accessed September 2, 2022, https://www.pewresearch.org/religion/religious-landscape-study/marital-status.

2. According to their analysis, 29 percent live in a household with extended family; 34 percent in a two-parent home; 11 percent as part of a couple with no children living with them; 6 percent a single-parent home. Cases of adult children living with a parent were treated separately. Stephanie Kramer, "Key Findings: How Living Arrangements Vary by Religious Affiliation around the World," Pew Research Center, December 13, 2019, https://www.pewresearch.org/fact-tank/2019/12/13/key-findings-how-living-arrangements-vary-by-religious-affiliation-around-the-world, accessed September 2, 2022, and "Appendix A: Methodology," December 12, 2019, https://www.pewresearch.org/religion/2019/12/12/appendix-a-methodology-11, accessed September 2, 2022.

3. Of the 196 who'd never been married, 126 (64.29 percent) wanted marriage. Twenty-seven (13.78 percent) weren't sure what they wanted, nineteen (9.69 percent) were celibate, and three (1.53 percent) were open to marriage but not necessarily seeking it. Only twelve (6.12 percent) didn't want marriage but weren't necessarily celibate. The remaining nine (4.59 percent) didn't clearly express their views on possible marriage.

4. These included thirteen Catholic priests, eleven Protestant pastors, and four celibate Orthodox clergy. Of the Orthodox priests, only one had chosen celibacy; two were widowed, and one was divorced. Beyond clergy, I also interviewed one Protestant ministry leader, two Catholic monastics, and two Catholic women who had taken vows of celibacy but weren't in communities. Two of the celibate people I interviewed were also same-sex attracted, but both said their celibacy was not related to their sexuality.

5. Eastern Catholic churches allow married priests but not married bishops. Msgr. Robert L. Stern, "Ecclesial Biodiversity," *ONE Magazine*, September–October 1998, https://cnewa.org/magazine/ecclesial-biodiversity-30805; Peter Galadza, "Eastern Catholic Christianity," in *The Blackwell Companion to Eastern Christianity*, ed. Ken Parry (West Sussex: John Wiley & Sons, 2010), 302–304. The 1980 Pastoral Provision of Pope John Paul II also allows "for the priestly ordination of married former clergymen coming from the Episcopal Church," according to the Pastoral Provision website. "The History of the Pastoral Provision," The Pastoral Provision, accessed October 28, 2022, http://www.pastoralprovision.org/history.

6. I don't fully understand the hierarchy, but it sounds like subdeacon is the lowest level at which you have to choose your life's course before you get ordained.

7. Orthodox tradition confirmed in interviews with priests and by reviewing the clergy listings on the Orthodox Church in America website, www.oca.org, accessed August 24, 2022. Eastern Catholic tradition cited in Stern, "Ecclesial Biodiversity," accessed October 28, 2022.

8. See, for example, "About Saint Brigid's Monastery," Saint Brigid of Kildare Monastery, accessed October 28, 2022, https://www.kildaremonastery.com /about-the-monastery.html.

9. See, for example, "Who Are We?" Communauté des Diaconesses de Reuilly, accessed October 28, 2022, https://www.diaconesses-reuilly.fr/qui-sommes -nous, translated via Google Chrome's built-in translator; Ngwa Anyele Eugene and Mother Evangeline Vié, "The Sisterhood of Emmanuel" booklet (2007), 7, accessed October 28, 2022, https://www.yumpu.com/en/embed/view /3bEQMTt2BfblZUGb.

10. "Matushka: Lots of Titles for the Priest's Wife," *The Catalog of Good Deeds* (blog), Catalogue of St. Elisabeth Convent, May 3, 2018, https://catalog.obitel -minsk.com/blog/2018/05/matushka-lots-of-titles-for-priests-wife.

11. The older male virgin is a classic joke in American culture, as in *The 40-Year-Old Virgin*. It's the same reason "Where the white women at?" works as both distraction and joke in the movie *Blazing Saddles*. Such jokes usually point out unpleasant truths about us.

12. In fact, marital status discrimination is illegal in at least seventeen US states, according to Workplace Fairness, "Marital and Parental Status Discrimination: State Law," accessed February 16, 2023, https://www.workplacefairness.org /marital-status-state-law. Their analysis, which doesn't have a date, says the following states all prohibit marital status discrimination: Alaska, California, Connecticut, Delaware, Florida, Minnesota, Montana, Nebraska, New Jersey, New York, North Dakota, Ohio, Oregon, Virginia, Washington, West Virginia, and Wisconsin.

    However, Myron Steeves of Church Law Center told me via email, January 15, 2023, that religious liberty usually trumps antidiscrimination. He cited *Hosanna-Tabor Evangelical Lutheran Church and School v. EEOC* (2012). In that case, the Supreme Court unanimously voted that the state couldn't tell a religious entity how to choose a leader, even if they violated antidiscrimination laws in doing so. See https://www.supremecourt.gov/docketfiles/10-553.htm.

13. John married a year after our interview.

14. See, for example, Lyman Stone, "Baby Blues: How to Face the Church's Growing Fertility Crisis," *Christianity Today*, August 8, 2022, https://www.christianity today.com/ct/2022/august-web-only/birth-rates-church-attendance-decline -fertility-crisis.html. At the end, the author writes, "For reasons I've described in length elsewhere, religiosity in America is declining. . . . However, this decline is not inevitable: Achieving growth again would not require American churches to

do impossible things. Having one more child on average, successfully integrating a modest share of immigrants into the US, or achieving higher conversion rates could all stave off decline."

15. Miguel Ruiz-Prada, Samuel Fernández-Salinero, Cristina García-Ael, and Gabriela Topa, "Occupational Stress and Catholic Priests: A Scoping Review of the Literature," *Journal of Religion and Health* 60, no. 6 (August 2021): 3807–3870.

16. The COVID-19 pandemic made this abundantly clear. Had I finished even a few months later, I could have been stuck who knows where. And had I wrapped up even a few weeks later, I might not have been able to drive to Alaska in my elderly car. Again and again, the details show God's exquisite timing for all parts of this project.

17. Dana Gioia, "Summer Storm," in *Interrogations at Noon: Poems* (Saint Paul, MN: Graywolf Press, 2001); and at https://danagioia.com/summer-storm. Used with permission.

CONCLUSION | TOWARD MEANING AND COMMITMENT

1. In this step, a native speaker translates the new Bible draft back into the source language (often English) to verify the accuracy and meaning of the translation. Back translation usually happens toward the end of the process.

2. Since our interview, Robin has come out as nonbinary but consented to my use of the interview as accurate at the time. When we last spoke, Robin was still grappling with how to reconcile faith and sexuality now. Such a journey echoes many people's stories in the Bible, especially the Old Testament.

   For years, I've struggled with the course of my own journey. Why couldn't God take me on a more direct route? Then Priscilla Shirer's Elijah study pointed me to Exodus 13:17-18. There, we learn why God *didn't* take the Israelites along the shortest route to the Promised Land. That passage shook me deeply.

3. God is God. And Paul calls His will "good, pleasing and perfect" (Romans 12:2). Who knows where Robin and I will find ourselves five, ten, and twenty years from now, should we live so long?

4. Almaz and her husband did get a mortgage, but paying it off caused them to struggle financially.

5. "History and Impact," Ekklesia Good News Ministry to the Poor, accessed September 4, 2022, https://ekklesiagoodnews.org/history-and-impact.

6. Wesley Hill, *Spiritual Friendship: Finding Love in the Church as a Celibate Gay Christian* (Grand Rapids, MI: Brazos Press, 2015).

METHODOLOGY

1. By American standards, I started the trip with middle-class assets. I paid off my last debt in 2012. With frugal living, I had saved about half a year's salary by 2018. Between many people's hospitality, a few financial gifts, and continued frugal habits like cooking whatever meals I could, I had perhaps 20 percent of my savings left once I moved to Alaska.

2. Groups accounted for 64 of the 345 people with whom I spoke for this book; interviews accounted for 279. I include in the demographic breakdowns the two friends whose stories I also used. Of the people I interviewed or know more about, 208 have never married (74 percent). Another 28 (10 percent) were widowed; 23 divorced (8 percent); 5 were separated (2 percent); and 16 were married (6 percent).

3. My research included interviews with forty Catholic, Protestant, and Orthodox clergy, twelve of whom (30 percent) were married. Nearly half—mostly Catholic—were celibate.

4. Particularly with topics like food, however, I believe it also captures aspects of single life more broadly, religious or not.

5. These include all three of the interviewee groups in Tanzania.

6. For all the Spanish interviews with delayed translation, I found a native speaker from the same country as the interview. For the Swiss interviews, I worked with a German woman, since I had learned "hoch Deutsch"—slightly different from Swiss German. She occasionally couldn't understand a word or the accent.

7. Number based on Open Doors's annual World Watch List ranking of the world's most dangerous places to follow Jesus. Rankings take into account both violence and pressure in several spheres of life. Seven of the countries I visited appear on the 2018 to 2021 lists: China, Colombia, Egypt, Ethiopia, India, Kenya, and Nigeria. Two more were on the 2018 and 2019 lists: Mexico and the Palestinian Territories. The final two entered the list in 2019 and remain for 2020: Russia and a country I won't name for the sources' safety. Open Doors, *World Watch List Report 2021: The Persecution of Christians: Key Facts. Key Trends. Key Actions.* (Orange, CA: Open Doors, 2021), 32; Jayson Casper, "The Top 50 Countries Where It's Hardest to Be a Christian (2020)," *Christianity Today*, January 15, 2020, https://www.christianitytoday.com/news/2020/january/top-christian-persecution-open-doors-2020-world-watch-list.html; Open Doors, *World Watch List 2019: The 50 Countries Where It's Most Dangerous to Follow Jesus* (Orange, CA: Open Doors, 2019), 8–9; Sarah Eekhoff Zylstra, "The Top 50 Countries Where It's Most Dangerous to Follow Jesus (2018)," *Christianity Today*, January 10, 2018, https://www.christianitytoday.com/news/2018/january/top-50-christian-persecution-open-doors-world-watch-list.html.

8. My Europe stops also included family visits in Albania and Germany, but I did no interviews there. I do include them in the total number of countries visited, however. And even these stops involved some work for future research stops.

9. Of the 268 people whose religious tradition I could identify, 129 (48.13 percent) were Protestant, 67 (25 percent) were Catholic, 33 (12.31 percent) were Pentecostal or charismatic, 21 (7.84 percent) were Orthodox, and 18 (6.72 percent) were independent. This last number includes some Chinese Christians, who didn't tend to identify with one of the three main traditions, and Messianic Christians—ethnic Jews who believe Jesus is the Messiah.

10. Some people were friends of friends of friends. Occasionally a pastor or priest made an announcement about my work and told anyone interested to talk to me. With nearly three hundred people I interviewed individually, it's hard to remember how I met all of them.

11. As a result, I talked to eighteen people who were seventy or older (nearly 7 percent of the 263 who gave me their ages). I also talked to eleven people who reported disabilities and fourteen who identified as a sexual minority.

ACKNOWLEDGMENTS

1. See https://www.instagram.com/explore/tags/nihongazuhause for some of our stops. Makoto Fujimura's writing includes *Silence and Beauty: Hidden Faith Born of Suffering* (Downers Grove, IL: InterVarsity Press, 2016).

2. "Stop Telling Christian Singles What They Can't Do," *Christianity Today*, February 14, 2013, http://www.christianitytoday.com/women/2013/february /stop-telling-christian-singles-what-they-cant-do.html; and "God Didn't Make Our Bodies Only for Sex," *Christianity Today*, February 21, 2013, http://www .christianitytoday.com/women/2013/february/god-didnt-make-our-bodies -only-for-sex.html.

3. Dr. Rah's work includes *Prophetic Lament: A Call for Justice in Troubled Times* (Downers Grove, IL: InterVarsity Press, 2015). Khang's work includes *Raise Your Voice: Why We Stay Silent and How to Speak Up* (Downers Grove, IL: InterVarsity Press, 2018).

4. Dr. Zurlo's work includes *Global Christianity: A Guide to the World's Largest Religion from Afghanistan to Zimbabwe* (Grand Rapids, MI: Zondervan Academic, 2022). Dr. Bruner's work includes *How to Study Global Christianity: A Short Guide for Students* (Cham, Switzerland: Springer Nature, 2022).

5. I regret that I didn't get a couple of people's names.

6. Dr. Mazibuko has published several scholarly articles on gender-based violence. Dr. Lake's work includes *The Bible in Australia: A Cultural History* (Sydney, NSW: NewSouth Publishing, 2018).

7. I regret that I couldn't include more of their insights directly. Dr. Shelton's work (with Michael O. Emerson) includes *Blacks and Whites in Christian America: How Racial Discrimination Shapes Religious Convictions* (New York: New York University Press, 2012).

8. Mark Charles's work (with Soong-Chan Rah) includes *Unsettling Truths: The Ongoing, Dehumanizing Legacy of the Doctrine of Discovery* (Downers Grove, IL: InterVarsity Press, 2019). Dr. Aldred's work (with Matthew Anderson) includes *Our Home and Treaty Land: Walking Our Creation Story* (n.p.: Wood Lake Publishing Inc., 2022).

9. Dr. Emerson's books include the aforementioned *People of the Dream*. Dr. Hastings has published several scholarly articles.

NavPress is the book-publishing arm of The Navigators.

Since 1933, The Navigators has helped people around the world bring hope and purpose to others in college campuses, local churches, workplaces, neighborhoods, and hard-to-reach places all over the world, face-to-face and person-by-person in an approach we call Life-to-Life® discipleship. We have committed together to know Christ, make Him known, and help others do the same.®

Would you like to join this adventure of discipleship and disciplemaking?

- Take a Digital Discipleship Journey at **navigators.org/disciplemaking**.
- Get more discipleship and disciplemaking content at **thedisciplemaker.org**.
- Find your next book, Bible, or discipleship resource at **navpress.com**.

 @NavPressPublishing

 @NavPress

 @navpressbooks

CP1790